THE WISDEN
PAPERS OF
NEVILLE CARDUS

EDITED BY BENNY GREEN

GUILD PUBLISHING

LONDON · NEW YORK · SYDNEY · TORONTO

CONTENTS

ACKNOWLEDGEMENT

The author and publishers would like to thank the following for permission to reproduce copyright photographs in this book: Hulton-Deutsch Collection, Sport & General Press Agency, *Manchester Evening News*, Popperfoto, Associated Press and Patrick Eagar.

INTRODUCTION

Between 1922 and his death twenty three years later, Neville Cardus published twelve books on cricket, although it might almost be said that he published only one. The bulk of his bibliography consists of collated clippings from the then 'Manchester Guardian', and of the early publications only a slim volume contributed to the 'English Heritage' series in 1930 is a book in the sense that it has been conceived with a beginning, a middle and an end. That most picaresque of all publishers, Grant Richards, who had set up in business in 1896 with a capital of £1400, and who was as responsible as any man could be for Cardus's career as an author, has described in some detail the slapdash nature of Cardus's approach. In a revelatory book called 'Author Hunting', Richards, having given an account of the element of pure fluke in his launching of Thomas Burke's 'Limehouse Nights', compares Burke's fate with Cardus's,

> A like fate awaited a later book, Neville Cardus's 'A Cricketer's Book'. He sent it to me in a disshevelled state in 1922. It was one of those offers that do not immediately attract the publisher. The packet was made up of newspaper cuttings, and why, I asked myself, should I be expected to interest myself in a book which was to be made up of articles that had appeared in a daily newspaper, even though that daily newspaper was 'The Manchester Guardian'? However, I had published P. F. Warner's 'Cricket Reminiscences', and I knew that cricket had some devotees who read books, even though their number was not as great as one would expect; and anyhow, whatever came out of the 'Guardian' stable was worth backing on general principles. After a time, therefore, I brought myself to a consideration of Cardus's proposal; and although I knew nothing about cricket, I said I would publish. . . . Cricketers do not frequent bookshops, and neither Cardus nor I made a fortune. Nevertheless, I was proud of my share in the production. . . . Let me add that Cardus, my friend, is a most difficult author to handle. In spite of the fact that the first proposal came from him, the result, I suppose, of some friend's urging, he will not believe that his stuff is worth reprinting, and the getting of a second and third book out of him was as difficult as anything I have ever experienced. But what a writer!

There is another, more significant sense in which Cardus could be said to have written only one book about cricket, even though it was published by instalments, one volume at a time. From 'A Cricketer's Book' to 'Full Score', the volumes fuse through a uniformity of style and attitude, and as both are unique in the context of sporting journalism, it is not surprising that they should hold the key to the central paradox of Cardus's reputation.

He is widely regarded as a charming concocter of white lies whose technical insight is suspect, and whose aesthetic morality, as he would have put it, is elastic enough to accommodate distortion of the facts to fit the theses. Many other cricket writers have found him precious, and have seen in his prose technique an engine which cannot help but obscure the truth, perfectly geared though it may be for telling us, in character portraits, much about the man himself. Nobody who wishes to discover what actually happened, runs the indictment, had better read him, for his descriptions are no more than elegantly expressed fantasies of wish-fulfilment inspired by the spectacle he happens to be witnessing. And yet, in spite of this, Cardus has contrived to produce the only body of sporting prose in the twentieth century in England which has a reasonable chance of becoming a classic. In 1907, even as the adolescent Cardus was refining his sensibilities in preparation for the work which would occupy the rest of his life, the essayist, critic and cricket fancier Edward Verrall Lucas, idolater at the shrine of Hambledon, could write of John Nyren's 'The Cricketers of My Time', 'I doubt very much if any more really great literature will collect about the pitch'. By adapting Nyren's method, which was to bring to the reader's attention the quiddity of temperament of the cricketers fondly remembered from childhood, Cardus was to match, and, at last, to outmatch Lucas's great hero.

The books published by Richards, and later by Rupert Hart-Davies, usually consisted of two quite independent sections, the first culled from the 'Guardian', and consisting of brief sketches of men and matches, the second an account of a Test series, again taken from the newspaper columns. The most striking thing about them is their almost total disregard for statistics. In painting his portraits Cardus might never have been aware that batting averages and bowling analyses are the preoccupation of so many of the game's followers. He achieves his ends in quite a different way, by relating his purely subjective impressions to a range of experience utterly divorced from the world of sport. An innings by Woolley is 'full of the very brevity of summer', and a match between Lancashire and Yorkshire 'tells a plain tale of the stiff energy of North country life'. One of his reports of a day's play between England and Australia begins: 'John Stuart Mill argued that on another planet two and two might easily make five', and another ends: 'It was a Tower Hill stroke. You could almost see the axe and the block'.

Some readers, and most cricketers, must have found the analogies fanciful, perhaps even incomprehensible, but for those who gradually became acquainted with the mind that conceived them, the surprising truth began to emerge that from the raw material of a ball game Cardus is striving to fashion a complete philosophic system and that he sees the cricket field as an arena where the forces of Good and Evil are locked in the combat of an everlasting morality play. For him the prime virtues are courage, grace, humour and imagination, the despised virtues anonymity, pretension and meanness of spirit. Flair is what he looks for and drabness what he can hardly bring himself to look upon. The triumphs of the scoreboard do not often interest him, any more than a relief map interests a landscape painter. It is manner, not matter, which commends itself to him, which means that many of his judgments are likely to seem quixotic to the point of perversity to those readers inclined only to add up the runs on each side, subtract one total from the other and give three undiscerning cheers for the winner. To what extent did it enlighten the tosspots of the Lord's Tavern to be told, as Cardus once told them, that Charles Macartney was the Figaro of cricket, 'not Mozart's, but the drier-minded one of Rossini'?

The first impact of all this can be bewildering. If what Cardus says is correct, then the rest of us have been watching cricket all our lives with unseeing eyes. We have never been asked to believe that the game of cricket represents a microcosm of the human comedy and we are not at all sure that we wish to be asked. We find ourselves plunged into seas of the most fanciful analogy and, were it not for the consistency of Cardus's attitudes, we would be drowned in no time. But we sense, even in our confusion, that somewhere at the heart of all this apparent perversity is a passion strongly felt and resolutely expressed. Admittedly it is not quite the kind of passion we bargained for when first we picked up his books, but at least there is no denying either its intensity or its durability. The flavour of 'Summer Game' is still there half a lifetime later in 'Final Score', although the prose has become rather less effusive.

His detractors say that Cardus's writing is too self-consciously erudite for either its own or the general reader's good, that it depends for its effect on too many extraneous factors, obscures too many issues, attempts the shotgun wedding of too many incompatibles, and is in fact guilty of the very pretensions it seeks to expose. It is bad enough for Macartney to be defined as Figaro, worse when the definition is qualified to mean Rossini's rather than Mozart's, worst of all when in another piece the same Macartney is cast as 'a Mercutio whose every innings is a Queen Mab's scherzo'. These analogies between cricket and grand opera are suspect enough, but they possess at least the virtue of synthesising Cardus's two most passionate loves. But what of his accounts of the notorious verbal exchanges between cricketers on the field of play, which so brilliantly personalise the drama of a match? For years it occurred to nobody to question the authenticity of these entrancing little duologues. But eventually some sceptic realised that from his seat in the press box or the pavilion, Cardus could not possibly have heard what mid-off said to cover point. The issue is further complicated by the fact that the conversations in his reports are so diverting that there is a temptation to accept them as the truth even if we suspect them to be false. And if they are indeed false, then the structure of Cardus's writing on cricket is in danger of total collapse because it is largely through the wit and vividness of these exchanges that men like Emmott Robinson and Richard Tyldesley emerge from the page at all.

The essence of the case against Cardus, then, is that he makes false-hood more attractive than the facts, that he seduces the reader down his own particular primrose path at the expense of the game he is supposed to be writing about. In view of the frequency with which he has been caught redhanded tampering with the evidence, consciously or not, the critics have an unanswerable case – but only so long as it is agreed that factual truth was what Cardus was after. For there is one defence which would justify all, and it is this; that when it comes to cricket, Cardus has presented us with a view of things, not as they happened, but as they appeared to happen after being refined through the processes of his own sensibilities and then coloured with the hues of his imagination. To expect cold fact from a man of exquisite sensibility is madness and we make that mistake with reference to Cardus only if we misjudge utterly what it was he was writing about and why. As it happens, the battle had already been fought and won by an English writer whose life overlaps that of Cardus. This was Ford Madox Ford, whose literary and artistic recollections were to be dismissed as mischievous moonshine by all those among his contemporaries who were too dull to have thought of anything half so readable. Ford painted unforgettable portraits of the Pre-Raphae-lites at work and at play; in Cardusian terms, Dante Gabriel Rossetti was his Archie MacLaren, Millais his Herbert Sutcliffe, and his own beloved grandfather Ford Madox Brown a magisterial Doctor Grace-like figure hovering with comic irascibility over all the rest of them. The anecdotes Ford published about these men and dozens of others, once read are never forgotten. They are portraits in miniature, thumbnail biographies, dazzling cameos exhibiting quite remarkable fixity of vision. But are they true? Are they snapshots or fantasies, evidence or perjury, fact or fiction? In time Ford became bored by the recriminations, by the repeated cries of 'Liar', just as Cardus must have done. And at last he mounted his defence to which there is no effective response,

> Even as a little boy, I knew that I had the trick of imagining things and that those things would be more real to me than the things that surrounded me . . . Where it has seemed expedient to me I have altered episodes that I have witnessed but I have been careful never to distort the character of the episodes. The accuracies I deal in are the accuracies of my impressions. If you want factual accuracies you must go to . . . But no, don't go to anyone, stay with me. . . . A lie is a figurative truth and it is the poet who is master of these illusions . . . It is possible I romance.

And most memorably of all, 'Our geese MUST be swans'. Cardus's writing comprises a view of life seen through the prism of Ford's impressionism. Among dozens of notorious examples was the issue of Cardus's marriage to Edith King, whose incidence he deployed memor-ably in the cause of cricket reportage:

> I married the good companion who is my wife during a Lancashire

innings. The event occurred in June, 1921. I went as usual to Old Trafford, stayed for a while and saw Hallows and Makepeace come forth to bat. As usual they opened with care. Then I had to leave, had to take a taxi to Manchester, there to be joined in wedlock at a registry office. Then I – that is, we – returned to Old Trafford. While I had been away from the match and had committed the most responsible and irrevocable act in mortal men's life, Lancashire had increased their total by exactly seventeen – Makepeace 5, Hallows 11 and one leg-bye.

By writing this comic, revealing critical paragraph, Cardus had placed himself in the same kind of jeopardy to which the Reverend Dodgson had once exposed himself when claiming that on the day of the historic boat trip with the Liddell sisters which became immortalised by 'Alice in Wonderland', it had been 'a golden afternoon'. The time came, as it had to, when some dullard referred to the Meteorological Office and discovered that the afternoon of July 4th, 1862, when Dodgson and Liddells had set sail, had been 'cool and rather wet'. Cardus was to suffer the same fate at the hands of critics who appeared to have missed the point of the joke, which was at the expense of Lancashire's batting policy. It was proven that Makepeace and Hallows opened for the county only once in June 1921, in a different match on a different day. But it is revealing that for those who have become familiar with the passage about the Cardus nuptials, the policies of attrition favoured by Makepeace were made manifest. Cardus once told a story about a bumpy morning at the crease experienced by Dick Tyldesley at the hands of the Oxford University fast bowlers. Someone then published a book proving that Tyldesley had never faced those bowlers, that no such match had ever taken place, that there was no university at Oxford and no county called Lancashire. In response Cardus published one of his last 'Guardian' essays, pointedly giving it the title: 'Guilty, m'lud, to fiction if it serves higher Truth'. In this essay, one of the most fascinating he ever wrote, Cardus claimed that 'such cricketers as Parkin, Dick Tyldesley, Sutcliffe and Leyland, simply set the humorous or picturesque imagination free to go its way'. In explaining the process by which he put into Dick Tyldesley's mouth a profound remark about morality and Westhaughten Sunday School, Cardus asks a rhetorical question and then answers it,

Did he really say it? To fulfil and complete him, to realise the truth of his Lancashire nature and being, it simply HAD to be said. Whether he himself said it, or whether I put the words into his mouth for him, matters nothing as far as truth, as God knows it, is concerned.

Cardus explained his position a thousand times. Whenever faced with a direct accusation he had always admitted full guilt and revelled in it, as Dickens must have revelled in Dick Swiveller and Mr. Tulkinghorn. He would agree with you when you suggested that in his own mind fact and fancy had mingled to form a personal mythology so thoroughly integrated that the literal truth was no longer discernible. In old age he had spun his yarns for so many years that he was no longer sure whether an incident had taken place or whether he had invented it. Once in conversation with me he began praising the imp of mischief which animated his beloved George Gunn. The story that afternoon was to do with George being not out overnight and sleeping late at his hotel with his wife who had to remind him that he was due at the crease at start of play. It seems that George had simply forgotten that he had been batting at close of play the previous evening. But in recounting the anecdote, Cardus became confused in his own mind between Gunn and a later Notts eccentric, Charlie Harris. It made no difference to the savour of the story, but it did indicate that sometimes the personalities merged into each other. It was no longer possible for him to remember whether the voices he had once heard had been those of Dick Tyldesley and company or his own. In one of his published defences Cardus quotes part of his own apocrypha with reference to the personality of Herbert Sutcliffe, and then asks, 'True? How could I have invented something so penetrating to the quiddity, the essence, of the Sutcliffe presence and temperament?'. Cardus knew the answer to that question as well as we do and, once we grasp its implications, we begin to understand what kind of writer he was. In the light of the evidence, it is comical that for fifty years he should have been regarded as a cricket reporter, or indeed as a reporter of anything. The contradictions are too overwhelming to miss.

The first great paradox about Cardus the writer on cricket is that he had no interest in the sporting life:

> I am not a man who is interested in sport. I have attended only one race meeting in my life. I have never seen an English Cup Final. I have seldom known that it was Derby Day until the next morning's newspapers. I cannot play any card games; I do not at first sight pick out a spade from a diamond. I am a member of the Savage Club and have never entered the billiard room. And I have not once in my life owned a single golf club.

Apart from a single reference to the twinkling feet of Billy Meredith glimpsed as a boy, and the recollection of the pathetic ambitions of a schoolboy friend called Clegg which were, astonishingly, to be fulfilled in the Manchester City colours, there is nothing either in the cricket books or in the volumes of autobiography to indicate that any game apart from cricket even exists. Winter for Cardus is either a long hiatus between seasons, to be beguiled by attendance at concerts, or a time of distant battles for the Ashes in Sydney and Melbourne. Addiction to one ball game usually implies a like addiction to some of the others or, at the very least, a passing interest. Most of Cardus's companions in the Press box stayed there once the season was over, to report football or rugby without the slightest feeling of incongruity or anti-climax. And even if we accept Cardus's total disengagement from all other sports and games, it would at least be expected that his curiosity would have been tempted once or twice by cricketers who spent their winters excelling in other games. Having observed that Hendren's strokes had about them 'the smack of the place in which he was born and bred', might not Cardus have speculated whether the same indigenous expression of style was part of Hendren's technique as an outside right? Having noted Denis Compton's ability to convey joy as a batsman, might he not have underlined the point by noting Compton's like ability to convey joy as an outside left? Having settled on William Gunn the cricketer as a symbol of Victorian orthodoxy, was there no inclination to explore the contradiction of William Gunn the footballer as a symbol of Victorian romanticism? In all his writings on cricket Cardus omits to tell us the most astounding thing of all about R. E. Foster, which is that he is the only man who ever captained the full England side at football *and* cricket. Even the deep friendship with C. B. Fry, which recurs like a leitmotif through Cardus's entire output, never prompts him to a review of that athlete's remarkable versatility as a football international and Cup Final medallist, very nearly a rugby blue, and holder of the World long jump record. We can only conclude that it was never the man who interested Cardus so much as the man in a specific setting. In any understanding of his work, it is of vital importance to remember this fact, that it is this setting and the rules of one highly idiosyncratic game, which so profoundly engaged his sensibilities. Once we understand this, once we learn how and why it happened as it did, Cardus the cricket reporter disappears, to be replaced by a very different kind of animal indeed. As always, the clues are buried deep in childhood.

* * *

So far as a later age can judge, the Lancashire side around the turn of the century was an unusually brilliant one, in temperament as well as technique. By a pure fluke of circumstance, it was this gallery of rampant originals to which Cardus's ripening schoolboy sensibilities were first exposed; the graceful Spooner and the staunch Tyldesley, the tragi-comic Briggs, who laughed his puckish way through a successful career to an asylum, and Mold, whose bowling action was so dubious that one reporter of the period lost patience altogether and wrote, 'Mold opened the attack, and at three o'clock Briggs came on to bowl the first overs of the day'. It is essential to remember that these men were not only the first cricketers Cardus ever saw, but the first artists of any kind. It was not cricket alone that they revealed to him, but human nature expressing itself through action or, perhaps in the case of Barlow, inaction. It might easily have been Dickens or Keats or Mozart who first bestowed upon Cardus what he was later to call the grace of art. By pure chance this act was performed not by any novelist or musician but by the unlikely crew which represented Lancashire cricket of the period, and one member of this crew in particular, its captain:

The first cricketer I saw was A. C. MacLaren. Lancashire were beginning an innings when I sat down on a hard wooden seat. MacLaren
drove a ball far to the distant boundary, straight and powerfully. I
cannot remember the bowler's name; he has passed with all other
details of the match into limbo, but I can still see the swing of
MacLaren's bat, the great follow through, finishing high and held there
with body poised as he himself contemplated the grandeur of the
stroke and savoured it. Then the clouds over Old Trafford burst, and
the rain fell in torrents. No further play occurred at Old Trafford that
day.

Notice how from the very beginning Cardus cannot resist rearranging
the amorphous mass of reality into an artistic shape, how the name of
the bowler is erased from the record, how the convenient arrival of rain
places that one memorable stroke in glorious isolation, a glimpse of
genius on a day's play consisting fantastically of only one shot. As
the years passed and the magic glimpse of MacLaren receded, Cardus
embellished the tale, adjusting the choreography almost without realising
it. In the last months of his life, exchanging recollections with another
distinguished ex-Mancunian, Alistair Cooke, he amended MacLaren's
stroke and incorporated into the anecdote another of the great Lancashire heroes:

> . . . and I saw MacLaren play a hook stroke like Greek sculpture, a
> beautiful sweeping hook stroke. And then it rained and rained and
> rained. I saw no more. I stood outside that ground, as little boys do,
> thinking there was going to be a miracle. The sky would clear and the
> dove would come. But no. I waited and waited, and out of the gates
> came a man in blue serge wearing a watchchain. I said, 'Aren't they
> going to play?'
> 'No, they've finished long since. Here. Here's sixpence for you'.
> And that was J. T. Tyldesley, and I never spent that sixpence for
> weeks. I showed it to my ragamuffin pals: 'Johnny Tyldesley gave me
> that'. And do you know, such was their scepticism that none of them
> believed me.

With that closing remark Cardus is winking at posterity, confessing for
the umpteenth time to the crime for which he was so often arraigned,
of gilding the lily. Yet it would be impossible to exaggerate the importance of this apparently minor event in his life. It could be said quite
literally to have brought him fully to life for the first time, to have
endowed him with an ambition and a philosophy, to have told him what
kind of person he was, and to hint at what he ought to be doing about
it:

> This brief sight of MacLaren thrilled my blood, for it gave shape and
> reality to things I had till then only vaguely felt and dreamed about.
> I did not think of cricket. I knew next to nothing of the rules and
> technique.

This is Cardus writing nearly fifty years after the event, when he had become a master of the art of rationalising the excesses of his own imagination. But for a moment there was only a small boy goggling at the sumptuous banquet of character. One stroke on a rain-ruined day, but enough to start him in pursuit of his god-figure, a pursuit lasting the forty years to MacLaren's death and beyond.

There is no question that he was in desperate need of the salvation which shone down at him from the Olympian heights occupied by MacLaren and company. Born in obscure circumstances in the Manchester suburb of Rusholme, he was raised in that threadbare no-man's-land between abject penury and the compromises of working-class deprivation. Cardus has not been altogether fortunate in his biographer, a civil servant who, evidently having been shielded by circumstance from any direct experience of the biting poverty known to Cardus, has called into question the degree of hardship of daily life at Summer Place, where the small boy was raised in the matriarchal society of a mother and an aunt who contrived to cheat their own wretched destiny by taking a succession of lovers with enough funds to subsidise living expenses. Cardus described his mother and his Aunt Beatrice as prostitutes without hinting at any moral judgments, but his biographer takes leave to doubt if his protectresses actually walked the streets in search of trade. To be sure, much of what Cardus tells us about his background is as suspect as his dithyrambs about the Lancashire cricketers. He is maddeningly disingenuous about his own origins, asking us to believe, for instance, that his mysterious father was a man called Cardus who married a girl whose name was also Cardus. He is accused of overstating the case regarding his mother's morality, even though the yellowing pages of 'The Daily Dispatch' for April 1902 bear him out in lurid detail. Certainly he rigged many of the facts about his origins but what is unusual about the rigging is that it seems to have been undertaken for neither of the two usual reasons, neither to conceal the shame of the family skeleton, nor to render the climb upward all the more heroic by overstating the lowliness of its beginning. When Cardus describes his grandfather mourning the death of his wife by renouncing 'The Sporting Chronicle Handicap Book' forever, in defiance of the fact that his grandmother outlived her husband by seven years, he is endowing the chaos of his childhood with the shapeliness of fiction and was no more lying about his grandfather than James Thurber and Ford Madox Ford were lying about theirs. Cardus loved his family so desperately that he transmuted them into the golden deities of his emergent years – which is precisely why they disappear from his annals once he has become a man. The adults observed by an intelligent, sensitive child seem to move across the face of the earth like so many giants and giantesses because that is exactly what they are. Steadily they shrink until at last they are no larger and no grander than the child regarding them, at which point they surrender the lustre of romance. Having served their purpose by stimulating the emergent imagination of the writer, supplying him with his first set of archetypes, their usefulness is done, and the writer moves on. Cardus's biographer has taken him to task for this, confusing the writer's loss of interest in his mother and his aunt as characters with his loss of affection for them, which was hardly the case in a man who, when all the objects of his childish love are dead, takes such great loving care to render them immortal.

To the schoolboy, MacLaren and his men were gods whose fortunes you prayed for. Indeed, Spooner became an object of devotion so passionate that Cardus confesses that perhaps he never actually saw Spooner play the ball at all because, unable to chance the possibility of seeing his hero cut down, he always closed his eyes at the moment of impact. And there was Johnny Tyldesley, his D'Artagnan, who so many times held off the enemy single-handed. There is one extraordinary episode in the autobiography which, imagined or not, tells us all we need to know about the love of cricket. Perhaps more than any other fragment of recollection this century it conveys the extent to which a game can become the focus of a small boy's powerful imagination, assuming for him the proportions of a myth, a mission, a private religion.

It is the August Bank Holiday of 1904 and Cardus is living in Summer Place. Across the Pennines the feared enemy Yorkshire is pressing the beloved Lancashire side towards its first defeat of the season. Cardus frets alone in the streets of Manchester, committed utterly, pathetically, to the outcome of this insignificant struggle which, on the face of it, has nothing to do with him at all. And yet it does, even though the cricketers locked in battle are not even aware that he exists, and exists only through them:

> I went into the city of Manchester, where I could be on the spot when the different editions of the newspapers came out with later and later details of the match. Outside the office of 'The Manchester Evening News' I waited, while the hours stood still. I looked at the Town Hall clock and willed the fingers to move, screwing my eyes to see the slightest sign of motion of them. I performed various acts to get the gods on my side and Lancashire's side. I stood over a grid in the gutter and told myself that if I could spit through it without touching the bars, Lancashire would after all be spared.

Madness perhaps, yet a madness not uncommon among small boys, although it makes a sorry mess of Cardus's proud claim never to have cared about the result of a match. Meanwhile the forlorn idolater continues his vigil:

> The city streets were more or less vacant, save for a few stragglers. Everyone was away, at the seaside or in the country. The August sunshine was full of dust and melancholy. Stray cats made themselves thinner and more pliable as they struggled to get through iron palings in deserted areas. Two o'clock and three o'clock and four o'clock; J. T. Tyldesley was still not out; MacLaren and Spooner had gone

early. Four o'clock, five o'clock, to half past six, close of play, then the coming of the news that paid for everything and lifted chains of staggering time from me and rendered me as happy as ever in my life – or as relieved – for Lancashire's day was saved by a century by Tyldesley – yes, even this horrible abyss of hours was bridged somehow for me.

Cardus is not joking. Tyldesley was to him as Achilles was to the Greeks, and a match against Yorkshire as vital as any Trojan War. And so, contemplating his boyhood down the perspective of forty years, burrowing through faded impressions and half-remembered faces, Cardus arrives not at a bereavement or a crushing disappointment or a romance, but at this long-forgotten cricket match.

From all contemporary accounts it seems likely that the hero of the anecdote was a more accomplished technician than either MacLaren or Spooner, in fact one of the game's great masters. Perhaps even as a boy Cardus sensed this because he never tells us he closed his eyes during an innings by Johnny Tyldesley. Among the Tyldesley feats he saw and remembered, Cardus preserves one curiously brilliant glimpse of a dead time with such clarity that it becomes difficult for us to admit that we were not there too:

> Seven or eight Lancashire wickets were down and nearly twenty runs still wanted when a storm broke; for an hour black clouds had rumbled up. Suddenly great spots of rain fell; you could hear the smack of them on the grass; then a flash of lightning was seen across the Stretford sky. Tyldesley, quicker than the storm, hit four or five fours in one over from Buckenham; square cuts, flicks high over the slips, death-and-glory strokes as forked as the lightning. Before the players could reach the shelter of the pavilion, Old Trafford was a lake or an archipelago.

In the lurid light of such poetic recollection, it is a sort of aesthetic justice that it was this same Tyldesley who was to act as the unwitting instrument of Cardus's second and more enduring love affair with cricket.

Cardus watched the pageant of the Lancashire side with a rapturous sense of discovery. But he also watched Henry Irving and read Dickens. Soon the images were hopelessly confused, or perhaps subconsciously arranged into neat composite portraits. Nor was it the cricketers who were the beggars at the extraordinary feast gathering inside Cardus's head. He was to insist that 'for character and gusto of life, only Sir Thomas Beecham is fit to compare with A. C. MacLaren'. And he makes the point that in his dual role of cricket writer and music critic, it is among the cricketers that he has rejoiced in the more interesting manifestations of character.

Today that claim would be ridiculous, but during the period to which Cardus refers, it was very probably true enough. Edwardian cricket was a world in miniature, the most beguiling Lilliput any social historian could wish to find. Like all faithful microcosms, it reflected every nuance of the larger life it represented and it is the essence of Cardus's achievement that he was the first to perceive this and to render it whole. In England of those years, character was still being expressed through those two now discredited prisms, Class and County. The Yorkshireman Rhodes was as different in technique from the Kentishman Blythe as the Pennines are from the chalk hills of the South Downs and both were as alien to a contemporary like MacLaren as the Board School from Harrow. No two virtuosi of the Edwardian game were quite alike and there were few archetypes they did not seem to suggest as they ran unknowing across the grass. Classicism was Tom Hayward, Romanticism K. L. Hutchings. Jessop was pure melodrama and C. B. Fry was what Cardus somewhere defines as 'the dry light of ratiocination'. The oriental mysticism of Ranjitsinhji was balanced by the earthy intuitive genius of George Hirst, the quietism of Quaife by the fury of Kortright. Even those indispensable accoutrements of the Edwardian age, the seeds of decadence, were being sown, by the all-rounder Bosanquet, whose hyper-sophisticated deceptions as a spin bowler, proving that after all nothing was quite what it seemed, were at last to render the front-foot heroics of the English amateur as quaint as a cavalry charge.

As a boy Cardus imagined all these artists as gods at play, although it was not until the second fortunate fluke of his life that he appeared to realise it fully. His experience at the hands of these men, essentially aesthetic rather than sporting, was shattering enough, but its most profound effect was to be a retrospective one. Like wine, the experience had to be left in the cellars of memory for the bouquet to mature. And yet, when the lock is turned in the cellar door and its owner moves away to loftier concepts, as he had to do if the synthesis between intellect and imagination was ever to take effect, the shock to the reader is positively distressing.

What now happened to Cardus was what happens to countless thousands of young men, except that Cardus was fortunate enough to survive the experience. He caught a severe dose of what he later ruefully defined as the Higher Criticism, by which he means Wagner for Wainwright, Locke for Lockwood, and the Colossus of Rhodes for the backlift of Rhodes. He debated the New Drama with a fervour which would hardly have been justified had it been any different from the Old Drama. He puckered his brow over Nietzsche, fretted about Richard Strauss and wrestled gallantly for a while with the Metaphysical. The inevitable resulted. In the light of a concept as inscrutable as the Negation of the Negation, who in his right mind could afford to bother with the morality of Ranjitsinhji's leg glance? When Shaw was removing the boundary between villains and heroes, who cared about the boundary between Jessop and the spectators? So long as Schopenhaeur had implied the evil of the entire human race, how could any intelligent man care whether Spofforth really was a manifestation of wickedness, or just a colonial with bushy eyebrows?

There was a focus for all this aspiration, and by 1908, when Cardus was eighteen, it had ousted Old Trafford from his affections and dragged him, all too willingly, back into the centre of Manchester. And now that the location of the temple had changed, the ritual changed with it:

> I would go and stand, fairly late on Monday nights, on the pavement at the corner of Cross Street and Market Street opposite the 'Manchester Guardian' building. I would look at the lighted windows and imagine that behind any one of them Montague was at work on a dramatic notice, that Agate was adding a finishing touch, that Samuel Langford, greatest of all writers on music, was meditating on Brahms over his desk.

Nine years later, after a series of misfortunes which left their scars, he was inside the fortress, waiting for the day when he would inherit Langford's job. At this point in his life cricket had vanished utterly, and he would no more have considered seeking it out again than reverting to short trousers and lollipops. Cardus the dedicated writer with the lily of aesthetic endeavour clutched firmly between his teeth, who writes essays on musical style, on literary technique, on the Dramatic Unities, never so much as thinks of writing a word about cricket. His five summers as a professional at Shrewsbury School had first begun to wean him from Old Trafford, and now, with his writing career under way at last, there seemed no likelihood that he would ever return. He was happy reviewing anything his editors threw at him, from Music Hall to Music Hall's adjunct, the law courts. With Maclaren and company dismissed and the name of Bosanquet now indicating the metaphysical philosopher rather than his nephew the spin bowler, Cardus busied himself with the significance of the Prince of Denmark – at which point there arrived the second of his two vast slices of good fortune.

In March 1919 he suffered a nervous breakdown possibly induced by overwork. For more than two years he had flung himself into his new life at Cross Street, abandoning with terrifying recklessness all his past loves although he must have been aware, even as he composed his notices, that the world in miniature first glimpsed through MacLaren's straight drive twenty years before was sinking, with a great many other things, into the mud of Flanders. Blythe and Hutchings had died in the trenches and most of the survivors were now too old to resume their cricketing careers. The rubric of the scorecard presented an unfamiliar spectacle. Even had he ever wished to recapture the first fine careless rapture, surely it was too late?

Fortunately, the 'Manchester Guardian' was being administered, then as always, with a comical blend of pride and parsimony, and when Cardus fell ill, the chieftains saw no reason to depart from their theory that the ailing writer does not exist who is too ailing to contribute the occasional paragraph or two. Crozier, the assistant editor, 'suggested' to Cardus that he might as well spend his convalescence by taking the air at Old Trafford, where, it was also 'suggested', he might feel inclined to compose a match report or two. In this fortuitous way, circumstances which had made him a theatre programme seller, an insurance clerk, a travelling salesman and a cricket professional at a boys' school, finally relented and sent Cardus tumbling into the arms of his destiny.

* * *

He returned to the Valhalla of his boyhood in June, 1919 and reacted in the most unexpected way. His first printed report of the cricket was so banal that it barely seems credible that he could have written it:

> Lancashire, batting first, completed an innings of 280, and dismissed Derbyshire for 236, causing them to go in again and lose two wickets for 35.

The bland anonymity of this sentence makes an entertaining comparison with an attempt by the same man twelve years later to convey the depth of his frustration at the ineffectual performance of the England fast bowlers in a Test match against Australia:

> I am afraid England's heavy guns were supplied with some dubious ammunition; I had a vision of spurious shells hitting the earth and burying themselves in the middle of the wicket. They will probably explode in some innocent match in the future between M.C.C. and Hampshire, and blow everybody sky high, scorers, pavilion cat and all.

Cardus's first sentence as a cricket reporter might have been scribbled by any agency hack; 'completed an innings', 'dismissed', 'causing them to go in again', three cliches in one sentence. But what is much more surprising about that first day back at Old Trafford is that not even the sight of his dearest hero was enough to stir him into full awareness of what was happening to him:

> Tyldesley began shakily, settling down soon afterwards, showing all his old mastery of the square cut.

Cardus calls this kind of reporting 'observing the unities'. In fact it was the precise opposite, an example of the utter disunity of his mind, torn between the intellectualism of Cross Street and the imaginative fervour of the days when his memorable Aunt Beatrice had given him a shilling to go to the cricket. And yet perhaps even this is untrue. Knowing what we do of the young Cardus, we have to consider the possibility that he was not so much incapable of reconciling the aesthete and the schoolboy, as uncertain that it was the right thing to do. Years of study had convinced him for the moment that the Higher Criticism must be reserved for the Higher Arts; perhaps for the moment he was deliberately repressing his own joy at returning to scenes of boyhood enchantment. Certainly in an essay written much later, in 1952, he describes his return in very different style:

> The prisoner in Reading gaol getting a sight of the sky did not suffer emotions more poignant than mine when, in May 1919, I saw again

the green circle of Old Trafford's grass after years in the confinement of Manchester, with apparently Cricket dead forever in my heart, usurped by music and 'other things of the mind'. I saw J. T. Tyldesley bring his bat down on an off-side ball from Bestwick and cut it square for four, exactly as I had seen him cut Richardson square in 1902. So it was true, I said; I hadn't exaggerated impressions of long ago; in this dazzling manner did indeed my boyhood's hero play.

Indeed he did, but for the moment Cardus appears to have been too bemused to say so. It is clear now that he was being granted a very rare privilege, the chance to savour for the second time a deeply cherished and remote past which had still not quite gone forever. Most men at some time in their later lives indulge in the pleasure of bemoaning the loss of a childhood paradise. Cardus is unusual in that, finding it again, he was able to embrace it with all the passion of a penitent lover. Johnny Tyldesley's enduring technique had remained constant throughout the time-warp into which the sternly intellectual young man had stumbled.

No wonder that when, after a few weeks, he did sense the old passions beginning to stir, he should have run amok, burrowing among his ragbag of literary analogy and philosophical abstraction with such determination to find profundity that years later he confessed an inability to read this early work at all. Nor, it seems, could the cricketers he was writing about. 'I wonder,' he asks himself, 'what Rhodes and all the other cricketers used to think about my apostrophes about them?' Possibly they regarded him as a sort of well-meaning lunatic, especially Rhodes himself, who must have been acutely embarrassed to wake one morning in 1928 to find the details of his career likened to 'the surge and thunder of "The Odyssey" '. But if these early effusions are not so finely balanced as the later works, neither are they half as bad as Cardus says they are. At any rate, for the moment he was perfectly content to sit in the pavilion of this strange metaphysical cricket ground into which he had stumbled, taking great care not to mix socially with the unsuspecting flesh-and-blood cricketers whose movements he was using as a springboard for his fantasies. Even as Makepeace and Hallows opened each innings in so very different a style to that favoured by MacLaren and Spooner, the ghost of his Aunt Beatrice must have haunted his brain, and the trains racketing past the far end of the ground must have recalled the days when he begged for sixpences at Central Station. The past and the present performed their uncanny dance, with the broadsword of Johnny Tyldesley the Excalibur of the whole romance. When, after a while, the inevitable happened and he began to mingle with the players, the cure was immediate, and the conventional abstractions in white flannels were replaced by the brilliant portraits of the Makepeace era.

However extravagantly it may have been expressed, the personal mythology which Cardus created in those first years as a cricket reporter proved durable enough to survive all his modulations of style. For the moment, he was involved in post-war cricket and thought he sensed in its tempo and spirit something missing which was vital to the game. He struggled ceaselessly to say what it was, and only later in life realised that what had vanished was not panache at the crease but his own boyhood and the world which had contained it. The truth of one of his most contentious beliefs, that nations get the cricket they deserved, was beginning to emerge. Not until Crozier sent him back to Old Trafford was he fully competent to understand the nature of that grace bestowed upon him by MacLaren in 1900. More than half a century later he was to write:

> Our pleasures need cellarage . . . Time is the winepress; ripeness is all . . . By all means let us attend as long as we draw breath to the vineyard of fresh experience, but the fruits must wait in the bin.

Cardus's joyous realisation when he returned to Old Trafford a lapsed votary was that 1900 had been an exceptionally good year. But the vineyards of recollection are notoriously lax in their book-keeping. Sometimes the wrong labels get stuck on the bottles. In 'Autobiography' Cardus placed his return to Old Trafford at May 1919. In 'Second Innings', published three years later, the key illness and convalescence are moved forward to 1921. The discrepancy is significant only in so far as it illustrates Cardus's blessed independence of facts and figures when writing of a game whose followers are often too preoccupied with the minutiae of the averages.

In 'Days In the Sun', published in 1922, the style is a shade over-ripe, but the preliminary sketches are already being entered for what will eventually become the comprehensive portrait gallery of an era. Woolley, Richardson, Gunn, Briggs, Tyldesley and Brearley make their bow. Seven years later, in 'The Summer Game', they are joined by Fry, Ranjitsinhji, Macartney and Macdonald, ten demigods lacking only a celestial wicket-keeper to make up a full eleven. Cardus was to stick to this nucleus for the rest of his life, with MacLaren always the first choice.

In his very first book there is a perfect example of the naive delight he was now taking in his ability to codify random impressions in terms of the Higher Criticism, a delight which is supposed to have embarrassed him later on. While writing about the fast bowler Walter Brearley, he is visited by the fancy that Brearley's true place would have been in the match between Dingly Dell and All Muggleton. Even as the thought occurs to him, he begins to develop a promising theme, drawing elaborate parallels between batting technique and literary style. He suggests that W. G. Grace demands the prose of Dr. Johnson, while the 'poised, fleeting charm' of a Spooner calls to mind 'the fugitive loveliness of a Herrick'. For Joe Darling, 'let us have a little of the rolling thunder of a page by Carlyle', and 'if Ranji is your theme, call on the muse that sent Coleridge his visions of Kubla Khan'. Macartney suggests flashes of Meredithian wit and Warwick Armstrong belongs to Rabelais, possibly because at the time he happened to weigh twenty two stone. Most predictably, MacLaren requires that 'a minor Gibbon must unloose a majesty of cadence'. Here is the great Archie attending his first fitting for the imperial robes in which Cardus will at last enfold him, a process which will embrace the whole of the writer's career. In May 1920 he writes: 'MacLaren played cricket as some proud Roman might have played it'. Thirty four years later he is still describing 'the majestic MacLaren'.

By 1934, with the publication of 'Good Days', he may be said finally to have shaken off all traces of the early precious period. In 'Autobiography' he admits the excessively modest suspicion that at least two of his books will endure beyond his lifetime; perhaps he was thinking of 'Good Days' as one of them. The seventeen essays grouped under the title 'The Style is the Man' include the famous piece on Woolley, customary devotionals at the shrines of Blythe, Spooner, and Macartney, but most important of all, an attempt to gather the random impressions of two of the finest creations in modern English fiction, Cardus's MacLaren and Cardus's George Gunn.

These two men are of the deepest significance in relation to Cardus's view of life in general as well as of cricket in particular, for they represent opposing poles in his philosophy of life; an equal love for romantic gesture and the earthiness which deflates it. As Cardus paints MacLaren and Gunn, each becomes a violent contradiction of the other, the nobility of MacLaren rendered totally absurd by Gunn's irrepressible impulse to lampoon his own greatness. To MacLaren, batting was all a matter of dignity. He made the extravagant gesture because it was part of his nature to seem heroic, and if it should cost him the game it mattered not at all, because no game's winning was worth the compromise of personal honour. Gunn, in stark contrast, batted only so long as that particular activity happened to interest him, which was by no means all the time, and he would think nothing of selling a long innings to a captain who needed it. There is a contradiction here that Cardus never resolves, or really wishes to resolve, because he is never quite sure which attitude he admires the more, one which elevates cricket to a great romantic art, or the other, which ridicules its pretensions by reducing it to a rustic knockabout comedy.

Cardus is by no means unaware of this confusion, and, at one point in his autobiography, attempts to explain it in genetic terms. Never having known the identity of his own father or, if he did, taking immense pains to conceal it and professing to know nothing about the gentleman except that he had been 'tall, saturnine of countenance and one of the first violins in an orchestra', he speculates that from this shadowy figure 'I suppose I inherited my feeling for music, and an unEnglish aestheticism. From my mother I inherited my less inhuman self and a very English love of the brave humours of the street . . . I am today austere and also a man of the world'. In other words, MacLaren and Gunn or, to put it in terms of the other half of Cardus's critical existence, Edward Elgar and Marie Lloyd.

In the MacLaren essay from 'The Style is the Man', every metaphor, every simile, strains to thrust home the analogy of the imperial idea. His hero is a man 'born to wear the imperial robe'; when at the wicket 'magnificence was enthroned', and he was England's captain 'by divine right'. He moved his field with 'a royal wave of the hand', and when he dropped a catch he gave 'a sign only of kingly frustration'. Even the way he plucks his trousers as he bends down in the slips is aristocratic. He is 'proudly eminent', has 'a haughty spirit and a fine scorn'. If it is not quite the subtlest piece of portraiture Cardus ever achieved, it does create the desired effect by sheer reiteration, and is a memorable example of how a single temperament may come to dominate the mind of the man who perceives it. In time Cardus gradually transmuted this vast item of imperial statuary into human terms, until we realise with a shock of surprise that it is a Lancashire cricketer who is the hero of Cardus's long life.

When we come to the astonishing figure of George Gunn we see the other side of the coin, that side which despises pretension and knows that its most effective antidote is outrageous irreverence. In the essay Cardus's Gunn gets off to a flying start. As early as his second paragraph he is deliberately killing off a promising innings because he finds the weather too hot for batting. By paragraph five he is a private tourist in Australia recovering from illness when he receives an SOS from an England side seriously depleted by injury. Obligingly he lifts himself out of his deckchair, cuts the Australian attack to ribbons, scores a dazzling century and then saunters back to the pavilion to describe the opposition as 'Saturday afternoon bowling'. The impression is of a kindly man touched with genius, always smiling gently to himself, never in a hurry, even against the most intimidating fast bowling, which he is able to reduce seemingly to half pace by some secret known only to himself. He can regulate the speed of his run-making to suit his whims, and is so maddening to others in his amused detachment that one Yorkshire opponent actually stops at the moment of delivering the ball and shouts frustrated abuse at him. To the leonine Macdonald, one of the most lethal fast bowlers of all time, he cheerfully remarks: 'You, Mac, you couldn't knock the skin off a rice pudding'.

Twenty years later, having had time to cogitate on this extraordinary problem in human temperament, Cardus is shrewd enough to perceive that the anomalies inherent in George Gunn perhaps run deeper than mere flippancy of approach or eccentricity of technique. Gunn's uncle was the great William Gunn, pillar of Victorian orthodoxy, who 'would have thought that a characteristic innings by George went near to blasphemy'. Is it not possible, asks Cardus, 'that George Gunn's whimsicality came . . . from some revolt against a tradition of decorum long respected in the family?' We accept this charming suggestion instantly, not because it is necessarily true or, if true, verifiable, but because it heightens the colour of Gunn's portrait, lending it a symmetry which reality probably forgot to bestow, bringing forward the central figure by shading in behind him the chiaroscuro of heredity. As for the issue of literal truth and

George Gunn's relation to it, Cardus had already made his confessional a long time before. In the 1934 sketch of Gunn, he begins one anecdote with the words: 'Another picture – and if it is not true it ought to be; it certainly observes the highest order of truth, which is truth of character' words with which the cricket reporter and the creative writer begin to part company. From now on all complaint about the factual inaccuracy of the Cardus portraits becomes not only irrelevant but frivolous.

For twenty years after 'Good Days' Cardus continued to tinker with his inventions, showing the same few temperaments from fresh perspectives, lovingly adding a splash of colour here, rounding off a line there, revealing – or creating – ever more intimate details in the lives of the characters in his gallery. They seem now to have stepped out of their frames and to be moving of their own volition. At first Cardus was merely describing their movements on a cricket field, but it is now rather as though he were repeatedly bumping into them as they go about their own quite independent affairs. Walter Brearley becomes an irascible old chap from Bolton, jumping on his hat in the Long Room at Lord's as he belittles the pretensions of the fast bowlers of the modern era. At the age of 62, Charles Burgess Fry stands up in the lounge of a Leeds hotel and plays again the stroke that cost him his wicket against Middlesex thirty years before. Johnny Briggs mops his brow after bowling out Australia in a spectral Test match taking place within the asylum walls: 'Eight for 52. Bring me half a pint, George'. Glancing back over the years, Cardus notices for the first time details he has overlooked and etches them in; the brass stud at the back of Rhodes' shirt collar, the watch-chain spanning the great divide of Harry Dean's waistcoat, the rippling of the grass in the long field as Spooner's shots race to the boundary, the fine spray of white paint powdering the turf by the pavilion fence as cut after cut from Johnny Tyldesley bangs against the wood. Gunn pats the grass affectionately with the bottom of his bat as he trots for a leisurely single, and Woolley dreams his way into another dimension, scoring one hundred and forty five centuries in the process.

Cardus never loses his affection for these figures, for to do so would be to lose affection for himself. He never tires of drawing their outlines and therefore never feels the need to further stimulate his imagination by immortalising more recent figures. The furthest forward he will agree to go is to the Lancashire side of the 1920s, the Professors he came to know so well. Makepeace and company are a kind of epilogue to the main text of the MacLaren era, although even here 'the fruits have to wait in the bin'. It is thirty years before he turns back to the Professors and, in the masterly 'Myself When Young', transmutes them into more portraits to adorn the walls of the anteroom to the Edwardian collection. Makepeace apart, Cardus remained a willing prisoner of his own early past and never gave the slightest hint that his fascination for these boyhood heroes had ever flagged. He returns to them again and again, never restricted by the narrow range he has imposed upon himself, always prepared to enrich his effects with one last brushstroke.

It is not uncommon for the gifted miniaturist – and that is what Cardus is – to keep returning in this way to the same few models rooted deep in a vanished, symbolic past. If that past is badgered enough, perhaps it may be induced to surrender its secrets, and, if it is true that first impressions are the richest, then it will provide the most fertile of all sources for the creative artist. Only when the lifeblood of the past has congealed into permanence can the artist get to work as Cardus did on the day he returned to Old Trafford. The most memorable precedent to Cardus's preoccupation with what is dead and gone is the identical attitude displayed by Max Beerbohm who whiled away his long, self-imposed exile at Rapallo by constantly caricaturing Edward VII, Disraeli, Balfour and George Moore. Cardus's monarch was MacLaren, his Disraeli Walter Brearley, his Balfour C. B. Fry and his George Moore George Gunn, except that his work was informed by affection rather than by spleen. There is one way in which Cardus was more fortunate than Beerbohm, who was able to preserve the ambience of Edwardian England only by fleeing from its ruins in the belief that there was nothing left of the life he remembered. The cricket fields of his youth remained unchanged. Cardus had only to step inside the gates at Lord's to feel the presence of every great player he had ever seen perform there. Cardus's exile, a purely temporal one, was to the cricketing era of the turn of the century and his devotion to its dominant figures whose quiddity mesmerised him.

Of them all, MacLaren stands supreme, a fact which is finally brought home in the autobiography, where he emerges as a dominant force in Cardus's life, eclipsed only by the heroine of the melodrama, Aunt Beatrice. At first MacLaren is a distant god, dimly glimpsed through pink clouds of hero-worship: 'My young eyes saw him clothed in glory'. Later he became an acquaintance, then a friend, until Cardus could write without any trace of affectation:

> Among exponents of the recognised arts in England, there is only Sir Thomas Beecham whom I have found fit to compare in character and gusto of life, according to a personal point of view, with A. C. MacLaren, on or off the field.

It was MacLaren who taught Cardus 'the meaning of epic romance, style, generosity of gesture', MacLaren who was 'incapable of paltry gesture', MacLaren who 'lighted a fire in me never to be put out'. And although Cardus never quite says so, we sense a strong implication that this MacLaren belonged to a breed which has disappeared from the English scene never to return. He came from what would then have been defined as the leisured classes, as his education at Harrow shows. He was just too old to fight in the first world war and died just before the outbreak of the second. He appears also to have been one of those men whose economic underpinning was shot away at some time before the first of the wars, otherwise, he would surely have moved on to Oxbridge. Instead he worked for a while as a schoolmaster, so it must have been financial rather than academic poverty which prevented him from executing the dainty educational quadrille of his class. Clearly some rupture occurred in the family affairs which exposed the son to pressures he had not been bred to expect. Cardus is too loyal to raise the issue; other writers have been more explicit:

> A. C. MacLaren was not a very rich man, but he had the air of one. He was for a time a schoolmaster, but through most of his career lived from hand to mouth. He had the grand manner. Once, after his cricket career was closed, he approached a friend on a newspaper and offered a cricket article. The deal was closed, the article appeared, and MacLaren asked his friend if he could be paid at once, as he was 'broke'. Arrangements were made, and the author received the then princely sum of £15.15s.0. Before the day was out he had moved from the cheap lodgings where he had been staying, into the town's best hotel, and gave a grand dinner party to his friends.

Perhaps the 'friend on a newspaper' was Cardus and perhaps also the article for which he received instant payment was the same one in which MacLaren was engrossed at Old Trafford one day in the 1920s when Cardus came across him. This last glimpse is the most curious of all. In none of the portraits are any of the subjects seen beyond the context of their own small buckskin-booted world. Apart from one absurd moment when George Gunn throws his own wicket away so that he may join his wife for tea, women are never mentioned, except in this last of the MacLaren anecdotes. The ageing Archie is at Old Trafford reporting a Test match for 'The News of the World'. Rain has stopped play, and Cardus wanders the scenes of his childhood, where he finds his hero sheltering with the crowd at the entrance to the tearoom. Cardus asks him why he is not in the pavilion 'with the mighty'. 'Oh', MacLaren replies, 'I'm quite all right. I didn't receive an invitation. Probably it's miscarried':

> At this moment a waitress emerged from the interior of the tea shed carrying a tray covered with a napkin. She was about to go through the rain to an adjoining enclosure for 'lady' members; but MacLaren stopped her, and he took off his raincoat and laid it over her shoulders; then, with a wave of his hand in the waitress's direction, he said, '*Now*, my dear'.

And so the great MacLaren, apotheosised at last into pure fiction, disappears from the annals. And as he recedes into the distance, the mind jumps back to Edwardian Manchester, when the fourteen-year-old Cardus boards a train after watching a Lancashire-Yorkshire match:

> To my awe, who should enter my compartment than A. C. MacLaren and Walter Brearley. I sat trembling as I gazed at these two gods come down for a while to walk the earth or rather to ride in an ordinary railway carriage. There was no other mortal being in the compartment

except myself, and I held my breath. And MacLaren said to Brearley, 'Well, Walter, you're a nice sort of bloody fast bowler', and Agamemnon answered Ulysses thus, 'And you're a bloody fine slip fielder, aren't you, Archie?'.

The year was 1904, two years after Victor Trumper's processional around the damp cricket grounds of England, four after Cardus's Aunt Beatrice had subsidised his visits to Old Trafford with the hard-won gains of her profession. A time to be preserved if it were at all possible. The great thing was that because of their eminence in a meticulously documented field, the symbolic heroes of Cardus's childhood could be made to stand still long enough for a portrait to be achieved. You simply took your subjects and examined them at leisure, not under the microscope of the small print in Wisden, but through the prism of imagination. With less exalted figures it was not so easy. With no quirks of greatness to distinguish them, they disappeared from the face of your earth, magically, suddenly, irrevocably. The continuity was lost forever. You found yourself unable to follow their progressions or to mark their fate. There is a moment in his autobiography when Cardus turns away from his imagined gods to contemplate the imperceptible passing of time. He remembers his first games of cricket on summer evenings, games in which he and his ragged companions would ape the mannerisms of the great players. Saddened by the realisation that the past must after all vanish, Cardus, the arch-preserver of yesterday, asks:

> Where are all the boys now that were my companions? – thin Smith, who bowled slow if he had that day seen Johnny Briggs, or bowled fast and all over the place and beyond his powers if the destruction of Lancashire had been wreaked by Arthur Mold. Where is Thompson now, who was fat for his years and could never be trusted not to run us all out? And where in the world between Australia and Summer Place is the boy who was one day given his first bat?

Smith and Thompson have disappeared from the annals, but at least Cardus has helped save MacLaren and company from the same terrible fate. If George Gunn had never existed, Cardus would have found it necessary to invent him. And if in the process he adjusted the facts in the cause of truth to character, what is that in a world where any agency hack can give us the scores?

Exactly how far from the truth did Cardus really stray? We can never know, but there remain a few fragments of evidence to suggest that romanticised as they undeniably are, Cardus's characters have a firm basis in truth. At one time in the tearoom of the Lord's pavilion there hung two photographs highly relevant to this issue, and although external evidence of this kind can be dangerously misleading, here it hints at certain conclusions about the men concerned which are not altogether surprising to an observer who has formed his impressions through Cardus's prose.

The first photograph is of the 1911–12 England side in Australia. A poignant portrait indeed, the last cricketers of the old world to sail away to Australia. There stands Woolley in his floppy hat like a dreaming poet, and R. E. Foster, within a year or two now of an early death, a fine sensibility draped in comically futuristic clothes. His hat is pure gesture and the cut of his jacket lapels is a broad statement which Savile Row is not to take up for a generation. But by far the most remarkable feature of this group photograph is to be found in the front row. There sits George Gunn, rendering an effect of complete uncanny relaxation. The casual pose and the amused smile hint at vast untapped reserves. As he sits there in the Pacific sunlight of a lost morning, he appears to be indulging a bunch of schoolboys he happens to have stumbled across on his morning stroll, and whose solemn skylarking offers him a useful means of passing an hour or two. Why does the expression on Gunn's face seem to mock the pretensions of the holy relics in the Long Room nearby? Why should the observer experience the not altogether comfortable feeling that cricket is after all a silly game hardly worth an adult glance? And how does Gunn contrive to convey the impression that he is acquiescing in all this foolery only because of his fundamental good nature? There are no answers to these riddles, or indeed to any riddles to do with George Gunn, but if there were, perhaps they would explain why he could throw his wicket away one day and bat for hours on end the next, why he could stonewall like a misanthrope on Monday and persecute the deep fielders on Tuesday. But then perhaps the Gunn in the photograph is smiling for a more prosaic reason. Perhaps he is thinking of that tour four years before, when he was not a member of the selected side at all, but only a poor invalid called in to perform a rescue act while enjoying a quiet convalescence. Even that breathless triumph had its funny side for George Gunn. He later complained to Cardus that throughout his famous 119 at Sydney, his sport was ruined because over in the corner of the ground where the brass band tinkled away during the cricket, there was a cornettist who blew consistently out of tune. Whatever the solution of the riddle, the photograph is not only a hypnotic glimpse of a banished past, but a remarkable confirmation of Cardus's view.

The other photograph, which used to stand at right angles to Gunn's, is again a touring team portrait, although of a very different kind. It records an unimportant and long-forgotten trip to the West Indies by the kind of semi-official, sub-standard side whose shortcomings were in nicely calculated deference to the modest ability of the locals. There in the centre sits A. C. MacLaren. It is the late 1920s and, as Cardus somewhere puts it, Archie has almost run his course. He is an old man now and he looks it, an Edwardian anachronism whose chortling whitened moustache evokes nothing more recent than the White Knight. Patently this man is a survivor from another age, unwilling ever to play his last game, and very possibly unaware that a small boy who once shared a railway carriage with him light years ago has already apotheosised him. The Noblest Roman? Hardly, but within the fading sepia world of the photograph a sad old gentleman.

There is another surviving fragment of evidence to support Cardus's portraiture, different in kind from the other two, and more troubling than either of them because of the way it half-contradicts Cardus's view even as it confirms it. Here is J. T. Tyldesley, Cardus's brave musketeer, explaining to a newspaper reporter the source of his powers of physical endurance and revealing in the process an aspect of his gallantry which is missing from Cardus's memory:

> Well, I think that social life is developing. There are far more whist drives and dances than there used to be years ago – even ten years ago. I have done my share of whirling buxom Lancashire lasses round a room, and that helps to keep a man light and quick on his feet. Now quickness in footwork has ever been one of my greatest assets. Dancing has helped to keep me fit and it is much more fascinating than using skipping ropes. At any rate, I am amply satisfied with the results of last season.

Which results Tyldesley has in mind remains uncertain – the cricket season or the dancing season? Whatever his meaning, we will not find it in Cardus. D'Artagnan at a whist drive? Broadswords on a timbered floor? But then the miniaturist has been captivated only by one special activity. The man in a specific setting.

Cardus, who had witnessed the decline and fall of the Noblest Roman, who had watched as the lissome heroes grew arthritic and faded away, himself grew old at last, although remaining loyal to 'The Guardian' until the very end, his living standard pinched by parsimonious rates of pay, his published pieces getting shorter and shorter as the result of stupid editorial policy. At last he became convinced that he had lost the gift of animated prose, even though one of his most sublime essays, 'The Most Beautiful Woman I Know', was written in his eightieth year. It was not very long before this that I heard the shocking rumour that he was short of cash. How much truth there was in the rumour I neither knew nor cared. If it were true somebody should put employment his way. If it were false, then employment should still be put his way. One day the B.B.C. commissioned me to compile a programme about Christmas with the Victorian Colonists. I suddenly remembered a particularly moving passage in the second volume of autobiography, 'Second Innings'. Why not get Cardus to read it himself for insertion in the programme? It would take him two minutes, it would put a small fee in his pocket and it would give me an excuse to visit him. He was agreeable. This was the passage:

> Snow on the roofs, in the streets and in the fields beyond, a mantle of peacefulness. Snow falling and snow dissolving, as imperceptibly as all these happy hours were vanishing and passing on their way. At no point could we detect a transition, increase or decrease; nobody ever

saw the first or the last flake of a snowstorm. So, like to the falling snow, in which no flake is different from another, or more laden with fate or change – so with our myriad lives and the whole of our world of those days. Peace on earth, goodwill towards all men. Where was the mortal heart that didn't believe it? No man envies another and would take his place; yet the years blow us here and there, and we are sent drifting on winds as wayward as those that swing the weather-vane on the snowy roof.

When he had read the passage, there was a long silence. Then he snapped the book shut, handed it back to me and said, 'You know that's not at all bad'. I murmured agreement. Then he said, 'Couldn't do it now, you know'.

Some years later I was writing, again for the B.B.C., a series about popular music in this century and, eager to put another ten guineas in the Cardus account, went to call on him again. Once again he was far too animated to suggest senility, giving a brilliant dissertation on popular music in terms of the English obsession with class, Johann Strauss representing the uppers, Gilbert and Sullivan the middles, and Gus Elen and company the working classes. It was at this meeting that I asked him if he cared to participate in a plot to raise several thousand pounds for him. Before he replied, he told me of the munificent gift presented to him by 'The Guardian' for fifty years of dedicated service. The presentation was made at a concert given in his honour, with Sir John Barbirolli as guest conductor. Barbirolli was to present Cardus with the cheque. While some other speaker was introducing the two heroes of the evening, Cardus pointed at the envelope which his friend was to present to him and whispered, 'One hundred pounds. Two pounds per annum', at which the startled Barbirolli looked incredulous at him and suggested informing the audience and the press of the size, if that is the appropriate word, of the gift. But Cardus shook his head, smiled and accepted the envelope while observing all the formalities of the occasion. I then reassured him that my plan was different. Did he realise how large a readership he still commanded? Had it never occurred to him that there were tens of thousands of readers like myself who would pay any price for a new book in the style of 'Good Days'? Had he never thought of anthologising his essays for 'The Guardian' during the 1928 West Indian tour, his responses to events in Australia, 1932–33? Did he not realise that those fifty years represented a gold mine in unearned royalties? He seemed astonished by the suggestion that he was not an extinct volcano and asked me if I were quite sure anyone was interested in accounts of old games of cricket. I suggested we compile two or three or four volumes and give them to one of several publishers in return for an advance of three, five or seven thousand pounds. He agreed but seemed dubious as to the likelihood of anyone wishing for more Cardus books. I then went to see a publisher and the response was eager. I felt joyous that I, who had received so much from Cardus, could now help to do a little in return. Two months after our conversation he died. He was in his 86th year. He had first entered the ground at Old Trafford as a small boy. Seventy years later he was made president of the club. He had scraped pennies in his infancy as a pavement artist and ended as a knight. But the really important achievement was in the portraits he conjured by synthesising what he saw with what he dreamed of. He peopled the cricket fields and pavilions of his imagination. To put into the mouth of Wainwright the famous comment on Ranjitsinhji: 'He never made a Christian stroke in his life' may not be strictly accurate, but it is inspired cricket reporting, which tells us everything we need to know about Wainwright as well as about Ranjitsinhji. Cardus no more told lies about Dick Tyldesley than Dickens did about Dick Swiveller. In his last years he was plagued from time to time by investigators who thought they had found him out. Sometimes Cardus reacted with a public apology. He need not have bothered. His defence was mounted most effectively of all by a fellow Mancunian, Alistair Cooke, who participated in a recorded dialogue with the old man. The interviewer had pressed Cardus to confirm or deny the truth of his stories. Before he could put his case, Cooke spoke:

> I think all journalists make up all quotations. And I think when you quote the victim, when you write about a politician, or a cricketer, they don't have the rhythm, the feel of cadence, that Neville Cardus has, and they usually say things wrong. And I am absolutely shameless – I can say this, having left the 'Guardian', because of course they're so ethical they would have looked it up and changed it. But I'm always saying, 'Somebody once said, and wisely', and then I quote something I just made up. Nobody ever changes it if it's in quotes, you see. If you say it on your own account, they may mess it up in the office, which some editors tend to do. The Higher Criticism? The Higher Criticism is what goes under your by-line.

In purporting to reveal the quintessential spirit of Archie MacLaren and Johnny Briggs and Johnny Tyldesley and George Gunn and the rest of them, Cardus was all the time revealing himself. It is a not unpleasing spectacle.

BENNY GREEN

LANCASHIRE [1926]

Cardus's Wisden debut took place in the most auspicious circumstances. For the first time in more than twenty years his beloved home county had won the championship. Ever since becoming the cricket correspondent for 'The Manchester Guardian' and a delighted habitue of Old Trafford, Cardus had awaited the triumph to come with a fierce, affectionate pride in the Lancashire cricketers at whose hands he had received the accolade of dressing-room acceptance. The last time the trophy had come to Manchester had been in the fast receding days of his boyhood when, with sixpences wheedled out of travellers arriving at Central Station or earned from selling newspapers in the street or as part of the largesse often scattered on him by the lady bountiful of his childhood, the boldly amoral Aunt Beatrice, he had been rendered tipsy with the wine of MacLaren's strokeplay, with the gentlemanly expertise of Reggie Spooner, with Johnny Tyldesley's broadsword of a bat. And if, after the passing years and the abyss of the Great War, there were no playing survivors from the 1904 championship side, there were at least intimations of dynastic consistency with the appearance in both lists of the names Hallows and Tyldesley. By 1926 Johnny Tyldesley had retired to run a sporting goods shop in Deansgate where, among the stock he dispensed, were copies of the same almanack in whose pages he had once featured so prominently. Dick, his podgy namesake who was unrelated, had yet to graduate into the side. But Johnny's brother Ernest had been the batting star of the 1926 side, scoring nine centuries and heading the county averages with nearly seventy runs an innings. Charlie Hallows finished in fourth place with a thousand runs and was to hit 52 centuries for the county. Charlie must often have evoked thoughts in Cardus's mind of his uncle, James Hallows, an epileptic who so overcame the frailty of his own constitution as to do the double in the 1904 championship year. Poor James had died, still a young man, in 1910, but his nephew was to retain his place in the county side until the early 1930s.

In old age Cardus looked back to this 1926 side and described the difficulties in which he found himself almost every time the Lancashire side went in to bat:

I found myself hard-pressed many days to cope as a writer with Lancashire's well-connived batting policy. First of all, the wearing-down process, so that at tea, after four hours, Lancashire's total was often not more than 150 for three. But I had now to telegraph a thousand words to the 'Manchester Guardian' if the match were being played miles away from Manchester. Then, at half-past six, I would send the remaining 800 words, to complete my daily portion. The first message was not once but many times a justifiably severe censure on

Lancashire's wasteful use of a perfect wicket. But after tea, Iddon or Ernest Tyldesley, or somebody or other, would launch the most vigorous attack, and at half-past six Lancashire's total had, after all, approached 350 or 400. It took much practice and instinct to get through my column and a half without exposing myself to the ribaldry of both the Lancashire players and those Lancashire supporters not on the spot. 'He's bin at that foony stoof agen'.

Despite the championship victory, 1926 must have been in one sense a sad year for Cardus, who watched in dismay as the Lancashire committee dismissed his favourite cricketer, Cecil Parkin. The misdemeanour was petty enough and insignificant enough to inflame the small minds of the committeemen who took offence at some journalistic peccadillo which appeared under Parkin's name. Too loyal to disclose the identity of the ghostwriter responsible, Parkin received his marching orders which he accepted with his usual breezy unconcern and spent the next ten years performing in the leagues. Cardus called him the first Jazz cricketer, by which, presumably, he meant that the rhythms of Parkin's temperament reflected the liberated ways of the new age. Certainly he never deferred to the amateurs who captained him and never lost an opportunity to poke fun at the ineptitude of his initialled betters. One who came in for the best of Parkin's derision was J. W. H. T. Douglas, his captain in the disastrous 1920–21 tour of Australia. Douglas enjoyed putting himself on and bowling for long spells. 'That's right, Mr. Douglas', Parkin would say, 'you go on and bowl 'em in and I'll go on after tea and bowl 'em out'. Once, with an innocent glance at an Australian scoreboard too huge not to be readable, Parkin gravely advised, 'Try the other end, Mr. Douglas, you can see your analysis from there'. A natural comedian who was also a gifted amateur magician, Parkin died, still only in his fifties, in 1943, while Cardus was far away in Sydney, Australia, composing an autobiography in which there was no room to mention the cricketer he had lovingly dubbed 'The Card'. But in 1952, composing the finest retrospective essay on youth ever achieved by any sporting writer, he had this to say:

A fellow of jest sadly finite! Witty, humorous, a stormy petrel, herald of the approaching times of irreverence and disrule, and all the more lovable for his delinquencies. A source of happiness to countless Lancashire men and women, and Lancashire lads and lasses. May the soil rest lightly on him.

Towards the very end of his life Cardus, in a radio conversation with fellow-Mancunian Alistair Cooke, revealed the richest of all Parkin's jokes. He had been born in Yorkshire.

For the first time since 1904 Lancashire are champion county. Their success was popular throughout the country, partly because cricketers felt that the best interests of the game would be served by a change, at long last, in the leadership. Lancashire's supremacy over Yorkshire could be challenged easily enough: Yorkshire were undefeated and amongst the teams they severely thrashed was Lancashire. Moreover, Lancashire had to bow the knee to so modest a county as Leicestershire. Invincibility ought to be one of the attributes of the conqueror; Yorkshire throughout the summer was certainly a harder side to beat than Lancashire. On the other hand, it must be admitted that towards the summer's end, Yorkshire lost much of match-winning ability, even at the same time that Lancashire went forward, match after match, in destroying vein. During August any team placed in a bad corner would have found it easier to force a draw against Yorkshire than against Lancashire.

Lancashire invariably begin a season in ambitious spirit – with eyes on the championship. But last summer there were periods during which it was a positive virtue to practice optimism at Old Trafford. Yorkshire won at Bradford in an innings, and Lancashire's batting in the game was deplorable. Then followed the dèbacle at Ashby-de-la-Zouch. Leicestershire won by 144; and there were not wanting pessimists in the Lancashire Eleven itself, who prophesied that at the end of the season Lancashire would be amongst the lower half of the championship table. The match at Ashby-de-la-Zouch has been called a blessing in disguise. The team thenceforward was new in temper and ability alike. Ernest Tyldesley ran into one of the richest veins ever struck by a batsman in this country. Of their last eleven matches Lancashire won nine outright; the other two were won on the first innings and one of these was against Yorkshire. At Old Trafford, on August Bank Holiday, the biggest crowd that has ever witnessed a single day's cricket in this country saw Lancashire make 500 against Yorkshire. In that handsome total, compiled in such a match, is perhaps Lancashire's strongest justification of their present lofty position. A thunderstorm at night, followed by an impossible wicket and some clever bowling by Iddon, saved Lancashire from defeat at Bournemouth. Had that game been lost, the championship could scarcely have come again to Old Trafford.

Lancashire's success was the more remarkable because it might be argued that the side was not as strong in bowling as in 1925. Parkin ceased to play for Lancashire after the fourteenth match, and, of course, Parkin had always been a 100 wickets bowler. Sibbles did not fulfil his promise of twelve-months previously; and Richard Tyldesley, though consistently steady, was rarely making the ball come from the pitch with his old keenness. Iddon and Woolley were merely useful change-bowlers. Watson could not bowl during August, owing to a strain. The side therefore must be described as short, on the whole, of the bowling strength we commonly get from a champion county. It was Macdonald, more than any other one player in the eleven who won the matches at the season's end, and so took advantage of those chances which came Lancashire's way – partly as a result of the ultra-cautiousness which hindered Yorkshire. Macdonald was rarely as fast as he was in 1921. None the less, he was far faster than the average English fast bowler.

His temperament seemed to thrive on any situation which gave his side a sporting chance; he won more than one game against time in a manner that did credit both to his imagination and opportunism. He is a bowler of varying moods – and varying paces. But, at a pinch, he can achieve true greatness, both of technique and temperament.

The batting was more reliable all-round than in recent Lancashire sides. The young players, Iddon, Sibbles and Woolley imparted some substance to the innings at its latter end, and even Macdonald made a century against Middlesex. But it was from Makepeace, Hallows and Ernest Tyldesley that authentic batsmanship came. Watson was again useful, but he is not exactly a stylist. Ernest Tyldesley had a wonderful summer. At one stage his consistency recalled the C. B. Fry of 1901. In nine innings from June 26, Tyldesley scored 1,128 runs with an average of 141. He scored seven centuries in consecutive matches – and four in successive innings. He was, at his best, as stylish as he was prolific. A big innings by Tyldesley will exhibit every stroke excepting the cut, all done with infinite grace and mastery. He had bad luck to play in only one of the Test matches. Makepeace was his true dependable self; on a bad pitch he still has few superiors in cricket to-day as a defensive batsman. Against Notts in the last crucial match of Lancashire's season, he transformed himself with the adaptability of genius into the quick scorer demanded by the situation. Hallows fell away a little in aggregate, and dependability. He often got out when apparently set, by sheer thoughtlessness. With more concentration, ball by ball, he would be one of our best left-handed batsmen. Major Green led his men with much tactical instinct, and better still, with understanding of character. He played many useful innings and is a cleverer batsman than he himself would seem to think.

Duckworth had many brilliant days behind the wicket, and, but for an inexplicable untidiness that sometimes comes over his work, he would be in the running for the position of Strudwick's successor. Sibbles ought to learn to spin the ball. Iddon advanced as a dashing maker of runs; he showed also much aptitude to exploit spin on a bowler's wicket. Other young cricketers likely to do well for Lancashire in the near future are Farrimond, a wicket-keeper with some utility as a bat; P. T. Eckersley, and Woolley – a useful right-handed batsman and bowler, though like Sibbles he depends overmuch on the new ball. A young player, named M. L. Taylor, a left-hander, may easily develop into a beautiful batsman; already he has style.

The season at Old Trafford was admirably managed and proved very prosperous. The balance sheet showed a surplus of over £10,000. A successful benefit was given to Mr. W. E. Howard, who for many years has done good work on the Old Trafford pavilion staff.

FIFTY YEARS OF LANCASHIRE CRICKET [1951]

Lancashire went on to complete a hat-trick of championship victories, and Cardus was to apotheosise the triumphant side with such inspiration as to render them immune to the usual process of decay which attends the later lives of once-eminent cricketers. Makepeace and Macdonald were preserved in their prime in the aspic of the most memorable literary style ever perfected in the cricket press rooms of the world. But a quarter of a century was to pass before Cardus returned to the pages of the Almanack, during which time the world and its ways had changed beyond recognition. The great men of the championship treble had long since disappeared from the field, Macdonald the victim of a road accident, the others into the dressing-rooms and pavilions of retirement. Between Cardus's debut in Wisden and his return twenty five years later, a second devastating world war had left Britain impoverished and about to dismantle the Empire. Careers had been shortened by the war, continuity breached, and the new Lancashire side, co-champions of 1951, were in no way comparable to the vintage side of the county's heyday. But Cardus does what he can to apply a roseate glow to his summary, even though it is quite clear that his heart abides in a time lit by lamps which no eye would ever see again.

In his review of half a century of Lancashire cricket, Cardus applies to the 1950 side the same canons of judgement as he had to Makepeace's champions, canons which had been formed in the raptures of boyhood, when the known world was encompassed by the boundary ropes at Old Trafford, and a comprehensive range of godhead represented by MacLaren, Spooner and Johnny Tyldesley. Twice in his recollections Cardus confuses the issue of his date of birth. In his opening paragraph he suggests that he was nine years old in July, 1899, and later he says that at Whitsun, 1900 he was 'rising eleven'. The notorious imprecision of Cardus's grasp of his own past may have been calculated, an attempt to touch up the self-portrait, or it may have been sheer carelessness. Whatever the explanation, his birth certificate tells that he was ten years old in July 1899, and at Whitsun of the following summer, rising twelve. Much more important to readers of a later generation was his ability to conjure an image which, once experienced, is never forgotten. Cardus described the comic effect of Walter Brearley's irascibility several times in his life but never better than in his description of beer glasses left undrained on the counter of the Long Room bar.

The most profound difference between the Cardus of the Wisden debut and the man who returned twenty five seasons later is a matter of the consummation of a life. Cardus spent the second world war in Sydney where he finally achieved the full-length self-portrait of his autobiography, a work of compelling artifice which presented him as he desired the world to see him. That work stands alongside the first seven chapters of Chaplin's 'My Autobiography' and the first volume of Wells' 'Experiment in Auto-biography' as the definitive account of the life of the urban poor in modern Britain. There had also been the collections of 'Manchester Guardian' pieces published as neat little hardbacks and the finest account of a tour ever published, 'Australian Summer', a witty narrative describing the fortunes and misfortunes of G. O. Allen's side which toured Australia in the winter of 1936–7 and so very nearly thwarted Bradman. The Cardus who summarised the Lancashire side of 1926 was a rising star. The Cardus who here looks back over fifty years of Lancashire cricket is an acknowledged master.

I FIRST saw Lancashire playing cricket one dull day in July 1899. I am at a loss to say why I went to Old Trafford at the age of nine, just as I am at a loss to explain where my gate-money came from. I wasn't interested in cricket then: my passion was football, which we played on the rough fields of Moss Side, with coats for goalposts. My heroes were Billy Meredith and Bloomer – I firmly believed that Bloomer had once split a goalpost in halves with a kick from just beyond the half-way line. I lived five miles at least from Old Trafford and, as I say, it remains a mystery that I should have entered Old Trafford in July 1899, in time to see G. L. Jessop come to the wicket to join C. L. Townsend, who scored 91, and very tall he looked, and graceful.

UNDER THE SPELL

Jessop left no indelible impression on me this time but I remember a beautiful innings by F. H. B. Champain, and with the naïve love of a boy to play upon words, I thought he was perfectly named. The only thing I remember about Lancashire from my introduction to the county is that one of the bowlers was named Lancaster, which also seemed appropriate to my dawning sense of the wonder of words and English.

Next year, 1900, I fell entirely under the spell of the game and of Lancashire cricket, once and for all and for ever. I saw – my second match! – Johnny Briggs take all the ten wickets against Worcestershire. After the ninth had fallen to him, Mold bowled wide; but for many overs Johnny couldn't pitch a ball in the danger zone. He was so excited; he bounced about as though uncontrolled and uncontrollable.

WHITSUN AT OLD TRAFFORD

My next match at Old Trafford took place on Whit-Monday 1900, and it was not Yorkshire. Believe it or not, Kent were playing Lancashire at Whitsun in 1900, when matches began on Mondays and Thursdays – so that often the great grounds of England – Old Trafford, Trent Bridge, Headingley, The Oval and Lord's – might any one of them be standing vacant on a sunny Saturday, the game having come to the end, or lost all interest, on the second day, the Friday. There's richness for you! . . .

Well on Bank Holiday at Whitsun 1900, I arrived at Old Trafford at
nine in the morning, paid my sixpence, and got a front bench directly
facing the pavilion. At twelve o'clock Lancashire took the field, and
C. J. Burnup and Alec Hearne began Kent's innings. Mold bowled from
the Stretford end, Briggs from the Old Trafford end – a very fast bowler
and a very slow bowler, each using the new ball (and there wouldn't be
another new ball available or permissible until the Kent innings was
finished, or until the 'old' ball had been – as John Gunn once put it to
me – 'knock'd in two').

In quick time Mold and Briggs began to ruin the Kent innings. Briggs
bowled Hearne for 2; Mold shattered all the stumps of W. H. Patterson
for 1; Mold uprooted a stump defended by B. D. Bannon for 0–11 for
3 and I gloated. I always liked to watch cricket alone these early years;
I could wallow better in my passions with nobody to intrude. Mold's
speed was so terrific that the Kent batsmen apparently couldn't see the
ball. With all of a boy's patriotic heartlessness, I derided the helplessness
of Hearne, Bannon and Patterson; and my ridicule and lust were intensified when J. R. Mason came in and played forward and missed Mold
three or four times, absolutely beaten, obviously 'out any minute'.

A GREAT INNINGS

At the other end of the wicket, a little man was putting his bat both to
Briggs and Mold in a way I didn't like at all; his name, as I say, was
C. J. Burnup. But there was no need to worry about him – surely! –
because Mold was about to send one or two or all three of J. R. Mason's
wickets flying this coming over. The truth is that Mason and Burnup
stayed in for nearly three hours and added 110 or thereabouts, and that
after Mason had been caught at the wicket off Mold for 68, another
Kent amateur named T. T. N. Perkins, cut and drove with an ease and
elegance which utterly spoiled my holiday; he scored 88. At half-past six
a disconsolate Lancashire boy rising eleven walked all the way home,
down Shrewsbury Street, past Brooks' Bar, all the way on foot to Rusholme, wondering why Mold had allowed such disappointments to
occur . . . Kent had batted all day – 408 or so for 7 or 8, and C. J.
Burnup was out in the last over, or almost the last, of the afternoon;
'c Smith b Cuttell 200,' an enormous total for one batsman – and such
a small and modest one – in those days when the currency of batsmanship
was not yet inflated but remained on the gold standard. I looked up this
match in the newspapers the other day and found that memory had not
played me false in a single important fact. One account of this day's play
said, describing Burnup's innings, 'it was a valuable effort, and though
slow at periods, an occasional lack of enterprise on Mr. Burnup's part
was excusable in view of Kent's bad start.' 'Slow at periods' – 200
compiled in a little more than five and a half hours by a batsman not
regarded one of the country's 'dashers,' and, moreover, after a furious
and successful onslaught by Mold! It would be regarded a quickish
innings to-day, if played uphill.

I received compensation next day for this bitter taste of adversity on Bank Holiday. I saw Johnny Briggs make a half-century in each of Lancashire's innings; he slashed skimming drives over cover-point's head, and frequently he 'blocked' a ball and pretended to risk a run, 'chancing it,' to use the period's expression. Such cricket would be regarded reprehensible from any famous contemporary England cricketer.

I was lucky to begin my long years of devoted attention at Old Trafford with three such grand games. Of course it was but seldom I could 'repair' to the great ground where not so long ago the run stealers had flickered to and fro. My pocket-money didn't run to sixpence a week. But I devoured the cricket scores and rejoiced in the 'cricket edition' and was afraid to turn to the 'close of play' scores. One evening I read in the stop-press: 'R. H. Spooner b Wilson 0.' R. H. Spooner was my favourite cricketer, and whenever he failed much of the savour went out of my life, not to say the purpose. But next evening, or the evening after, a worse blow befell me. Again I turned to the 'close of play' score and there, in cold print, was this announcement: 'R. H. Spooner b Wilson 0,' – a 'pair of spectacles' for him. I hadn't the heart, that summer evening, to play cricket with my schoolmates. I wandered the streets blighted.

MAJESTIC BATSMEN

It is commonly thought that Lancashire cricket has always expressed North-country dourness and parsimony. This is an error. In 1904 Lancashire won the County Championship without losing a match; and until an August staleness afflicted the team, the rate of scoring by Lancashire averaged 70 to 80 – some days 100 – an hour. No county has boasted three batsmen going in Nos. 1, 2 and 3 possessing more majesty than A. C. MacLaren's, more style and ripple of strokes than R. H. Spooner's, more broadsword attack and brilliance than Johnny Tyldesley's. In 1904 and 1905 the Lancashire XI was usually chosen from A. C. MacLaren, R. H. Spooner, J. T. Tyldesley, L. O. S. Poidevin, James Hallows, Sharp, Cuttell, W. Findlay, A. H. Hornby, Kermode, W. Brearley; and there were in those early 1900's Harold Garnett, and Heap, Huddleston and Worsley. The team was undefeated, not only in 1904 but until half-way through the summer of 1905, and then Surrey overwhelmed them at Aigburth. The 'unbeaten certificate' – to quote the metaphorical language of the Press of those years – was twice threatened in 1904, by Yorkshire at Leeds: a century by Tyldesley saved the day, and he batted more than four hours for it, one of the few slow innings of his life.

Again – I seem to remember – Surrey were winning easily at The Oval on a Saturday in 1904 – the third day, before lunch – but during the interval sun baked a wet turf and Huddleston's off breaks were unplayable. Given a 'sticky' pitch, Huddleston was a very dangerous spinner, but not the equal of 'Razor' Smith of Surrey, who could make the ball go the other way as well. Brearley was equal to the physical feat of bowling all day; he was nearly as dangerous to limb off the field as on it when he prodded you in the chest punctuating his story of what he had done to Victor Trumper. He was known to push people the whole length of the bar in the Long Room at Lord's, leaving their drinks far away, completely isolated.

DANGEROUS PITCH

Poidevin, from Sydney, would have played for Australia had he not settled as a doctor of medicine in Manchester. James Hallows, left-handed batsman and bowler, had rare gifts but poor health. He might easily have become one of the greatest of all-round England players; he was nearly that as it was. Cuttell at his best would to-day be one of the first choices for an England XI. MacLaren, Spooner, Tyldesley, and Brearley all played for England in 1905; and Jack Sharp joined them in the English rubber of 1909. In 1901, the wicket at Old Trafford was so dangerous that Sharp took 100 wickets in a season and C. B. Fry extracted from the turf some pebbles or foreign bodies which subsequently were exhibited to the public in the window of Johnny Tyldesley's sports shop in Deansgate; we looked at them in silent wonder like people who gape in the geological museum. Incredible that during this same season Tyldesley scored 3,000 runs, playing half his innings on this rude, rough turf at an average of 55 and more. I doubt if any batsman alive or dead has so strongly as this established his genius.

So far, I have been recalling the MacLaren epoch in Lancashire cricket. There was not one recognised and accredited 'stonewaller' in the XI, for Albert Ward – beautiful in forward movement, whether scoring or not – belonged to a vintage preceding the Championship summer of 1904 – and Makepeace came later. There was a subsequent A. H. Hornby period of some ebullience and insecurity, with A. Hartley sound as a rock and the skipper himself chafing on the leash for a drive over the rails. But hereabouts the bowling lost the axe-edge. Harry Dean persevered, and Frank Harry, off-spinner, was a willing horse. During the MacLaren supremacy the Lancashire attack had enjoyed rare resources, from the 'sticky' wicket terrors of Webb, who but for a sceptical view of himself might have scaled the heights, to Brearley, Dean and Kermode, not forgetting William Cook, who round about 1905 would have glorified the England attack with his fast bowling, but preferred the leagues.

Now comes a gap in my memory's frieze. In 1912, 1913 and 1914 I was playing as a professional at Shrewsbury School, and temporarily lost sight of doings at Old Trafford. I am vague about these three seasons; others and earlier ones I can live again in my mind's eye to a detail, as though they all happened only last year. In 1919 I picked up the broken thread, and this time I found myself *actually* paid to watch and delight in Lancashire cricket, as correspondent of the *Manchester Guardian*.

In 1919, a season of two-day games, Old Trafford discovered Charles Hallows, nephew of James, another superb left-handed batsman – one who might easily have served as England's reply to Warren Bardsley. Cecil Parkin, who as far back as 1914 had flickered a will o'the wisp light on one or two fields now rose to more than fame as a magnificent bowler; he won the love of that public that revels in a 'character'; he was a combination of Springheel Jack, merry-andrew and, on a damaged pitch, a master of a breakback quick as the execution blade. His 'googly' was his mocking cap-and-bells. 'Lol' Cook maintained the classical tradition of length; James Tyldesley exploited fast in-swingers to a leg-trap and Richard Tyldesley persuaded many batsmen to 'feel' for leg-spin real and imaginary.

TRIPLE CHAMPIONS

Myles Kenyon prepared the way to a Lancashire renaissance. Then, under the firm, shrewd and humour-loving leadership of Leonard Green, Lancashire surpassed even the Yorkshire of the Rhodes-Robinson dynasty or 'rump'. For three consecutive years Lancashire led the County Championship – 1926, 1927 and 1928 – and again in 1930 thanks a good deal to E. A. McDonald, most beautiful of fast bowlers of our time with his silent curving sinuous run to the crease, most deadly in pace and abrupt rise to the batsman's wrists and – now and then – higher still.

The batting policy was set by Makepeace; if the toss were won, the plan was to stay there all day for 300 at least and to wear enough sheen from the pitch for McDonald. On 'sticky' turf nobody has excelled Makepeace in the art of passive resistance with the 'dead' bat, left-hand lightly gripping top of the handle. But, at a pinch, Makepeace would reveal resource and strokes. At Trent Bridge in 1920, Lancashire lost two wickets for next to nothing against Barratt, bowling formidably on a 'green' pitch; the accredited stroke-players were out, so Makepeace was obliged to attend to the necessary job of making the runs. He was not defeated until after tea, for 152, scored in three hours fifty minutes, with eighteen fours. His left side and chest were black and blue from bruises.

The Lancashire 'ca canny' batting tactics told of the change in the economy and social life of Lancashire county at large. Gone the old Manchester cosmopolitan opulence and the piles of 'brass' in the hinterland, symbolised by the great amateurs, MacLaren, Spooner and the Brearleys, the Hollinses, and by Tyldesley, Sharp, and the rest. The county in the 1920's lived 'near the bone', and Lancashire cricket more than hinted of this transformation. The team became notorious as a spoiler of cricket festivals: at Eastbourne and Cheltenham, retired colonels turned pale when they heard that Lancashire were batting. At Old Trafford or in Yorkshire at Bank Holiday time, a Yorkshire innings was quite skittish compared to one by Lancashire. But there was organised technique during the Makepeace regime; the scoring was slow 'on principle', not because these fine players couldn't have scored quicker had they chosen.

GOOD COMPANIONS

There was vast humour in it all; to travel round the country with Lancashire in these years was an education in shrewd cricket sense as well as a revelation of North-country nature. Peter Eckersley, and later Lister, controlled a great if mixed company because they understood character as much as cricket. Under Eckersley, the County Championship was won once more in 1934. Ernest Tyldesley added aggression to Makepeace's Fabianism though he could, given the cue, be obstinate enough. At his best he was amongst not only the prolific run-getters of the period; he was one of the artists as well.

To-day Lancashire cricket is again – or was last year – in the ascendancy, sharing the honours with Surrey. There is surely an even more lustrous future ahead, for youth is there in plenty, commanded by a captain who every day gains strength as batsman and strategist. Few counties have so persistently honoured a proud tradition. A noble array of names can readily be chosen from Lancashire men fit to stand against Australia for England, chosen from teams of the last fifty years, teams of my time, in a match imagined, and because not ever to be played in Time and Space, seen in immortal sunshine – and cloud – at Old Trafford: – A. C. MacLaren, R. H. Spooner, Tyldesley (J. T.), Tyldesley (E.), Washbrook, Oldfield, H. G. Garnett (or W. Findlay) wicket-keeper, Jack Sharp, Parkin, Dean and Brearley. And I have been compelled to leave out – Heaven forgive me! – Makepeace, Cuttell, the two Hallows, 'Dick' Tyldesley, A. H. Hornby, Heap. I don't include McDonald because he was an Australian. And I am not forgetting Barnes, unearthed by MacLaren. Though he played at least one whole season for Lancashire – I saw him lay low the might of Surrey at Old Trafford in 1902 on a perfect wicket, until Vivian Crawford took charge of him, backed-up by Captain H. S. Bush – Barnes can hardly be said ever to have belonged to Lancashire. Barnes was a man born to possess, not to be possessed. And if I omit Tattersall from my Lancashire team representative of the best in the country over the span of half a century, it is not from want of enthusiasm about his talent, and not because I am unaware that in 1950 he was the most successful and omnivorous bowler since Arthur Mold (a Northamptonshire man, by the way), but because, being young, Tattersall has not yet had the chance to fix immovably his claims on the attention of history. That he will do so, we can be pretty sure, is only a matter of time.

A CALL FOR CULTURE [1952]

Safety First Can Ruin Cricket

Cricket has always endured cheerfully enough the strictures of greybeards who reject the heroes of the new age, whoever they might happen to be, and moan for the lost glories of their youth. In the years when Sobers and Barry Richards were rewriting the record books, there were those who sighed for the vintage days of Compton and Edrich. But even as the Middlesex Twins were performing miracles daily, aged gentlemen demanded the sweet orthodoxies of Hobbs. Hobbs himself had broken W. G. Grace's record of 126 first-class centuries, and by so doing reminded the Oldest Member of the lost Victorian leader. And yet there were men a hundred years ago who regarded W. G. as an impudent whippersnapper not fit to be compared with the really great players of Fuller Pilch's time. And so it will always be, a dance in reverse to the music of time, ever back and back again, until at last the only cricket ground worthy of the mention is at Broadhalfpenny Down. Raymond Robertson-Glasgow summed up the situation beautifully when he ended his poem about just such an old curmudgeon with the couplet:

I ceas'd, and turn'd to Larwood's bounding run,
And Woolley's rapier flashing in the sun.

Cardus's essay in the 1952 almanack smacks of the retrospective view, but with some justification. He was genuinely concerned because he believed he saw in the cricket he was watching a decline into drab efficiency. He was by no means alone in his doubts, but two factors distinguish the drift of his conclusions. He believes that unless the professional cricketers of England mend their ways, the game is headed for crisis. He can see, long before the event, a time when commercial expediency will eclipse style, when the result will be everything and everything else nothing, when cricket will be obliged to choose between the fleshpots and extinction. He implores the players, the committees, the groundsmen, to put matters to rights while there is still time. Tragically, his cry for the subtleties of a Blythe or a Rhodes was to go unanswered, although his dream of a new generation of genuinely fast bowlers was to be realised quickly enough with the sudden advent of Trueman, Statham and Tyson.

The other aspect of Cardus's prescience concerns the great placebo of a later age: coaching. The rhetorical question which he asks about the great stars of the past is unanswerable and, had he surveyed the product of the cricket schools a generation later, he might have been forgiven for murmuring 'I told you so'. It is revealing that Cardus, one of the first educated commentators to question the sense of mass coaching, should himself have been a product of the intuitive school, a consummate creative artist who had made the discovery that if a thing is really worth doing, then its essence cannot be taught. Having learned that nobody can teach you to write like Cardus, he made his deductions with Sherlockian relentlessness, concluding that nobody can teach any man to bat like Hammond, or bowl like Keith Miller, or field like Constantine. What a grim poetic irony that when the coarsenesses of the one-day game finally arrived, the scene of the debacle should have been Cardus's idea of heaven, the Lancashire county ground at Old Trafford. In 1952 his plea for brighter cricket was taken by most people to be the predictable rumbling of a man growing old too fast for his own liking. A generation later the cricket world was to eat its words.

CRICKET, more than any other game, is able at its best to rise above competitive appeal and results; it can show its fine arts entirely for our pleasure – our aesthetic pleasure. In fact as a game, pure and simple, dependent on who loses and who wins, cricket is often a poor substitute for football, tennis, racing or tiddly-winks. I am, of course, discussing first-class matches running to three days and more; the crowd is usually largest on the first day when there's no prospect of a decision. A third afternoon, promising a fight, is played to empty benches and to the apparently homeless ancients of the pavilion.

Obviously a game that absorbs so long a time for a match, so that the end is not clearly seen in the beginning, must, at bottom, depend on a spectacular and human interest; the players must possess something about them that allures us, apart from what the score-board says.

Cricket is in full attractive health when all its departments are being exhibited by exponents with a personal touch. We will gladly forget the clock and the fact that no finish is likely to be approached until tomorrow at the earliest, if all the time there are strokes to look at, good bowling of variety to look at, and good swift fielding in all positions to look at. No game equals cricket for range of technique and duration of scene. It cannot hope in the present age to hold its own with other and faster competitive games unless also the players are constantly interesting in themselves.

Of how many cricketers at the moment may we say that they are worth watching for distinguished individual skill? Of how many contemporary batsmen may we say that if they stay at the wicket an hour we are sure to see fine free stokes? I can't think of six. Hutton, the 'Master', is not certain in an innings of three hours not to bore us and deny his powers.

Nobody ever saw an innings by Woolley that, given half an hour's duration, was not glorified by at least three glorious hits. The same can be said of Duleepsinhji, Hammond, Barnett, Dacre, Cyril Walters, Bakewell, Bowley of Sussex, Ernest Tyldesley . . . but I could fill much valuable space with the list, all names more or less of cricketers in action in the same seasons.

Any organism to be really vital must function in all its parts. 'Masterful' batsmanship does not mean the ability, patience and endurance to amass runs. The art of batsmanship comprises strokes to all parts of the field. Everybody has heard of the square-cut But how many times do we get the opportunity nowadays to applaud the flashing beauty of it?

Years ago, J. T. Tyldesley of Lancashire scored 165 against Surrey at Old Trafford, and when he was out there was a streak of white powder in front of the rails of the pavilion (the pavilion at Old Trafford is square to the wicket). Tyldesley's square cuts had knocked the paint off. Is it argued that bowlers these times can't pitch to the off? Very well, then; genius is resourceful and discovers other ways and means.

Batsmanship signifies square cuts, drives, straight and to the on and off, on the ground or over the in-fielders' heads, leg glances and leg-hits; hooks and pulls. I do not exaggerate if I say here and now that it is possible to go to a cricket match in our present period and not in a whole day witness half the stokes that are the game's crown jewels; what is more, we won't see many attempts to perform some of them.

So with bowling. The art of bowling comprises pace, spin, medium and slow, left or right-handed, variations of flight, and all the rest. English cricket, as I write these lines, lacks a great fast bowler, lacks a great slow left-hand bowler. How, then, is it arguable that the contemporary cricket is 'as good as ever' and in a state of health, if in so many of its departments there is no life, no distinguished executant?

You wouldn't say of a man that he was proof that the human physique is as good as ever it was if he happened to be deaf, unable to walk well, but was sound of heart. You wouldn't maintain that an orchestra was as good as it might be if it didn't have any good brass nowadays, and no first flute.

And without strokes in all directions, fielding is bound to lose power to charm the eye for want of opportunity. And good fielding is essential to cricket as a constantly entertaining spectacle, guaranteed to convey pleasure to thousands, runs or no runs.

The tendency to put emphasis on cricket as competition, an affair of match-winning and percentages, is dangerous, and if it is not checked the game may easily, as a three-day matter, become obsolete after another decade. The result is important; we all want to win. But by its constitution, cricket must retain its unique fascination as spectacle, as pageant in summer time, and medium or vehicle for the expression of character in action.

I can't believe there is less innate talent for cricket in English boys and men to-day than in the past. But I do insist that the atmosphere and general governance don't bring the best out of a gifted player. The pressure of the spirit of the age hinders freedom and individuality. Life in this country is rationed. Can we blame Bloggs of Blankshire if in a four-hour innings he lets us know that his strokes are rationed?

The times we live in are against the bold extravagant gesture. Our first-class cricketers seldom are allowed to play for fun. Their 'committees' are shortsighted enough to imagine that the crowd will flock for ever to sit in silence while batsmen wait for the shine to wear off and then 'dig themselves' in; while bowlers wheel them up mechanically on the short and safe side. The multitude storms your gates in a season when your team is winning the County Championship. But you can't hope to win it every year. . . .

The future of the game in its present first-class shape and procedure is dependent on the revival of personal art and initiative. In 1905 the Australians discovered that Frank Laver had learned to swing the ball dangerously. The English air and the green turf helped his swerve, and for weeks he carried all before him. When he arrived at Old Trafford he clean bowled my hero, R. H. Spooner, for 0. Johnny Tyldesley came in next and he and A. C. MacLaren sternly watched the new ball 'demon' and defended with unusual asperity. After a quarter of an hour, though, nothing had been done to clear the atmosphere; the score-board stood menacingly at 7 for 1. Then, while the Australian field changed over, MacLaren and Tyldesley held converse in mid-wicket, and what they said was audible to everyone present, including Laver.

'Johnny,' said MacLaren, 'I propose to drive this fellow.' And Tyldesley replied: 'You'll, of course, do as you please, Mr. MacLaren; but I'm going to cut him.'

You see, they were free enough, and men and cricketers enough, to form an individual plan. Whether it would succeed rested with the hazards of sport. The point is that they did not intend to submit to bondage or negation. The style is the man himself, in cricket or in any other occupation. Too much is said to-day of the material setting and organisation of cricket; of schools and coaching.

But what is to be taught? Technique in the abstract, divorced from spirit, tradition and faith in the impulse (and native skill) of a born player of games? Was Woolley coached or Macartney or Compton or Gimblett or Keith Miller or Victor Trumper or McCabe? Or Grimmett?

More than all material factors, cricket is in dire need of a great personal example. Most young folk are imitative to begin with: they'll push from behind the crease, content to wait for the loose ball, if that's the way their 'betters' behave. They'll rub the new ball on their trousers, like so many bereft Alladins rubbing the lamp, for want of a better trick, for so long as no master of more artistic accomplishments is there to inspire them.

Where there is no vision . . . certain as to-morrow is it that, failing a renaissance of the game as art and spectacle, with character and the personal touch dictating and directing the competitive issues, cricket's days are numbered, or at any rate likely to be chequered.

Already it lives more or less on the profits which come from the Test matches. The first sign of the renaissance will be heralded when once more a Test match does not give us a different kind of cricket from that of a county match, but is an ordinary first-class match in apotheosis.

In the past, great players didn't think that in a Test match they were under an obligation to deny their best gifts and to inhibit themselves for safety's sake. Grace, MacLaren, Ranji, Trumper, Hobbs, Woolley – and on and on to yesterday – found the challenge of a Test match an incentive to their greatest deeds. What has been done in the past by mortal cricketer it is possible to do again, given the love and the desire. At least – as Pooh-Bah would say – a man might try.

A. L. HASSETT: A BORN CRICKETER
[1954]

By 1954 Cardus is adamant that not just cricket but the times themselves are out of joint. Societies really do get the cricket, and everything else, that they deserve. Using the personality of the visiting Australian captain Lindsay Hassett as a pretext, he introduces his theme by insisting on the unbreachable links between the climate of any particular age and the blossoms which flourish under its suns. He has not written more than two sentences before he has evoked yet again the gods of his youth. It is barefaced oldfogeyism, yet the embarrassing truth was that nowhere in the English game were there cricketers to compare with Ranjitsinhji and Jessop. But the apologist for a later age, while acknowledging the truth of that proposition, might have foxed Cardus with another, by asking him who in the Edwardian era batted more brilliantly than Denis Compton, or with more classic rectitude than Hutton. Cardus quickly acknowledges the uselessness of that sort of comparative judgement, but there is the unmistakeable implication, as his argument proceeds, that Britain, being a stern utilitarian sort of place these days, all buttoned up and grim-faced, offers those of us who crave for the vicarious romance and adventure of great cricket only disappointment.

In Hassett he sees a victim of circumstance, a natural hitter of the ball who has been obliged to exchange his elan for the lesser arts of attrition. The Hassett who first emerged was the product of an era whose memories of Trumper and Macartney were still fresh in the mind. But the Hassett of whom Cardus writes is a child of austerity who has learned to clip his wings. But the truth of the proposition ought not to obscure other truths about Hassett which may have been powerful factors in his retreat from attack to defence. When he brought his country's team to England in 1953, he must surely have sensed the danger of anti-climax. He had inherited a side rendered virtually invincible by Bradman, for which reason the tourists he led in 1953 looked very much like 'Hamlet' without the Prince. After a quarter of a century of relying on Bradman to cow the opposition, Hassett and his men found themselves obliged to get along as best they could. In spite of the fact that the English tourists of 1950–51 had been defined by Cardus as 'the weakest conglomeration of cricketers which has ever represented this country against Australia', Hassett's side had had moments of grave self-doubt. Although Australia had retained the Ashes by four matches to one, the margin at Melbourne had been a mere 28 runs and at Brisbane Australia had won by only 70 runs with Hutton, batting at number six, running out of partners with 62 not out. Four-One might so easily have been Two-Three. And yet in 1948 England had been no match for Bradman's side. The great difference was that Bradman had been removed from the equation and England could at last expect to dismiss the enemy for reasonable scores. Under such pressing circumstances it is no surprise that Hassett's batting throughout the 1953 series was canny rather than carefree. In the event, his average for the five Tests was no more than 36.50 but it was good enough to place him above all his colleagues. In that tour the Australians registered four centuries in the Tests; Hassett scored two of them. In composing his valedictory to one of the most popular captains ever sent to England by Australia, Cardus omitted one important fact. England won the rubber, a fact which has much to do with the affection in which Lindsay Hassett has always been held.

O NE of cricket's rare fascinations is the way it responds to atmosphere, and is quick to express scene or character and even a national spirit. After all, a great game is an organism in an environment, so we need not be surprised if players change according to the pressure of circumstances in which they find themselves, technical and psychological.

By no accident did men such as A. C. MacLaren, F. S. Jackson, C. B. Fry, K. S. Ranjitsinhji, R. H. Spooner and G. L. Jessop lord the green earth of our cricket fields in the opulent years of the Edwardian high noon and the glowing Victorian sunset.

Two wars have altered the economy of living, have altered the attitude to living. MacLaren and 'Ranji' and others of that breed played the game, even in a Test match, much in the same mood in which they went to Ascot or Goodwood; it was for them a summer pastime. They set the tempo of cricket, and it moved to the same rhythm as that of the privileged world they dwelt in.

The professionals had to go with them at the same pace – and how admirably they emulated the amateur tradition! Johnny Tyldesley, George Hirst, David Denton, Ernest Hayes, Frank Woolley, Jack Hobbs before 1914 – no batsman, not MacLaren himself, made strokes more splendid, more daring, more intensely infused with the true blood and spirit of cricket, than the strokes of these, all of them cricketers for a livelihood, in a period when sport was by no means the paying proposition it is to-day.

I once saw MacLaren drive the fifth ball in a Test match straight for four; an over or so later he was caught near the sight-screen, trying to repeat the hit, only aiming higher and farther. Such an extravagant gesture would scarcely meet the approval of the modern policies; indeed, I am certain that if MacLaren were playing nowadays he would be called 'ham' by the present generation, just as they would call Henry Irving 'ham'. (I find it ironical that in a half-starved rationed time of the troubled history of the world, the term 'ham' should have been used as a term of contempt to apply to any excessive sign of a generous and romantic nature!)

It is bad criticism to set the masters of one period against those of another and to blame, say, a Hutton or a Hassett for not indulging the gestures and points of view of a MacLaren or a Jackson. MacLaren and Jackson were representative men in a particular national scene and atmosphere; Hutton and Hassett each are, in relation to the contemporary environment, equally as representative. The style is the man himself. Nobody by evidence of statistics or by aesthetic argument can *prove* that Jackson was greater as a batsman than Hutton. All that a critic as seasoned as myself is entitled to say is that he preferred the richer and 'hammier' sorts of cricket to the scientifically-rationed products of later origin.

Lindsay Hassett might serve as a perfect example to point our moral: that cricket reacts to the social and economic pressure of life, and that inborn skill is very much swayed by external compulsion. Hassett, in his first seasons, promised to join the ranks of the quicksilver rapier-like users of the bat, kindred with Macartney, Tyldesley, Hendren, 'a little terror,' five feet six of aggression pertinacity and brilliance. I have seen Hassett 'lay into' W. J. O'Reilly even as Johnny Tyldesley once 'laid into' Colin Blythe and Warwick Armstrong.

When Hassett arrived fresh to England in 1938, he at once became renowned for combined consistency and beautifully-poised swiftness of stroke-play, an enchanting late-cutter and a vehement hooker. Following 43 at Worcester, he scored 146, 148 run out and 220 not out in consecutive innings. At the crisis of the Leeds Test match the same summer, Australia in their second innings had lost four wickets for 61, needing 105 to win on an unpleasant pitch, in a dreadful light. Douglas Wright, bowling then with nothing less than genius, overwhelmed Bradman and McCabe. With thunder in the air and in a tension unbearable, Hassett drove and pulled with the ease and confidence of nature. He won the match, plucked the brand from the burning – though as a matter of course, all in the afternoon's work.

Hassett was born in 1913, and therefore the foundations of his technique and approach to cricket were laid during a time still enlivened and ennobled by traditions and memories of Australia's greatest stroke players. Not yet had Test matches lost the fresh impulse of pleasure and sport from the first ball bowled. The idea never occurred to Trumper, Macartney, McCabe, MacLaren, Tyldesley, Woolley to play in a Test match extending over several days 'a different game' from the one they played in three-day matches. It is generally forgotten that all Test matches in Australia, until the second war, were played to a finish. But because there was no time-limit Victor Trumper did not dawdle at the wicket; it was not in his nature to do so.

No great cricketer compromises his true character or his instinctive technical capacity. And if his technique doesn't work by instinct, he isn't a master. Hassett was born to natural elegance and boldness as a batsman; he found himself caught after 1939 in a tremendous transition, both in cricket and world environment.

Nothing could have signified more emphatically his resources, as a man of character and cricketer of innate flexible skill, than his adaptation to an altered scheme of things, a changed and less individually enterprising view of Test cricket, a view putting value primarily on security and team-work. He never lost lightness of touch, though, no matter how for the cause's sake, he controlled himself, bat in hand, often seeming to hide himself behind it, over and over.

There was no sullenness about his slow scoring; we could get the flavour of a humourous principle behind it all; it wasn't himself that was bearing the cross of long patience stonewalling but the crowd! And he knew it! I once stopped him in North Terrace, Adelaide, after he had batted all day on a perfect wicket, scoring about twenty runs an hour, mostly in singles, and, weary in my soul I asked him: 'Good gracious, what's the matter, Lindsay? . . .' With a twinkle he replied: 'Wore out. Just wore out!'

In his career he scored 16,890 runs, average 58.24. Against England, here and in Australia, his figures are 42 innings, 1,572 runs, average 38.34. But to discuss Hassett statistically is a waste of time and sense. He played cricket with the wit of his mind. At Melbourne in 1951, when England won a Test match after years in the wilderness, Hassett went on to bowl at the finish, just to provide generously the winning hit in a kissing-cup, so to say. With eight wickets in hand England wanted only another three or four. But Hassett set his field very mathematically, moving men about to an inch. Then he solemnly measured out his run. And then, before bowling – an old ball, of course – comic inspiration visited him; he rubbed it vigorously on the right side of his stomach.

Australia has sent to these shores no captain of cricket who shared Hassett's secret into our English ways – knowing it without any surrender of Australia's own related yet not entirely similar ways. He could be open-hearted, apparently casual, even complying. But, at the pinch, he would put on his poker face – and now – not Armstrong himself could have been more obstinate. It is because of Hassett's influence that Test matches between England and Australia are emerging from the mechanically stupid to a condition not unconnected with volatile sport as conceived by the present generations.

An Australian of Hassett's vintage likes to win, we may be sure, and, moreover, does his damndest to win. But should the luck go the wrong way, there's always the consoling thought that, come to think of it, we've been playing a game; and none of us is the worse for it and some of us much the better. And there are friends as well as runs to be got out of it. Lindsay Hassett goes into retirement to the good wishes of far more friends all over the globe than all the 16,000-odd runs he accumulated, at his leisure and according to his own sweet will, at the wicket.

SOUTH AFRICA OFFER
SERIOUS CHALLENGE [1955]

*Cardus's account of South African Test history is a masterly affair, con-
cise, witty and perceptive, and so disinterested that at one point even A. C.
MacLaren is made to look foolish. Predictably the heroes of the piece are
the opening batsmen Herbie Taylor, for having defied the genius Barnes
on matting wickets, and Aubrey Faulkner, the great all-rounder who came
to such a pathetic end. Although as the years passed, Cardus was more
and more called upon to compose obituary notices on the lions of his
young manhood, he generally tended not to mention anything tragic unless
it could be softened by anecdote. Johnny Briggs and Albert Trott are
examples of sad endings which Cardus evidently felt comfortable describing because of the whimsicalities of both of those unfortunate men. But
the case of Faulkner was so enigmatic that Cardus ignored it altogether,
confining himself to the cricket. After he retired, Faulkner opened a cricket
school in a disused garage in Richmond, and among his protégés was
the Middlesex spin bowler Ian Peebles who later composed the most
comprehensive sketch of Faulkner left to us. Peebles describes him as
'enigmatic, lusty and highly sexed'. The son of a drunken wife-beater, he
had one day taken his revenge on his father and beaten him up. 'I nearly
killed him', he told Peebles. At the end of the 1930 season, Faulkner went
to his school, wrote a note saying 'I am off to another realm via the bat
room', went into the store-room and gassed himself. Faulkner had no
close friends and the reason for his despair has never been disclosed. It
may be that Cardus's reticence was due at least in part to the niggardly
ration of space he was offered by the editors of the almanack. While Sir
Pelham Warner's 'Twilight Reflections' went on for ten pages in this
edition, Cardus was allocated only three. With more space he might have
been able to tell the odd tale of how C. Aubrey Smith preceded George
Lohmann as an influence in the formative years of South African domestic
cricket.*

For more than a quarter of a century the field or arena of international
cricket was occupied almost exclusively by England and Australia,
until in 1905–06, South Africa, winning four out of five Test matches
against England, rushed in almost with the rude violence of the gate-
crasher. South Africa had emulated Australia's example and learned first
principles from an English player, namely George Lohmann; even as
Australia had learned them from Caffyn. Lord Hawke contributed to
South African education in cricket when he took teams to play in a
country much agitated at the time by the Jameson Raid, but not so much
agitated as to overlook the genius and Attic handsomeness of C. B. Fry.
Pioneers of the game born or bred in South Africa included Sir Donald

Currie, the Hon. J. D. Logan, and in more recent times, Sir Abe Bailey. Another asset to the awakening cause was Frank Mitchell, not unknown in Yorkshire during the county's greatest seasons.

In 1905, the M.C.C. sent a very good team to South Africa, under the leadership of P. F. Warner. It was soundly thrashed in the rubber; it was indeed routed by the new weapon of the period – the 'googly.' Two years afterwards South Africa arrived full strength in England, with the greatest 'googly' bowlers ever seen in action in one and the same match: Vogler, Schwarz, Faulkner and White. In those days cricket was played on matting in South Africa, but none the less these artists in spin caused much mental confusion amongst some of our finest batsmen, notably A. C. MacLaren, who wrote to the Press arguing that the new-fangled stuff would put an end in time to all scientific and even to decent and gentlemanly behaviour in cricket.

The 'new fangled stuff' certainly caused a revision of if not a revolution in the principles of batsmanship. Back-play began to supersede forward-play; and the right foot began to move across the wicket, so that pads might be used as a second, and perhaps as a first line of defence. Here beginneth the deplorable two-eyed stance. But the truth is that the superb and original spin of Vogler, Schwarz, Faulkner and White was first frustrated, not to say mastered, by batsmen who seldom employed pads self-consciously, but used their feet for stroke-making purposes. In 1907 the South African attack was countered and conquered by Jessop, Fry, Braund, Tyldesley, Spooner and others to whom a cricket bat was an instrument to be exercised freely, almost instinctively. At Lord's, Jessop scored 93 in not much more time than 90 minutes; and he per-suaded the South African captain Percy Sherwell to place four men on the boundary while Kotze was bowling; and Kotze was one of the fastest of all fast bowlers. It was in this Lord's Test match of 1907 that Sherwell himself played an innings of memorable heroism and brilliance. Against England's first innings total of 428 (in a three-day match), South Africa followed-on and lost a wicket for nothing. Sherwell, who often went in nearly last, opened the innings, and in an hour and three-quarters of cricket of rare power and precision reached a century.

The 'new-fangled stuff' and the accomplished batting of Shalders, Sherwell, Nourse and Faulkner, plus the electric pace of Kotze, could not win South Africa a rubber in England.

Indeed not until 1935 did South Africa lower the England colours in this country. But on the matting at Cape Town, Johannesburg and Durban, South Africa were often nearly unbeatable and victorious between 1907–10. It was in 1910 that a team from South Africa first challenged Australia in Australia. The beautiful wickets there defeated even Vogler's spin; and South Africa lost four out of five Test matches, yet enjoyed increase in batting prestige, mainly through the remarkable performances of G. A. Faulkner, whose average in the Test matches was 73. Faulkner at his best was one of the greatest all-round cricketers of all time; and Vogler at his best was nearly the most dangerous of all bowlers. The most dangerous bowler of them all, living or dead, was none other than S. F. Barnes, who in the South African season before the war of 1914–18 played in South Africa under the captaincy of J. W. H. T. Douglas, and on matting made a cricket ball spit fire, gyrate and describe angles unknown to geometry. In the second Test match of this rubber, he took 17 out of 20 wickets; on matting Barnes was undoubtedly the most difficult bowler ever evolved by cricket and a peculiar substitution for turf. Yet at his deadliest Barnes met a worthy opponent in H. W. Taylor, who played with ease and assurance in each Test match, and for Natal at Durban in 1913–14 scored 91 and 100 out of totals of 153 and 216. The annals of the game provide no proof more convincing than this of supremely great batsmanship; for how possibly could any mortal batsman be subjected to a severer ordeal – Barnes on matting, with wickets falling at the other end all the time? H. W. Taylor must be counted one of the six greatest batsmen of the post-Grace period.

As time passed and South African cricket suffered natural and inevitable ups-and-downs, the fact became more and more obvious that until turf was cultivated in South Africa, and matting discarded, even the best talents of the country would suffer frustration on English and Australian wickets. After the end of the 1914–18 war England needed to battle hard to win in South Africa; Taylor in 1922–23 scored 176, 101, 102 and 91 in the Test matches, and two spinners, Nupen and Hall, were formidable, with Blanckenberg a splendid bowler-batsman. But when South Africa came again to England in 1924, Nupen found our turf unresponsive to his spin, so that an almost veteran South African leg-break and googly bowler was recalled to service, S. J. Pegler, another fine artist in the 'new-fangled stuff'. A lean year or two for South Africa served as a 'lying fallow' season. H. G. Deane, one of South Africa's several cricket captains of rare personal appeal, led the gallant team which won friends everywhere in England in 1929, a team which included 'Jock' Cameron, magnificent as wicket-keeper and hard-hitting batsman; and Mitchell, Owen-Smith (whose century at Leeds and a last-wicket stand with 'Sandy' Bell worth 103 are deathless) and Morkel, not to forget the fast bowler Ochse and Christy. South Africa yet again were unable to win a Test match in England, but had the satisfaction of declaring an innings closed at Kennington Oval with the score 492 for eight.

The writing was on the wall; sooner or later justice would be done, a long ploughing of the furrow and the soil (and sand) would surely yield the desired fruit or crop. Chapman led England's team of 1930–31, and South Africa won the only finished match in the rubber by 28. Significantly enough, South Africa held their own on the turf wicket that had by now been planted at Cape Town. At last, in 1935, and at Lord's, most blessed of all places for anybody's first victory, South Africa beat England in England; and it was poetic justice to the ghost of the old spinners, Vogler, Schwarz and the rest, that the first South African victory on English turf was achieved largely by the leg-breaks and 'googlies' of Xenophon Balaskas. Other heroes of South Africa in this great inaugural game were Cameron, Crisp, Langton, Eric Rowan and Bruce Mitchell, with Wade the unobtrusive but omnipresent captain and planner. In recent times, only yesteryear in fact, we have had proof once more of the resilience of South African cricket, following spells not at all prosperous, with old masters all falling by the way in a heap. The youthful team that forced a drawn rubber in Australia, inspired by J. E. Cheetham, heralded a fresh epoch, rich in a great off-spinner, Tayfield, and at least one batsman of brilliance, McLean. The challenge of South Africa to English cricket today is serious and likely to call for a strenuous answer. The pioneeer work of years is about to receive fitting rewards and prizes – and what worthy pioneers! – Tancred (a lovely player!), Shalders, Hathorn, J. H. Sinclair (handsome giant of a hitter and bowler), Sherwell, White, Faulkner, Llewellyn, Catterall, Noah Mann, the Nourses (father and son), Viljoen, Zulch, Siedle, the Rowans, with Alan Melville as a stylist fit to compare with Taylor, the master of them all.

LEN HUTTON: THE MASTER [1956]

In the 1956 edition of the almanack, once again the only serious fault with Cardus's essay is its brevity. In assessing the career of Len Hutton, he writes little more than a thousand words; the preceding article, a symposium on 'The Growing Pains of Cricket', spreads to fifteen pages. The sketch of Hutton, as far as it goes, is a Cardusian delight, from which we learn something of Cassandra, Bach, Paganism, the Zeitgeist, Caesar and the Battle of Austerlitz. But it hardly goes far enough. In referring to Hutton's captaincy of England, Cardus suggests that the sergeant-major eventually graduated to commissioned officer. But he does not quite make enough of the fact that Hutton's appointment marks a turning point in the social history of England. Before he was appointed captain, that post had never been offered to a professional cricketer, on the assumption that only a man educated at a university possessed the necessary qualities. The fact that no credible amateur alternative presented itself to the selectors is telling proof of the extent to which the lives of Englishmen had been altered. Hutton's appointment proved to be a selectorial triumph, a bold stroke justly rewarded. But the achievement of beating the Australians at home and away in successive rubbers is perhaps no more noteworthy than the fact that while he was considered civilised enough to captain his country, he was never acceptable as a captain of his own county. Yorkshiremen who may wonder sometimes why the rest of the world sometimes laughs behind its hands, need only recall that the snubbing of their greatest cricketer was and remains a contemptible act.

LEN HUTTON was the only batsman of his period to whom we could apply the term 'Old Master', referring in his case not to his number of years but to the style and vintage of his cricket. He followed in the succession of the classic professional batsmen who each went in first for his county and for England: Shrewsbury, Hayward, Hobbs and Sutcliffe – though Sutcliffe wore his classicism with a subtly Sutcliffian difference.

As Old Masters go, Hutton was young enough; the sadness is that physical disability put an end to his career in its prime. He had all the classic points of style when, not much more than 19, he came to Lord's in 1936 and scored fifty-five. I then wrote of him in this strain of Cassandrian prophecy: 'Here is a young cricketer who is already old in the head and destined to enliven many a Lancashire and Yorkshire match of the future.'

If by means of some Time-machine capable of television we could today see a picture of Hutton batting twenty years ago, and one taken of him during his maturity, we would notice no fundamental difference in technique. We would see that his cricket had grown in experience and finish, that is all. Like the music of Bach, Hutton's batsmanship in its evolution from an early to a late period presented no marked divisions; it was never raw, unprincipled or embryonic. He batted grammatically from the start, choosing his strokes as carefully as a professor of logic his words.

Even when he first played for Yorkshire, beginning with 0, he seemed to begin an innings to a plan, building the shape and the duration of it to a blue-print in his mind, and to a time-table. But once in the greenest of his salad days he fell into error. He opened a Yorkshire innings on Saturday at Bradford with Arthur Mitchell, dourest and most unsmiling of the clan. After a characteristically Yorkshire investigation of the state of the wicket, the state of the opposition bowling, the state of mind the unpires were in, the state of the weather and barometer, and probably the state of the Bank of England itself, Mitchell and Hutton began to score now and then.

Young Hutton was feeling in form, so after he had played himself in he decided to cut a rising ball outside the off-stump. Remember that he was fresh to the Yorkshire scene and policies. He actually lay back and cut hard and swiftly, with cavalier flourish. He cut under the ball by an inch, and it sped bang into the wicket-keeper's gloves. And Mitchell, from the other end of the pitch, looked hard at Hutton and said, 'That's no . . . use!' This was probably Hutton's true baptism, cleansing him of all vanity and lusts for insubstantial pageantry and temporal glory.

He observed the classical unities; that is to say, he did not venture beyond reliable and established limitations of batsmanship learned in the traditional school. Geometrical precision in the application of bat to ball, each movement of the feet considered until the right position was found almost instinctively, not bringing him merely to the ball and, as far as possible and if necessary over it, but also with body at the proper balance.

Never, or hardly ever, did Hutton play a thoughtless innings; his mind usually seemed to move a fraction of time in advance of his most rapid footwork and sudden tensions of limb, sinew and nerve. It is, of course, wrong to suppose that Hutton was at any time a batsman slow in his mental and physical reactions at the crease.

The score-board may have told us that he was not getting runs feverishly, but the vigilance of Hutton was eternal; the concentration in him was so intense that it frequently exhausted his not robust physique much sooner than did the more obvious toil and burden of the day. In the most austerely defensive Hutton innings we could feel a mental alertness; purpose in him suffered no weariness.

And whether or not he was putting into practice his wide repertoire of strokes, he was the stylist always; rarely was he discovered in an awkward position at the crease, rarely was he bustled or hurried. Once at Kennington Oval, Lindwall knocked Hutton's cap off in a Test match. Such an outrage could be equalled in a cricketer's imagination only by supposing that Alfred Mynn's tall hat was ever likewise rudely removed.

On a bowler's wicket, when the ball's spin was angular and waspish in turn, he could maintain his premeditated technical responses, often using a 'dead' bat, the handle held so loosely that when the ball came into contact with the blade's middle it was as though against a drugged cushion: the spin was anaethetised into harmlessness.

But Hutton was, when grace descended upon him, a versatile and handsome stroke player. Old Trafford will remember that in 1948 he made a century of a brilliance which, in the circumstances – Bank Holiday and a Lancashire v. Yorkshire match – was almost pagan.

He drove Lindwall with Spooneresque charm and panache at Brisbane in December 1950; at Lord's in the Test Match of 1953, he played one of the most regal and most highly pedigreed innings ever seen in an England and Australia Test Match on that hallowed ground. And he has contributed to a festival at Scarborough.

If Hutton had lived and played in the Lord Hawke epoch, when even Test cricketers in England had somehow to adapt themselves and their skill to matches limited to three days, he would have been a different batsman in his tempo and mental approach. But he could not possibly have been greater.

Any artist or master of craft is an organism in an environment; he is very much what circumstances and atmosphere make of him. His very greatness consists in how fully he can sum up the technique of his day as he finds it, and how representative he is of his day's spirit. MacLaren, lordly and opulent at the crease, was a representative man and cricketer in a lordly opulent period; Hutton's cricket has been as true as MacLaren's to the Zeitgeist, to the feeling, temper and even to the economy of the age which shaped his character and his skill, both conceived as much as in integrity as in joy.

As a captain he was shrewd but courteous; he knew the game's finest points, and though never likely to give anything away, was too proud to take anything not his due. Sometimes he may have allowed thoughtfulness to turn to worry; but this is a natural habit in the part of the world which Hutton comes from.

Hutton certainly showed that a professional cricketer can wear the robes of leadership in the field of play with dignity. At first, no doubt, he appeared at the head of his troops not wearing anything like a Caesarian toga, but rather the uniform of a sergeant-major. But he moved up in rank and prestige until he became worthy of his command and defeated Australia twice in successive rubbers, wresting one from the enemy at the pinch and looting the other after a series of Tests which were, if I may be free with my allusions and metaphors, the Australian's Austerlitz.

One of Hutton's most winning characteristics – and his personality is extremely attractive – is his smile, a smile with a twinkle in it. He had many occasions in his distinguished career on which to indulge this smile, many provocations to it, and he never missed the joke. A Yorkshireman has his own idea of humour, and Hutton, as great or famous as any Yorkshireman contemporary with him, relished his laugh all the more because very often it came last.

C. B. FRY [1957]

The saddest of all duties to befall Cardus as a contributor to the almanack came with the 1957 edition, to which he contributed an obituary of his old friend and dialectical sparring partner, Charles Burgess Fry. No more remarkable character ever stepped on to a cricket field than Fry, the greatest all-round player of ball games produced by the British this century. As a batsman who scored 94 first-class hundreds, including six in successive innings, and who in 1901 scored over 3000 runs in the season, Fry brought Aristotelean principles to bear on the art of making runs. As a captain of England he was never on the losing side and excelled in everything he did, seemingly without effort, certainly without payment. In 1901, at the very apex of his fame as a batsman, he was capped for England against Ireland at Association football. A year later he played full back for Southampton in the F.A. Cup Final. At Oxford in 1892 he broke the World long jump record with a leap of over twenty four feet, a mark which remained unsurpassed for more than twenty years. He was a foregone conclusion to get his blue for Rugby, but an injury deprived him of the honour. As Liberal candidate in a by-election at Brighton he polled over 20,000 votes and, acting as Ranjitsinhji's aide at the League of Nations in Geneva in 1919, was given the chance to rise to Rassendyllian heights when a convocation of bishops offered him the throne of Albania. He was a successful editor of boys' papers who once commissioned a short story from P. G. Wodehouse, wrote some cricketing novels, became a star cricket reporter. He is credited with two epigrams on the game: 'Batting is a dance with a stick in your hand' and, when reproached for being a batsman with only one stroke, 'Yes, but I could make the ball go to ten different parts of the field'. Photographs bear out the opinion of his contemporaries that he was a physical specimen so perfect that Phideas would have rejoiced.

Although during his life Cardus wrote vividly of his friend, nowhere does he describe how, where or when they met, nor does he tell us of any association between them away from cricket. In the obituary, reprinted from 'The Guardian', he stays with the bare facts. To get any impression of the warmth of his affection for Fry, we have to turn to 'Second Innings', where we find the pair of them on board the 'S.S. Orion', bound for Australia for the 1936–7 Test series:

> We voyaged to Australia together in 1936–37; and every morning Fry held court amongst the deck-chairs on the 'Orion', as she ploughed patiently through the seas. He dressed differently every day; some-times with topee and short leather trousers, as though about to trace the source of the Amazon; or in a scaled green sort of costume which made him look like a deep-sea monster; or in a bath towel worn like a toga. One day, to tease him, I said, 'Good morning, Charles. No hemlock yet? Give us your ideas about the Iambic'. In full spate came a swift survey of the origin and development of the Iambic, with quotations from all periods and writers, every sentence ending with 'You see what I mean' or 'However'. A sort of intellectual Jack Bunsby; an original and fascinating man.

Indeed, so remarkable was Fry that the appended tributes from the editor of Wisden and others add to the interest of Cardus's recollections.

CHARLES FRY was born into a Sussex family on April 25, 1872, at Croydon, and was known first as an England cricketer and footballer, also as a great all-round athlete who for a while held the long-jump record, a hunter and a fisher, and as an inexhaustible virtuoso at the best of all indoor games, conversation.

He was at Repton when a boy, where at cricket he joined the remark-able and enduring roll of superb young players emanating from the school – Fry, Palairet, Ford, J. N. Crawford, to name a few. At Oxford he won first-class honours in Classical Moderations at Wadham, and it is a tribute to his calibre as a scholar and personal force that most of the obituary articles written after the death of Viscount Simon named Fry in a Wadham trinity with Birkenhead. Not the least doughty and idealistic of his many-sided achievements was as a Liberal candidate for Brighton, where he actually polled 20,000 votes long after he had ceased to live in Sussex and dominate the cricket field.

With all his versatility of mind and sinew Fry himself wished that he might be remembered, as much as for anything else, by his work in command of the training-ship *Mercury*. For forty years he and his wife directed the *Mercury* at Hamble, educating youth with a classical sense of values. He once invited the present writer to visit Hamble and see his boys play cricket and perform extracts from 'Parsifal'! Hitler sent for him for advice during the building-up of the 'Youth Movement' in Germany. He was a deputy for the Indian delegation to the first, third, and fourth Assemblies of the League of Nations, edited his own monthly magazine more than half a century ago, and was indeed a pioneer in the school of intelligent and analytical criticism of sport. He wrote several books, including an autobiography, and a *Key Book to the League of Nations*, and one called *Batsmanship*, which might conceivably have come from the pen of Aristotle had Aristotle lived nowadays and played cricket.

Fry must be counted among the most fully developed and representative Englishmen of his period; and the question arises whether, had fortune allowed him to concentrate on the things of the mind, not distracted by the lure of cricket, a lure intensified by his increasing mastery over the game, he would not have reached a high altitude in politics or critical literature. But he belonged – and it was his glory – to an age not obsessed by specialism; he was one of the last of the English tradition of the amateur, the connoisseur, and, in the most delightful sense of the word, the dilettante.

As a batsman, of course, he was thoroughly grounded in first principles. He added to his stature, in fact, by taking much thought. As a youth he did not use a bat with much natural freedom, and even in his period of pomp he was never playing as handsomely as his magnificent physical appearances seemed to suggest and deserve. He was, of course, seen often in contrast with Ranjitsinhji, who would have made all batsmen of the present day, Hutton included, look like so many plebeians toiling under the sun. Yet in his prime Fry was a noble straight-driver. He once said to me: 'I had only one stroke maybe; but it went to ten different parts of the field.' But in 1905, when the Australians decided that Fry could make runs only in front of the wicket, mainly to the on, and set the field for him accordingly, he scored 144 in an innings sparkling with cuts.

In his career as a cricketer, he scored some 30,000 runs, averaging 50, in an era of natural wickets, mainly against bowlers of great speed or of varied and subtle spin and accuracy. From Yorkshire bowling alone he scored nearly 2,500 runs in all his matches against the county during its most powerful days, averaging 70, in the teeth of the attack of Hirst, Rhodes, Haigh, Wainwright, and, occasionally, F. S. Jackson. In 1903 he made 234 against Yorkshire at Bradford. Next summer he made 177 against Yorkshire at Sheffield, and 229 at Brighton, in successive innings. Ranjitsinhji's performances against Yorkshire were almost as remarkable as Fry's; for he scored well over 1,500 runs against them, averaging more than sixty an innings. In 1901 Fry scored six centuries in six consecutive innings, an achievement equalled by Bradman, but on Australian wickets and spread over a season. Fry's six hundreds, two of them on bowler's wickets, came one on top of the other within little more than a fortnight.

The conjunction at the creases of C. B. Fry and K. S. Ranjitsinhji was a sight and an appeal to the imagination not likely ever to be repeated; Fry, nineteenth-century rationalist, batting according to first principles with a sort of moral grandeur, observing patience and abstinence. At the other end of the wicket, 'Ranji' turned a cricket bat into a wand of conjuration. Fry was of the Occident, 'Ranji' told of the Orient.

Cricket can scarcely hope again to witness two styles as fascinatingly contrasted and as racially representative as Fry's and Ranjitsinhji's. Between them they evolved a doctrine that caused a fundamental change in the tactics of batsmanship. 'Play back or drive.' 'Watch the ball well, then make a stroke at the ball itself and not at a point in space where you hope the ball will presently be.' At the time that Fry was making a name in cricket most batsmen played forward almost automatically on good fast pitches, frequently lunging out full stretch. If a ball can be reached only by excessive elongation of arms and body, obviously the pitch of it has been badly gauged. Fry and Ranjitsinhji, following after Arthur Shrewsbury, developed mobile footwork.

It is a pungent comment on the strength of the reserves of English cricket half a century ago that Fry and 'Ranji' were both dropped from the England team at the height of their fame. In 1901 Fry scored 3,147 runs, average 78.67; in 1903 he scored 2,683 runs, average 81.30. In 1900 Ranjitsinhji scored 3,065, average 87.57. Yet because of one or two lapses in 1902, both these great players were asked to stand down and give way to other aspirants to Test cricket.

As we consider Fry's enormous aggregates of runs summer by summer, we should not forget that he took part, during all the extent of his career, in only one Test match lasting more than three days, and that he never visited Australia as a cricketer. For one reason and another Fry appeared not more than eighteen times against Australia in forty-three Test matches played between 1899, when he began the England innings with W. G. Grace, and 1912, in which wet season he was England's captain against Australia and South Africa in the ill-fated triangular tournament. By that time he had severed his illustrious connection with Sussex and was opening the innings for Hampshire. The general notion is that Fry was not successful as an England batsman; and it is true that in Test matches he did not remain on his habitual peaks. None the less, his batting average for Test cricket is much the same as that of Victor Trumper, M. A. Noble, and J. T. Tyldesley. The currency had not been debased yet.

Until he was no-balled for throwing by Phillips – who also 'called' Mold at Old Trafford – Fry was a good fast bowler who took six wickets for 78 in the University match, opened the Gentlemen's bowling against the Players at The Oval, and took five wickets. Twice he performed the hat-trick at Lord's.

He played Association football for his university, for the Corinthians, Southampton, and for England.

In his retirement he changed his methods as a writer on cricket and indulged a brisk impressionistic 'columnist' style, to suit the running commentary needed by an evening paper: 'Ah, here comes the Don. Walking slowly to the wicket. Deliberately. Menacingly. I don't like the look of him. He has begun with a savage hook. He is evidently in form. Dangerously so. Ah, but he is out. . . .' Essentially he was an analyst by mind, if rather at the mercy of an impulsive, highly strung temperament. He sometimes, in his heyday, got on the wrong side of the crowd by his complete absorption in himself, which was mistaken for posing or egoism. He would stand classically poised after making an on-drive, contemplating the direction and grandeur of it. The cricket field has seen no sight more Grecian than the one presented by C. B. Fry in the pride and handsomeness of his young manhood.

After he had passed his seventieth birthday, he one day entered his club, saw his friend Denzil Batchelor, and said he had done most things but was now sighing for a new world to conquer, and proposed to interest himself in racing, attach himself to a stable, and then set up 'on his own'. And Batchelor summed up his genius in a flash of wit: 'What as, Charles? Trainer, jockey, or horse?'

It is remarkable that he was not knighted for his services to cricket, and that no honours came his way for the sterling, devoted work he did with the training-ship *Mercury*.

MR. HUBERT PRESTON writes: Charles Fry secured a place in the Repton XI in 1888 and retained it for the next three years, being captain in 1890 and 1891. In his last season at school his average reached nearly 50.

When he went up to Oxford, Fry was captain of the cricket and Association football XIs and president of the athletic club, acting as first string in the 100 yards and the long-jump.

He also played a good deal of Rugby football, and his friends insisted that but for an unfortunate injury he would have added a Rugger 'Blue' to his other honours. Charles Fry was also a fine boxer, a passable golfer, swimmer, sculler, tennis player and javelin thrower. But it was on the cricket field that he achieved his greatest triumphs. He represented three counties – Sussex, Hampshire and Surrey – scoring altogether 30,886 runs in first-class matches, average 50.22. His total of centuries reached 94 and five times he scored two separate hundreds in a match.

Fry's best season was 1901 when his aggregate reached 3,147, average 78.67. In that summer he scored 13 hundreds and made six in successive innings – a feat equalled only by Sir Donald Bradman. In 1899, 1901, and 1903, Charles Fry hit a century for the Gentlemen against the Players at Lord's, his 232 not out in 1903 remaining the highest individual score for the Gentlemen at Headquarters.

His one three-figure Test innings against Australia was 144 at The

Oval in 1905, when the rubber had already been decided. Two years later he made his only other hundred for England, 129 against the South Africans, also at The Oval. Fry shared with Vine (J.) in thirty-three opening partnerships of 100 for Sussex.

Considering the very high rank he attained among batsmen, Fry, at the outset, was a stiff ungainly performer and was still somewhat laboured in stroke-production when he went up to Oxford. But from the time he began playing for Sussex with 'Ranji' his game improved. He was a natural on-side batsman with a powerful straight drive and many useful leg-side strokes.

The records contain very few details of Fry's achievements as a bowler. Yet he figured in a somewhat heated controversy in the 'nineties about 'unfair deliveries.' Cricket writers generally regarded him as a 'thrower.' Fry was equally insistent that all his deliveries were scrupulously fair.

In his writings, Fry recalled how Jim Phillips, an Australian heavy-weight slow bowler turned umpire, was sent to Hove specially to 'no-ball' him.

'A bright move,' commented Fry, 'because, of course, I rolled up my sleeve above my elbow and bowled with my arm as rigidly straight as a poker. The great Jim, sighting himself as a strong umpire, was not deterred. Large as an elephant, he bluffly no-balled me nine times running. It was a farce and the Sussex authorities and players were very angry.

'However, I bowled often afterwards unscathed, even in Gentlemen v. Players' at Lord's and in a Test Match.'

Outside sport, Fry's greatest work was accomplished as director of the training ship *Mercury* which he saved from extinction and to which he devoted forty-two years of unsparing effort entirely without remuneration. He was assisted by his wife, formerly Miss Beatrice Holme-Sumner, who died in 1941. In recognition of their work, Charles Fry was given the honorary rank of Captain in the R.N.R. and Mrs. Fry was awarded the O.B.E.

In his absorbing autobiography, *Life Worth Living*, published in 1939, Fry told of how he 'very nearly became the King of Albania.' His association with Ranjitsinhji led him to occupy the position of substitute delegate for India at the Assemblies of the League of Nations at Geneva, where he composed a speech delivered by Ranji which 'turned Mussolini out of Corfu.'

The Albanians sent a delegation and appointed a Bishop, who bore a striking resemblance to W. G. Grace, to find 'an English country gentleman with £10,000 a year' for their King. Fry had the first qualification but not the second; but Ranji certainly could have provided the money. 'If I had really pressed Ranji to promote me,' said Fry, 'it is quite on the cards that I should have been King of Albania yesterday, if not today.'

In collaboration with his wife, he wrote the novel *A Mother's Son* which was published in 1907.

Other tributes included:

SIR PELHAM WARNER: 'His style was stiff, but he had a cast-iron defence and played well off his pads. He put his great mental powers into improving his cricket, and that he developed into a very great batsman there can be no question. Ranjitsinhji's opinion was that he was "the greatest of all batsmen of his time on all wickets and against every type of bowling." . . . Perhaps his greatest innings was his 129 at The Oval in 1907 against the famous South African googly bowlers – Vogler, Faulkner, Schwarz and White – on a wicket which *Wisden* says "was never easy" and on which "the South African bowling was very difficult and the fielding was almost free from fault." '

SIR JOHN HOBBS: 'I played with "C. B." in my first Test against Australia in this country. The year was 1909 and we both got blobs in the first innings. "C. B." persuaded Archie MacLaren, our captain, to let him go in first with me in the second innings, and we knocked off the 105 runs wanted for victory. . . . Later he was my skipper and we always got on well together. He was a great raconteur, and my wife and I have spent many happy hours just listening to him. I saw him at Lord's this season.'

SIR LEONARD HUTTON: 'He was a fine judge of a cricketer and he always took the keenest interest in the progress of young players. I had a number of letters from him when I was still in the game. They were kindly, encouraging letters which contained much sound advice which I greatly appreciated.'

FRANK WOOLLEY: 'He was one of the most solid batsmen I ever bowled against. He had a tremendous amount of determination, especially on difficult pitches, and the patience to play the type of game required. I remember once bowling to him on a "sticky" when the ball was turning a lot. I beat him several times in one over without getting his wicket. Next over, to my surprise, he demonstrated that I was not pitching the ball on the right spot and it was going over the stumps. That was typical of him. He was a great theorist.'

LAKER'S WONDERFUL YEAR [1957]

There was something else which happened in the 1956 season which the editor of the almanack deemed, with some justification, worthy of Cardus's attention, the freakish achievements of the Surrey and England off-spinner Jim Laker. Early in their tour the Australians had come to the Oval looking for their first victory over a county side. Their hopes were quickly destroyed by Laker who took all ten of their first innings wickets in 46 overs for eighty eight runs. The last time any Australian touring side had suffered so rare an indignity had been in 1878 when another Surrey bowler, the slow left-armer Edward Barratt, representing the Players at the Oval, took all ten for 43 runs in twenty one overs. What was doubly extraordinary about Laker's annus mirabilis was that in the championship he took only 57 wickets. In six matches against the tourists – the five Tests and the Surrey match – he took a further 58. The feat for Surrey had stretched the credulity of the cricketing world, but what was to follow was to surpass the bounds of earthly possibilities, reducing the Oval triumph to the mundane.

Before England went out to bat in the fourth Test at Old Trafford, with the series poised at one win each, Laker had been the outstanding slow bowler of the rubber, with twenty wickets at a cost of just over thirteen runs per wicket. But at Manchester, after Cowdrey and Richardson had laid the foundation of a huge total of 459, Laker proceeded very nearly to eclipse the miracle at the Oval by taking nine for 37. The visitors now followed on, facing the hopeless task of making 375 to avoid an innings defeat. This time Laker, writing himself into the history books with so firm a hand that so long as records are kept his name will be familiar, returned these figures:

Overs	Maidens	Runs	Wkts
51.2	23	53	10

His match figures were:

Overs	Maidens	Runs	Wkts
68	27	90	19

This fantastical feat established five new records:

1) *Nineteen wickets in a match, the most in any first-class game. The previous best had been 17, achieved twenty times. The most in a Test match was 17 for 159 by S. F. Barnes for England against South Africa at Johannesburg in 1913–14.*

2) *Ten wickets in an innings for the first time in a Test match. The previous best for England against Australia was eight for 35 by G. Lohmann of Surrey in 1886–87. The best for England in any Test innings, nine for 28, Lohmann against South Africa in 1895–96.*

3) *Ten wickets in an innings twice in one season for the first time.*

4) *Thirty nine wickets in four Test matches, equalling the record of A. V. Bedser as the highest number in an England-Australia series, with one match to play.*

5) *Fifty one wickets in five matches against the Australians to date in the season.*

By taking a further seven wickets in the fifth Test, Laker established another record, of 46 wickets in a series.

Nobody was better qualified than Cardus to place Laker's miracles in the context of the past. Only in his brief closing sentence does he seem not quite willing to acknowledge Laker's fitness to breathe the same air as S. F. Barnes and the beloved Cecil Parkin.

A GAINST the Australians in 1956, J. C. Laker bowled himself to a prominence which might seem legendary if there were no statistics to prove that his skill did indeed perform results and deeds hitherto not considered within the range of any cricketer, living or dead.

No writer of boys' fiction would so strain romantic credulity as to make his hero, playing for England against Australia, capture nine first innings wickets; then help himself to all ten in the second innings. Altogether, 19 for 90 in a Test match. If any author expected us to believe that his hero was not only capable in one chapter of a marvel as fantastic as all this, but also in another chapter, and our earlier chapter, bowled a whole Australian XI out, 10 for 88, the most gullible of his readers would, not without reason, throw the book away and wonder what the said author was taking him for.

Yet as far back as 1950 Laker was hinting that he possessed gifts which on occasion were at any moment likely to be visited by plenary inspiration and accomplish things not only unexpected but wondrous. At Bradford, five miles from his birthplace, Laker, playing for England v. The Rest, took 8 wickets for 2 runs in 14 overs – a feat which probably the great S. F. Barnes himself never imagined within mortal bowler's scope – or even desirable. Against Nottinghamshire at The Oval in 1955, Laker took 6 wickets for 5.

Between 1947 and 1953 he did the 'hat trick' four times.

Obviously the gods endowed him in his cradle with that indefinable power which from time to time generates talent to abnormal and irresistible achievement. And he has done his conjurations – they have been nothing less – by one of the oldest tricks of the bowlers' trade. Not by the new-fangled 'swing' and not by 'googlies' or Machiavellian deceit by flight through the air, has Laker hypnotised batsmen into helpless immobility, but by off-breaks and of the finger-spin type which would have been recognised by, and approved by, cricketers who played in Laker's own county of Yorkshire more than half a century ago. He really follows the great succession of Yorkshire off-spinners – from Ted Wainwright, Schofield Haigh, not forgetting F. S. Jackson, to George Macaulay, reaching to Illingworth of the present day.

Laker's actual finger spin probably has seldom been surpassed on a 'sticky' or dusty wicket, in point of velocity and viciousness after pitching. I can think only of Ted Wainwright, Cecil Parkin and Tom Goddard who shared Laker's ability to 'fizz' the ball right-handed from the offside. There was more temper in Macaulay's attack than there is in Laker's, more vehemence of character. But for sheer technical poten-

The President of Lancashire County Cricket Club in repose

TOP LEFT The wrist turns, the fingers roll, the ball twirls on its apparently innocent way. Jim Laker at Lord's, 1952

TOP RIGHT Sydney Barnes, malevolence personified. The greatest of all bowlers, whose every nerve and sinew is tensed in the moment of delivery

BELOW Lancastrians who loomed so large in Cardus's imagination – artist–cricketers who reflect the Edwardian lust for boaters and bicycles

Johnny Tyldesley, D'Artagnan at the crease

TOP Lord's, 1951. Len Hutton, the youngest of the old masters, demonstrates the poise of classic batsmanship
BELOW Denis Compton, 1947. *Annus mirabilis*, records shattered, history rearranged. None suffered more
than the South African tourists, who conceded five hundreds, including this innings of 163 for England at
Trent Bridge

TOP LEFT George Gunn (1879–1958). Scion of a great cricketing dynasty, a nonchalant vituoso, seen here grinning benignly, as usual

TOP RIGHT Herbert Strudwick, whose youthful wicketkeeping style was so adventurous that the Editor of Wisden suggested a series of fines to temper his exuberance

BELOW The Gentlemen, 1894. Back row (left to right): J. Douglas, J. R. Mason, G. J. Mordaunt, A. C. MacLaren. Middle row: S. M. J. Woods, H. T. Hewett, W. G. Grace, H. W. Bainsbridge, F. S. Jackson. Front row: G. MacGregor, A. E. Stoddart.

LEFT Cardus whiles away the *longueurs* of a life on the ocean wave by playing deck quoits. It will do, but it is certainly not cricket
RIGHT The great master walks out to bat at Melbourne serenely en route to nearly 60,000 runs and 197 centuries

The *nonpareil* Victor, seen in a moment of sublime self-absorption at The Oval, 1899, when the juvenile Cardus first became besotted. This photograph has probably adorned more cricket pavilions around the world than any other

TOP Bradman puts the English attack to the sword at Trent Bridge, 1930. The slaughter is destined to continue for another 18 years
BELOW Monday, 17 August 1925. Hobbs punishes the Somerset attack on his way to a century which will bring him level with Dr Grace's record of 126 hundreds. On the following afternoon Hobbs scored another to become the most prolific batsman in history

tiality, often for sheer actual spitefulness, Laker's off-spin must be regarded as entirely out of the ordinary, and very much his own.

Any great performer needs to be born at the right time. If Laker had begun to play for Surrey in the 1930's, when wickets at The Oval and on most large grounds were doped and rolled to insensibility, he might have made one or two appearances for Surrey, then vanished from the scene. Or maybe he would have remained in Yorkshire where pitches were never absolutely divorced from nature and original sin.

Laker was clever, too, to begin playing cricket and bowling off-spin after the alteration to the lbw rule dangerously penalised batsmen who had brought to a fine art the use of the pads to brilliant off-breaks pitching off the stumps and coming back like a knife – as Cecil Parkin's frequently did. Laker has been quick to adapt his arts to the deplorably unresourceful footwork of most batsmen of the present period; moreover he has, with the opportune judgment of those born to exceptional prowess, taken advantage of the modern development of the leg-trap.

On a good wicket, his attack naturally loses sting. His tempting slowish flight enables – or should enable – batsmen to get to the pitch of his bowling. He thrives on success in perhaps larger measure than most bowlers. He likes, more even than most bowlers, to take a quick wicket. There is sometimes an air of indolence in his movements, as he runs his loose lumbering run, swinging his arm slowly, but with the flick of venom at the last split second. At the end of his imperturbable walk back to his bowling mark he stares at the pavilion as though looking for somebody, but looking in a disinterested way. He is entirely what he is by technique – good professional technique, spin, length and the curve in the air natural to off-spin. He does not, as Macaulay and Parkin did, assert his arts plus passion of character and open relentless lust for spoils and the blood of all batsmen.

He is the Yorkshireman, at bottom, true enough; but Southern air has softened a little the native and rude antagonism. Even when he is 'on the kill' on a wicket of glue there is nothing demonstrably spiteful in his demeanour; he can even run through an Australian XI in a Test match, as at Manchester in his 'wonderful year', and seem unconcerned.

His bowling is as unassuming as the man himself and on the face of it as modest. That's where the fun comes in; for it is fun indeed to see the leisurely way Laker 'sends' his victims one after another, as though by some influence which has not only put the batsmen under a spell, but himself at the same time. Somebody has written that all genius goes to work partly in a somnambulistic way. Jim Laker is certainly more than a talented spinner.

DENIS COMPTON: THE CAVALIER
[1958]

Denis Compton represented a fascinating problem for Cardus to resolve. The belief that the spirit of cricket, and indeed of everything, must necessarily be conditioned by the temper of the times would seem to be contradicted by the amazing cricket played by Compton in the immediate post-war years, cricket which would have been hard to credit even in the Edwardian golden age, which had been marked by the heroics of Gilbert Jessop and Major Poore. Cardus deploys this apparent contradiction of his ideas as the exception which proves his rule. After the euphoria of unconditional surrender and the return of millions of serving men and women to civilian life, a disinterested observer might have convinced himself that the British were subsiding into a disenchantment brought about by the realisation that the good old days, if ever they had existed, were not going to return. The world was too much changed for that. In the meantime, rationing persisted, the mark of utility was still everywhere in evidence and in the arctic English winter of 1946–47, fuel shortages had reduced the conquerors to shivering misery.

At a deeper level, the childlike faith of the mass of voters in the omniscience of the first Labour government ever to rule with an overall majority was speedily corrupted by debacles like the Ground Nuts scheme and the first spectacular corruption case, in which the defendant accused of bribing a government underling jabbered his way into the dictionaries of quotations by protesting to his inquisitor, 'Don't confuse me with the truth'. The cadaverous Chancellor of the Exchequer, Stafford Cripps, demanded with messianic fervour that the British continue to tighten their belts and was obeyed. Wealth, thundered the Chancellor, was immoral, and it was perhaps a pity that by the time his widow died leaving one third of a million pounds, nobody cared enough any more about the hypocrisy of Socialist moneybags even to make jokes about it. So the nation suffered and shivered, and prepared to dump its last unsullied political ideal. Is it taking Cardusian beliefs too far to suggest that this mood was borne out with depressing accuracy by much of the cricket of the immediate post-war years? Too many county games as well as Test matches tended to be pointless little wars of attrition and Cardus was only one of the more prominent among countless onlookers who dared to wonder if the Welfare State, for all its good intentions, might not have a stultifying effect on the expression of quiddity of temperament in all walks of national life.

And yet, laughing gaily in the face of all this glumpot theorising, there was Denis Compton who, if Cardus was right in his assumptions, had defied the zeitgeist with astonishing brilliance. For this reason, and because of his connoisseur's relish for an inspired executant, Cardus chose

Compton as a hero, rightly suggesting that to crowds wearied by the deprivations of war, and now frustrated by rules and regulations and the filling out of forms drawn up by illiterate bureaucrats, Compton was better than a tonic. Cardus draws our attention to the fact that in an age of rationing and shortages, Compton batted like a profligate. In 1947 one of the few commodities in plentiful supply were runs. Compton scored nearly 4000 of them, including eighteen centuries, leaving all existing records far behind. But it was not the quantity but the quality which mesmerised those who ran to watch the deeds being performed. No more exhilarating batsman of true class had ever been seen before and it seemed altogether too cruel that this paragon should have been rendered mortal after all by something as mundane as a knee injury. The troublesome kneecap was eventually removed and, although Compton's batting survived this trauma, there is no question that the handicap shortened his career by several seasons. When he writes his appreciation for the 1958 almanack, Cardus expresses the pious hope that perhaps there is more to come. His optimism was sadly confounded when Compton bowed out of the first-class game in 1958 at the age of forty. Hobbs had scored more than half of his 197 centuries after the age of 40.

D ENIS COMPTON counts amongst those cricketers who changed a game of competitive and technical interest to sportsmen into a highly individual art that appealed to and fascinated thousands of men and women and boys and girls, none of whom possessed a specialist clue, none of whom could enter into the fine points of expert skill. He lifted cricket into an atmosphere of freedom of personal expression. The score-board seldom told you more than half the truth about what he was doing on the field of play. In an age increasingly becoming standardised, with efficiency the aim at the expense of impulse – for impulse is always a risk – Compton went his unburdened way, a law to himself.

Most cricketers, even some of the greatest, need the evidence of the score-board to demonstrate their gifts over by over; if they are not scoring, if they are compelled by steady bowling or by force of adverse circumstances to fall back on the textbook, they are certain, in such moments, to wear out the patience of all who are not vehemently partisans, or students of academic zeal and watchfulness.

Even a Sir Leonard Hutton or a Peter May needs to do well to convince the lay onlooker that he is really worth watching for hours. Compton fascinated all lovers of cricket, informed or uninformed, whether he was making runs or not, or whether he was taking wickets or not.

In fact, whenever Compton seemed seriously in trouble and under the necessity to work hard he was then even a more arresting spectacle than usual. As we watched him groping and lunging and running out of his ground before the ball was released, we were more than ever aware that here was no merely talented cricketer; here was one under the sway and in the thrall of incalculable genius. For it is certain that Compton often was as much in the dark as the rest of us as to why and how he came by his own personal achievements, how he added to a fundamentally sound technical foundation an unpredictable inspiration, as though grace descended on him.

Once in Australia he ran into a new bowler of curious variations of spin; I think the bowler was Iverson. Compton was momentarily visited by one of his moods of eccentric fallibility. He played forward as though sightless; he played back as though wanting to play forward. He apparently didn't quite know where he was or with what he was coping. At the other end of the wicket a comparative newcomer was batting steadily, but runs were not being scored quickly enough. So the young novice approached Compton between overs for instructions. 'You go on just as you are,' was Denis's advice. 'You're playing well. I'll get on with the antics.'

At his greatest – which is really to say most days in a season – he made batting look as easy and as much a natural part of him as the way he walked or talked. Versatility of stroke-play; swift yet, paradoxically, leisurely footwork; drives that were given a lovely lightness of touch by wristy flexion at the last second; strokes that were born almost before the bowler himself had seen the ball's length – all these were the signs of the Master. Yet the word 'Master' in all its pontifical use was not applied to him but, in his period, reserved for Sir Leonard. The reason is that Compton's cricket always looked young, fresh and spontaneous. The resonant term 'Master' implies a certain air of age and pompousness, a Mandarin authority and poise.

When cricket was begun again, after the Hitler war, Compton in his wonderful years of 1946–1947 expressed by his cricket the renewed life and hopes of a land and nation that had come out of the dark abyss. In a period still sore and shabby and rationed, Compton spread his happy favours everywhere. The crowd sat in the sun, liberated from anxiety and privation. The strain of long years of affliction fell from all shoulders as Compton set the ball rolling or speeding or rippling right and left, as he leaned to it and swept it from the off round the leg boundary, as he danced forward or danced backwards, his hair tousled beyond the pacifying power of any cream or unguent whatsoever . . . yes, the crowd sunned themselves as much in Compton's batting as in the beneficial rays coming from the blue sky. Men and women, boys and girls, cheered him to his century, and ran every one of his runs with him.

As I say, his batting was founded on sound first principles – nose on the ball, the body near to the line. But he was perpetually rendering acquired science and logic more and more flexible. He was a born improviser. Once a beautiful spinner from Douglas Wright baffled him all the way. He anticipated a leg-break, but it was a 'googly' when it pitched. To adjust his future physical system at the prompting of instinct working swift as lightning, Compton had to perform a contortion of muscles which sent him sprawling chest-flat on the wicket. But he was in time to sweep the ball to the long-leg boundary.

It is not enough to remember his brilliance only, his winged victories, his moments of animation and fluent effortless control. He has, in the face of dire need, played defensively with as tenaciously and as severely a principled skill as Hutton commanded at his dourest. Compton's 184 for England at Trent Bridge in 1948 must go down in history among the most heroically Spartan innings ever played. . . . England batted a second time 344 behind, and lost Washbrook and Edrich for 39. Compton and Hutton then staved away disaster until 150 was reached, and Hutton was bowled.

In a dreadful light Compton defended with terrific self-restraint against Miller at his fiercest. It is possible the match might have been snatched by him from the burning. Alas, at the crisis, a vicious 'bumper' from Miller rose shoulder high. Compton instinctively hooked, thought better of it too late, slipped on the greasy turf, and fell on his wicket. For six hours and fifty minutes he mingled defence and offence in proportion. He did not, merely because his back was to the wall, spare the occasional loose ball. At Manchester, in the same rubber of 1948, Compton again showed us that there was stern stuff about him, the ironside breastplate as well as the Cavalier plume. He was knocked out by Lindwall. Stitches were sewn into his skull and, after a rest, he came back when England's score was 119 for five. He scored 145 not out in five hours twenty minutes.

These two superbly heroic innings, in the face of odds, may be taken as symbolical of a life and career not all sunshine and light heart, although Compton has lavished plenty of both on us. Nature was generous with him at his cradle; she gave him nearly everything. Then in his prime and heyday she snatched away his mainspring, she crippled him with many summers of his genius still to come.

In his fortieth year he is as young at heart and as richly endowed in batsmanship as at any time of his life. There are ample fruits in his cornucopia yet – if it were not for 'that knee'! Still, we mustn't be greedy. He has shared the fruits of the full and refreshing cornucopia generously with us. He will never be forgotten for his precious gifts of nature and skill, which statistics have no power to indicate let alone voice. Perhaps there is more of him to come. It is hard to believe that nature is any readier than we ordinary mortals are to see him at last reposing with the authentic 'Old Masters'. Whatever his future, our hearts won't let him go. Thank you, Denis!

CHARLES MACARTNEY AND GEORGE GUNN [1959]

A year later Cardus was faced once more with the paradox which was to become his constant companion for the rest of his life. He liked nothing better than to indulge in fond reveries on the past, to rhapsodise about long-lost afternoons in the sun when the cricketers of his youth had come to embody that youth by sporting in the field as he watched. He was provided with a legitimate excuse for indulging himself in this way each time one of the old giants passed on. The 1959 almanack carries his double obituary on two of the abiding passions of his life, Charles Macartney, the great Australian batsman known as the Governor-General, and another GG, the beloved George Gunn who, it could be said without a trace of exaggeration, and in whimsical contradiction of any death notices, has been immortalised in the pieces which Cardus never tired of writing about him. There was a certain symmetry about the lives of these two great players. Gunn (1879–1958) and Macartney (1886–1958) made their Test debuts in the same match at Sydney in December 1907, and although they went on to highly contrasting careers, this coincidence on occasion coupled them in Cardus's mind.

Macartney remains one of the very few international cricketers whose larger fame is due not just to Cardus. He figures intermittently in the memoirs of Cardus's whimsical friend James Matthew Barrie, whose idolatry of so great a Test star quickly mellowed into a sort of tutorial solicitude. Once, when Macartney, having lunched, taken tea and dined with the rest of the Australian side at Stanway, the country house rented by Barrie each summer, declined the offer to stay the night, his excuse was that he had to write a letter home to his wife. Barrie offered to write the letter for him, which he did. When Macartney went home, he found that Barrie had arranged free tickets to be provided for the cricketer and his wife for all Australian productions of Barrie's plays. As for Gunn, Cardus rejoiced in that remarkable man's indifference to statistics and the fate of matches generally. R. C. Robertson-Glasgow took the same view as Cardus, and wrote of Gunn:

> I see that, apart from his 62 centuries, an average of 26.71 stands against his name. 'How very funny', I can hear him say. 'Why not 267.1, or 2.671, or 2671?' In genius, in pleasure given and enjoyed, the last figure is about the truth.

CHARLES MACARTNEY and George Gunn were two great individualists amongst batsmen, alike in their determination to occupy the crease on their own terms. But they were independent with a difference. Macartney revelled in constant aggression. He played a defensive stroke as a last resort. A maiden over to him he received as a personal affront and insult. George Gunn would one day make runs quickly and as audaciously as Macartney, but he never appeared to bustle. Next day, in fact, it might happen in the same innings, he would suddenly change mood and gear, and indulge in stonewalling obviously at his own whim, no credit to the bowler. George took little notice of the scoreboard. A few days before his death he came to Lord's last summer, and he told me that he had 'always batted according.' It would have been beside the point if I had asked him 'according to what?'

In June 1913, at Trent Bridge, Yorkshire went in first against Nottinghamshire and scored 471, leaving Nottinghamshire with only a draw to play for. Gunn scored 132 in six hours, so wilfully slow that Yorkshire bowlers taunted him, asking 'Hast lost thi strokes, George?' And George replied, 'Oh, you'd like to see some strokes, would you? Well, next innings I'll show you some.' Yorkshire declared their second innings closed and Nottinghamshire's total, when rain washed out the day, was 129 for three wickets. The score-card, preserved in silk at Trent Bridge, reads as follows:

Gunn not out	*109*
Lee b Haigh	*4*
Hardstaff run out	*3*
Alletson c Booth b Rhodes	*0*
Gunn, J. not out	*8*
Extras	*5*
	129

Gunn scored his 109 in 85 minutes. 'I decided to play swashbuckle just to show 'em,' he explained. In another match at Trent Bridge, in August 1928, Nottinghamshire, playing Kent, wanted only 157 to win on a perfect wicket on a beautiful third afternoon. There was heaps of time left and the crowd settled down to watch Gunn and Whysall jog home comfortably. But George scored exactly 100 in an hour and a half, so that the game came to an unnecessarily abrupt end, with an hour or two of sunshine wasted. I asked Gunn afterward, 'Why did you hurry? And on such a lovely afternoon.' 'Well,' he replied in his amiable, indulgent way, 'when "Dodge" (Whysall) and me were coming down pavilion stairs, a member spoke to me and said something he shouldn't have said. I can't tell you what it was, but it annoyed me. So I went and took it out of Kent bowlin'.'

Macartney on the kill was as the tiger with his prey. George played with bowling, the best in the world, like cat with mouse. He didn't eat it after he'd killed it. Macartney put the attack unmercifully to the sword. In 1926 Armstrong's conquering team feared Macaulay of Yorkshire. Macartney decided to knock Macaulay out of the rubber at Leeds, the third Test, and Macaulay's first that year. A. W. Carr, captain of England, won the toss and sent Australia in on a soft but not difficult pitch. (Charles Parker, deadliest of left-arm spinners, was 'drink-waiter.') Warren Bardsley fell to a slip catch off the first ball sent down by Maurice Tate and Macartney was missed by Carr in the slips off the fifth ball of the same over. Macartney, not at all interested in his good or Carr's bad luck, immediately annihilated the England attack. He scored a century before lunch, incidentally removing the menace of Macaulay once and for all out of Australia's way.

In 1921 at Trent Bridge, he scored 345 in three hours fifty minutes. He was missed when 9 in the slips by none other than our other hero – George Gunn. Macartney cut and drove with a blinding swiftness and so utterly demoralised the Nottinghamshire attack that A. W. Carr decided to make a gesture which would convey to the critics in the Pavilion some idea that he, at least, was keeping his head. He decided to change his bowlers round. 'It wouldn't have mattered a damn to Charles which end Fred Barratt or Tich Richmond was bowling from, but the move would be proof that I was still in charge.' He decided to bowl the odd over himself to enable the change-round. 'It'll look all right in the score-sheet in all the slaughter,' he thought. 'A. W. Carr 1–1–0–0.' If my readers will consult *Wisden* of 1922, they will discover that Carr's single over was plundered to the extent of 24 runs. 'And I pitched 'em wide where I thought he couldn't possibly reach them,' said Carr. No bowler, no tactics, no kind of field could tame Macartney.

In the 1926 Test at Old Trafford against Fred Root's 'Leg theory' inswingers, Macartney took three hours to reach a century. Though he hit 14 boundaries in that time, he assured me afterwards that he had hated the innings. ' "Rootie" knew he couldn't get me out, so he bowled wide. Only fools get out that way.' He often batted in a temper. In the Triangular Tests of 1912 when England played Australia at Lord's, somebody in the dressing-room teased Charles as he was putting on his pads. 'Cripes, Charlie, "Barney" (Barnes) and Frank Foster are goin' to do it again.' (It was the season following the great Barnes-Foster triumphs in Australia.) 'Cripes, Charlie, "Barney's" pitchin' 'em on the leg and only just missin' the off.' When Charles went out to bat he was, so I was authoritatively informed, 'livid with rage.' He scored 99; D'Artagnan and Mercutio in one. Barnes took none for 74.

In Test matches Macartney scored 2,132 runs, average 41.80. George Gunn, in two rubbers, both against Australia in Australia, scored 843 runs in nineteen innings, with an average of over 44.

Only once was he invited to play for England in England – at Lord's in 1909, when he was lbw Cotter 1, and b Armstrong 0. Nobody to this day knows why George Gunn was not called into action for England in 1921 against Gregory and McDonald. He liked fast bowling and used to walk out of his crease, in leisurely fashion, to play it. 'If I stayed in crease for it,' he explained to me, 'it comes up too 'igh, because I'm not tall. So I goes out to meet it on the rise, where I can get on top.' A young Lancashire wicket-keeper who had not seen George before was astounded to see him 'walking-out' to McDonald. 'Ah,' thinks the young wicket-keeper, 'if ah can stump him off "Mac" ah'll sure get me county cap.' So next ball, as George sauntered forth while McDonald was still gliding into action, the young wicket-keeper risked stealing up to the stumps. Gunn played down a nasty kicking express to his toes, then turning round, saw the young 'keeper's nose near the bails. 'Good mornin', young feller,' he said. 'Nice day, isn't it?'

He celebrated his 50th birthday in June 1929 by scoring 164 not out against Worcestershire. He promised me, weeks in advance of the event, that he would thus celebrate it. There was nothing, in fact, that he couldn't do with a cricket bat. He once said to me, 'Ever since I played the game – and I began in "W. G.'s" time – batters have always made two big mistakes. First of all, they take too much notice of the state of the wicket, pattin' and pokin' – it only encourages bowlers. Then – and this is more serious – they take too much notice of the bowling.'

Often he stonewalled with obvious self-determination, seldom because he was compelled to by the attack. 'I never hurry,' was his motto. 'Either on the field or off it.' When he made runs swiftly, he was still apparently taking his own time with ample ease and leisure to enjoy himself. He was a shortish, well-built but not at all a sturdy man, a little bandy in the legs, quizzical of eye and face, and slow and humorous in his talk. In 1906 he suffered a haemorrhage of the lungs and was obliged to winter in New Zealand. He happened to be in Australia in December 1907 when A. O. Jones's M.C.C. team were there. He was called on for the Test matches and scored 119 in his first Test innings at Sydney. Though he seemed to improvise strokes and do all sorts of original things with the best bowlers, he was at bottom faultless of style; he owed much to instruction when young from the scrupulously classical Arthur Shrewsbury. It is true that Gunn totalled 35,190 runs in first-class cricket, average 35.90 with 62 hundreds, but statistics tell little of his genius. We might as well add up the quavers and crotchets in Rossini's operas. He was himself, delightful and lovable; and he 'always batted according'.

Macartney's resource and brilliance were vehement. His innings often plundered the attack savagely. His strokes might flash at times all round the wicket, but there was no yeilding humour in them. He was after the blood of Englishmen. As the bowler prepared to run, Macartney would raise his bat above his head, legs apart, as though stretching himself loose for action. From under the long peak of his green Australian cap gleamed two eyes bright as a bird's. The chin was thrust out in defiance. His shoulders were square, and he also was below medium height. His arms were powerful, wrists as steel. He was not born commanding; only after hard service did he earn his nickname 'The Governor-General.' He was self-taught, never coached. To begin with he had few strokes at all. In his first Tests – during 1907–1908 rubber, the same in which Gunn first had international honours – Macartney's place in the order of going in varied. Twice he was seventh or eighth. He was known then less as a batsman than as a left-handed slow spinner. In England, his first trip here, he took 11 wickets for 85 against England at Leeds, in July 1909.

In the same rubber, at Birmingham, in England's first innings, he went on first and in a few overs he got rid of MacLaren, bowled for 5, Hobbs lbw for 0 and C. B. Fry bowled for 0. No spinner has enjoyed so impressive a haul at so little expense. In those days his spin and length were superb.

Macartney goes down in the game's history side by side with Victor Trumper. He did not share Victor's effortless and chivalrous poise. For all his dazzling sword play and footwork, Macartney was an ironside cavalier. None the less, he belongs to the great immortal and decreasing company of cricketers who, while they are attending to the duty to their team – and the first duty of any player is to try to win – combine serious intent with personal relish, thus winning not only our admiration, but our affection, remaining warm in our memory for years.

FIVE STALWARTS RETIRE [1960]

The Cardus essay for 1960 was something of a departure, a farewell wave on the occasion, not of death, but of that lesser cricketing death, retirement. The five outstanding players who ended their careers at the end of the 1959 season were all gifted cricketers, well-known to Cardus through his summer duties for 'The Guardian'. He had studied their art from the perspective of every Press Box in the country and had drawn his characteristic conclusions. The opening section, devoted to Godfrey Evans, invokes the spirit of Jazz as Cardus attempts to convey the acrobatic ebullience of his subject – at which point he leads us once more back into the lush pastures of the past, drawing a contrast between the leaping, gambolling Evans and the classic self-effacing serenity of W. A. Oldfield, whose wicketkeeping style had been so polite, even to the brink of the apologetic, that Cardus had memorably defined him as the Claude Duval of keepers.

The second sketch reminds the writer that he had spotted Washbrook as a teenager certain one day to play for England. Yet again he takes his chance of measuring the present against the past by linking the apprentice Washbrook with the great Makepeace, who here receives a brand new line of dialogue. The wave goodbye to Dennis Brookes is a pretty tribute to a cricketer who year by year amassed many thousands of runs and dozens of centuries without ever quite being considered among the top rank of batsman. As Cardus observes, 'It is sometimes a mad, unjust world'. The essay on George Tribe chronicles the career of a different kind of unTest player, a brilliant Australian immigrant who, like Fred Freer, Bruce Dooland and Colin McCool, forewent the chance of a distinguished international career by throwing in his lot with an English county. Had Tribe been English-born he would have walked into the national side of the period and Cardus is quite justified in nominating him as one of those players who never succumbed to the merely mechanistic. The Laker essay is very brief and to the point; Cardus had already had his say on Laker's classic purity of style in the 1957 edition. But there is one tiny but oddly pleasing additional touch here, the invoking of Kingsley Amis's bestseller of the 1950s, 'Lucky Jim', to apostrophise a great bowler.

The most striking aspect of the five farewells is one no more than hinted at by Cardus. In the postwar years, the convention was being established of what the great heroes of the past would have regarded as early or even premature retirement. Laker was 38 when he walked off the field for the last time. Evans and Tribe were 39. How would their defections have struck indestructibles like Frank Woolley, Jack Hobbs, Philip Mead and Wilfred Rhodes who, at the age of fifty, all remained accomplished players? In the 1960s the advent of the one-day game certainly made life more rigorous for the professional cricketer but the decision to stop playing by artists like Evans and Tribe came as a sad shock to thousands of their devotees who had looked forward to several more seasons of enjoyment watching their heroes.

Tribute is paid here to five personalities who have recently given up English first-class cricket: Godfrey Evans, Cyril Washbrook, Dennis Brookes, George Tribe, Jim Laker. We would remind our readers that Mr. Cardus devoted a whole article to Laker in the 1957 *edition of 'Wisden.'*

GODFREY EVANS

GODFREY EVANS must be counted amongst the very few cricketers of his period who did not possess a birth and residential qualification to play and become a life member of the Anonymities C.C. When he was on the field he was unmistakably a character expressing himself without reserve. A wicket-keeper, of course, is so placed that the eyes of the spectators are drawn to him; he occupies a main centre of attraction. But there have been wicket-keepers – and quite good ones – who have seemed not much more than accessories to the bowlers' violence and craftiness. They have caught the catches obviously coming to them, and they have kept the byes down to a reasonable minimum.

Godfrey did not just wait for chances which any competent keeper could take. He was creative. With abnormal anticipation and agility he could turn a brilliant leg-glance, a certain four most times, into a batsman's fatal error.

Three marvellous catches by Evans remain in my memory; and I imagine that Neil Harvey cannot forget them either – for in each case he was the astonished batsman. At Brisbane in December 1950, he turned Bedser beautifully to leg, a swift low glance perfectly timed, and he was then 74. Evans apparently saw the stroke even as Harvey was positioning himself to perform it. So rapid was the sideway swoop of Evans that he made the catch look easy. Then at Melbourne in January

1955 when Australia wanted 165 to win with eight wickets left, Harvey flicked the seventh ball of the morning (from Tyson) round the corner and this time Evans dived full length to the right, clutching the ball in his out-stretched glove. Many people were of the opinion that the destination of the Ashes – won by Len Hutton's team – hung on that catch for England went on to win the match by 128 runs. Likewise at Lord's, in June 1956, he flung the whole of himself at another lightning glance, this time off Bailey, and changed an artistic stroke into an impulsive error on Harvey's part. Three truly sinful catches. Evans was constantly bringing off catches which caused even the bowler to question his own eyesight and credulity.

Such a wicket-keeper is a positive force in the attack. With Evans behind the stumps, the greatest batsmen hesitate to attempt strokes which, with stumpers of average ability behind them, they would have put into execution confidently. Alec Bedser would be the first to give evidence on behalf of Evans's sure and avaricious opportunism. By the way, it was only compensatory justice that in the Old Trafford Test of 1953, Harvey when 52 not out was sensationally missed by Evans off Bailey, after which cornucopia of luck Harvey proceeded to score 122.

Evans was not a keeper in the classic style, not all quiet balanced outlines, like Bertie Oldfield, who used to catch or stump in a flash and yet appear the embodiment of politeness and almost obsequious deportment, as though saying to his victim: 'Awfully sorry, but it is my painful duty – Law 42, you know.' Evans was modern in the most surrealistic patterns achieved by his motions. He seemed to get to the ball by leaving out physical shapings and adjustments which ordinary human anatomies have to observe. He was a boneless wonder.

Did he play to the gallery? If he did so the quicksilver snapdragon leapings, dartings and flickerings of him was second nature. Nobody could pose with Evans's accuracy and get away with it. An old master stumper of the 1900's once told me that Evans broke the rules of the wicket-keepers' technique, that his preliminary position could be classically questioned. I could not follow his pedantic arguments; but I replied to the effect that genius usually walks according to its own 'laws.'

Evans belonged to the present age in his genius for a sort of 'jazz' or 'swing' of the traditional procedure of his calling. Basically he was sound, scientifically prepared for the right and rapid movements to which he added his own mental and muscular conjurations. He was perky, jaunty, in a way a 'comic,' with method in his cavortings. It is no surprise to learn that he was not a man of Kent by birth but of Finchley; he was in fact the 'Cockney' keeper in *excelsis*. Nobody ever saw Godfrey Evans look bored or uninterested on the field or off it. At the end of the longest day he remained alive in every nerve. And his flesh, apparently, was inexhaustible. It was a vitality of spirit, reinforced by humour.

The crowd hailed him with glee as he walked out to bat. He won the usual and easy laughs by darting in and out of his crease, pretending to go for unsafe runs. As a fact, he could be a very dangerous and even a beautiful driver, as the West Indies discovered at Old Trafford in 1950, when he came to the crease in England's first innings with the score 88 for five.

While Bailey defended, he attacked and scored his maiden Test century of 104 out of 161 put on for the sixth wicket. As proof that Evans is not all 'fun and games' but a true cricketer, we can point to his wonderful adaption and self-discipline at Adelaide in January 1947. In England's second innings England had lost eight wickets for 255, Compton not out. Evans actually did not score a run until he had driven Bradman and the Australian attack almost to desperate measures for ninety-five minutes. In all, Evans obstructed for two hours and a quarter. He and Compton scored 85 together and, without being separated, saved the match, Evans not out 10, made from seven of the 98 balls he received. The innings was evidence of the serious side of Evans who, as with every born and skilful man of comedy, knew, and still knows, how to time a laugh.

Cricket is the poorer for his retirement at the early age of 39. Most of us had thought that time would toil and pant after him in vain.

CYRIL WASHBROOK

CYRIL WASHBROOK, at the age of 18, scored 152 in his second match for Lancashire at Old Trafford in June 1933. But before he had scored as many as 20 it was clear that we were watching an England batsman in the making; and I did not think I was being prophetic but merely anticipatory when that day I wrote of him in the *Manchester Guardian* as a boy destined for the highest honours. I fancy that I warned him against his tendency to risk lbw by hitting across the line of the ball to the on. He has in his career fallen a victim to obstruction as frequently as any other cricketer of his period. But Cyril was never willing to deny himself a brilliant hook or a swinging on-drive simply because the ball might be well on the way to the stumps when it collided with his pads.

At Nottingham against Australia, in June 1948, he was caught at long-leg from a hook off Lindwall and his score was half-a-dozen when he took his liberty. In the same rubber, at Manchester, he was twice dropped at long-leg by Hassett, who then borrowed a hat from a spectator. Washbrook learned his first-class cricket in a period when Old Trafford was in the inevitable slump which usually follows a lengthy victorious sequence, though losing only one match,in 1933. Washbrook for the season made 518, average 28.77. Next year, 1934, Lancashire won the County Championship again but Washbrook, for all his promise, was allowed to play in only six games. In 1935 Lancashire receded to fourth place in the tournament but Washbrook totalled 1,724 runs, average 45.36. Yet in the season of 1936 I was obliged to make a protest in my newspaper because he was left out of the Lancashire team at Trent Bridge. It will be understood, then, that Washbrook was brought up in a hard school. Makepeace, though no longer dourly opening the Lancashire innings, was the brain centre at Old Trafford. If a young player was clean bowled by an off-break Makepeace would meet him in the dressing-room and scornfully ask, 'Where *was* your legs?'

Washbrook had not celebrated his 25th birthday when war broke out in 1939, taking from him years of opportunity in the game just as he was arriving at mastery. With the return to peace, he asserted himself in unmistakable fashion by scoring 2,400 runs in the season, averaging 68.57. Naturally he went to Australia in 1946–47. And now began the Hutton-Washbrook first-wicket partnership for England – and such was the bad luck of both of them – they had to face the very hot music of Lindwall and Miller. I doubt if any cricketer – Hobbs, Sutcliffe, MacLaren, Hayward, Trumper or Duff – faced an opening attack more menacing, more challenging to eyesight, nerve, skill and breastbone than Lindwall's and Miller's, with Lindwall's subtlety and the modern use of the new ball thrown in. We often forget, when we are trying to estimate a batsman's quality, the power of the bowling he has been called on to face. Twice did Washbrook get a hundred in the face of the Lindwall-Miller barrage; and at Old Trafford in 1948 his 85 not out was cut and hooked from Lindwall and Miller at their most desperately short and fast. In all, Washbrook played 66 innings for England for 2,569 runs, average 42.81. Perhaps of all of them he most gratefully remembers his 98, played with an autumnal serenity at Leeds in 1956, when at the age of 41 and a few months he was recalled to the England XI. Three England wickets had fallen to Archer for 17 in an hour when Washbrook came in. Peter May was in dire trouble. Washbrook, nearly lbw straight away, calmly piloted the innings through the storm. In five hours and a half he scored 98.

At his best he was a batsman of panache. He always looked the born cricketer, whether at the wicket or in the field, where at cover-point he was brilliant, yet somehow relaxed as he stood there while the bowler walked to his starting place; Washbrook had about him a casual wandering sort of air, even if indifferent, until the moment came for action; then he was as galvanic as graceful. I liked the way he wore his cap; no cricket cap looked so jaunty of peak as Washbrook's. His shoulders were the true cricketer's shoulders. At the wicket he would thrust out his chest reminiscent of a pouter pigeon. Whenever he clamped his right foot on the crease, those who knew him well – Lancastrians, of course – knew that he was about to put the bowlers to the sword. He could, in the mood, cut an attack to ribbons.

On other days strangely passive moods came over him. He could seem almost strokeless and unsmiling. At Lord's in 1950, against the West Indies, he reached a century at close of play and next morning made not another run from Ramadhin and Valentine in half an hour. Sometimes I think he was unlucky to come into cricket when he did – in the epoch of MacLaren and J. T. Tyldesley his swordlike stroke-play would have been encouraged; for in his uninhibited form he could have stood comparison even with MacLaren and Tyldesley. I have seen Washbrook bat with a really majestical command and contempt. He had on his day the grand manner and who – since Wally Hammond – has shared the imperial secret?

DENNIS BROOKES

DENNIS BROOKES is one of the finest in all that splendid company of cricketers who somehow have not played for England as frequently as they were entitled to by reason of first-class gifts of skill and of character. In a period in which our Selection Committee have looked far and wide for batsmen accustomed to facing the new ball at the opening of an innings, Brookes has been passed by, though in fairness to the said Selection Committee, the fact must be pointed out that Brookes was nearing his fortieth year when the Hutton-Washbrook combination came to an end. He was also far too long neglected by Lord's in the Gentlemen v. Players match. Only once has he played for England – in the West Indies in 1948 when he chipped a bone in a finger in the opening Test and was out of the game for the tour, with a century to his credit v. Barbados.

He was born in Yorkshire, ten miles from Leeds, yet the County inexplicably never heard of the schoolboy, though he scored 145 not out for his local team. Northamptonshire got to hear of him and gave him his chance in 1934 when he was not yet 18. Against the county of his birth – his first match – the boy shaped promisingly enough, scoring 19 not out in a Northamptonshire total of 100 against Bowes and Verity in good form. But not until 1937 did he impinge on the critical eye; that season he scored 1,285 runs, average 26.77. The war sadly interrupted his cricket, as with many other young hopefuls, after he had headed the Northamptonshire players in the first-class batting list – 1,531, average 36.45.

In a county not until recently blessed with confidence, Brookes has perhaps enjoyed a position which could be envied by many of his colleagues who are always in the limelight. He soon proved himself not only a sound and cultured craftsman with the bat, but better still, he became known and admired as a man of modesty and conscience. His appointment to the Northamptonshire County C.C.'s captaincy in 1954, succeeding F. R. Brown, had the approval of all his friends. Brookes never sought honours, but when last season he was chosen for the first time to represent the Players against the Gentlemen at Lord's, he had the honour of captaining the side, he was obviously a proud man.

In his career Dennis Brookes scored 30,874 runs, average 36.10, with 71 centuries. And only one Test match – and none in England! It is sometimes a mad, unjust world. He took his toll of boundaries from the touring sides – 93 off the West Indies (including Constantine and Martindale) in 1939, and a brilliant 144 not out against the Australians in 1957. He was never a batsman trying to catch the uneducated popular eye; but for the connoisseur he was always good to look at, in control of a technique firmly based on first principles, with modest touches of grace added. Few cricketers have served their counties and the game more faithfully than Dennis Brookes – or have got as much pleasure, a reason for pride, from it.

GEORGE TRIBE

GEORGE EDWARD TRIBE, like Bruce Dooland, found opportunities to display his skill in English county cricket after Australia, apparently, had turned a blind eye to it. He was born in Melbourne, learned the fundamentals there and actually played for Australia in three Tests during the rubber of 1946–47, when W. R. Hammond's team were the opponents. I saw him bowl in the Tests at Brisbane and Sydney, and though he took only the wickets of Ikin and Voce in six innings for 330 runs, the discerning watcher had reason to write optimistically of his future as a left-hand wrist spinner, in the style of the erratic but on his day inspired Fleetwood-Smith. After successes in Lancashire League cricket, he qualified for Northamptonshire; and he accomplished the 'double' in his first season of 1952 – in all matches. For Northamptonshire he scored 969 runs, average 29.36, and took 116 wickets, average 25.46. In all he achieved this all-round performance in seven of his eight summers in English cricket.

Like all bowlers who flick the ball from the back of the hand, Tribe was constantly fascinating to watch. When the wrist-spinner is bowling 'tosh' he is worth watching as closely as when he is on the spot. At any moment he might send along the unplayable ball that leaves the batsman standing. Tribe on his day was extremely difficult to play, though maybe his 'wrong-'un' was not as deceptive as Fleetwood-Smith's. But day by day he was the more accurate of the two – I compare him with Fleetwood-Smith because of his left-handed action. He could, of course, lose pitch and direction at times, and become a batsman's gift from heaven. All wrist-spinners must pay this price. It is much easier to rub a new ball on your thighs and let the seam and shine bowl for you.

Tribe was not only a great wicket-taker and a batsman of sound defence and strong stroke-play; he was a cricketer who enhanced the charm and variety of a game which seemingly is, more and more, developing into a routine standardised efficiency. Not only will he be missed by the county of his adoption, his retirement from the English scene at the early age of 39 is premature; and deprives the game of skill, entertainment value and genuine sportsmanship, whether luck was smiling at him or frowning.

JIM LAKER

The passing from first-class cricket of 'JIM' LAKER must be regarded as truly historical. For long The Oval will look rather empty in his absence; the England XI is already feeling the pinch, for lack of his off-spin. He was not only a craftsman in a great tradition; also he had his obvious character, his personal touch. Never did he appear to hurry; not always did he seem eager to bowl. When he was at his best and batsmen were hopping around the crease as though on hot bricks, he went about his destructive work casually, as though it were all in the day's work and the sooner the day was over the better. His performance of taking 19 wickets in a Test match is not likely ever to be equalled. Almost miraculous circumstances are needed to arrange for the taking of so many wickets in the same match. The fortunate bowler has to be at his very best throughout the game; and all the other bowlers – Test match bowlers, mind you – have all the time to be at their most helpless.

O Lucky Jim! – but only skill of the rarest order ever wins the approval and aid of the invisible good fairies! Laker goes down in the history of cricket as a classic exponent of off-spin – the most classic of all kinds of bowling.

HUBERT PRESTON [1961]

Hubert Preston, a one-time editor of Wisden, who had more than once commissioned Cardus to contribute, died in his 92nd year on August 6th, 1960. There was nobody better qualified to compose a valedictory than Cardus, who well remembered the slightly forbidding presence of Preston in the Press Boxes during his beginnings as a cricket writer. Preston's death broke the last surviving link with the emergent days of the almanack under the command of the remarkable Pardon brothers: Charles took over the editorship at a time of crisis in 1887, and retained his command until his death in 1890, when he was succeeded by his brother Sydney, whose run of editorship, from 1891 to 1925, remains the longest in the history of the publication. Under the Pardons, Wisden climbed to a position of great eminence among the world's annual publications. Among their most loyal assistants was Hubert Preston, who was recruited by them in 1895 and remained for 56 years, the last eight of them, from 1944 to 1951, as editor.

The pricelessness of Cardus's memoir lies in its evocation of a lost time, when there was a telegraph office at the nursery end at Lord's, when the reporters bowed greetings to each other and when a young English hopeful might try his hand at a bit of pioneering in the Colonies before coming home to settle down to the really important things in life, like reporting cricket matches.

Born on December 16, 1868, Hubert Preston died on August 6, 1960, aged 91. He spent the greater part of his life reporting Cricket and Association Football. He helped in the preparation of Wisden *from 1895 to 1951, being Editor for the last eight years.*

WHEN I entered the Press Box at Lord's some forty years ago, Hubert Preston sat next to Sydney Pardon at the end of the front row, near the steps leading to the exit. It was a different Press Box then, far different from the large place of accountancy which today is metallic during the summers with typewriters. I doubt if Sydney Pardon would have allowed anybody to use a typewriter in his presence at Lord's or any other cricket ground.

I didn't dare go into the Lord's Press Box during my first season as a cricket writer for the *Manchester Guardian*. I was shy, provincially raw. I wrote my reports sitting on the Green Bank. I wrote them on press telegram forms, and at close of play handed them in at the telegraph office under the clock at the Nursery end.

One afternoon, Hubert Preston saw me as I sat on the Green Bank scribbling my message. 'Why don't you come into the Press Box?' he said, in his own brisk, rapidly articulated way. He took me by the arm and led me up the steep iron steps. The tea interval wasn't over yet. Preston introduced me to Sydney Pardon, who then introduced me to the other members of the Press Box, some of them life-members – Stewart Caine, Harry Carson, Frank Thorogood and others. Each made a courteous bow to me; it was like a *levée*. Pardon pointed to a seat in the back row. In time, he assured me, I would graduate to a front place among the elect.

Hubert Preston was, with Pardon and Stewart Caine, the most courteous and best-mannered man ever to be seen in a Press Box on a cricket ground. Stewart Caine would actually bow to me and give me precedence into a gentlemen's lavatory. Hubert's deafness was the reason why, now and again, the aristocratic Pardon was obliged to raise his voice. Pardon once apologised to me for an occasional voice crescendo. 'You know,' he said, 'Hubert is quite sensationally deaf.' At The Oval, a match was beginning on a superlative wicket in the 1930's, a shaven lawn, reduced into an anaesthetic condition by a ten-ton roller. As we watched, we made our several comments on this batsman's paradise. 'Not fair to bowlers.' 'Ought to be stopped, this doping.' 'Bound to be a draw – no life in the pitch.' 'Not fair to bowlers – doped – killin' the game' and so on.

Hubert, unable to hear a word of all this, sat concentrating on the cricket. Then he spoke: 'This wicket is playing funny already. J. T. Hearne would have 'em all out before lunch. Too much water in the preparation.' What is more, Hubert's prophecy, uttered in the silence surrounding him, was soon proven right. The wicket *did* very soon help the bowler.

Hubert was so modest, so reticent of his own talents and history, that not until his death did I learn from the obituary notices that his first job in London as a journalist was with my own paper, *The Guardian*. Or that he farmed for some time in Canada, from 1893–1895. Or that he had played cricket on the sacrosanct turf of Lord's and had performed the 'hat-trick' there, for the Press v. The Authors. Or that he had played soccer for Lyndhurst v. The Royal Arsenal, forerunners of *the* Arsenal.

He was naturally a man of few words because of his deafness. But his sparkling eyes could talk. I have seen him chastise a poor stroke on the field of play by means of a facial expression far more eloquent than any word, written or oral. He was alive in every nerve and muscle. If responsive life had departed from his ears, the more sharply vital his other faculties seemed to grow. In no sense did he become an 'old man.' And though he extolled the great players of the past, he was, to the end of his career as a cricket journalist, quick to recognise young talents of quality. Almost to the last hours of a life extending from December 16, 1868, to August 6, 1960, he remained mentally active and curious. He was apparently tireless, and a continuous enjoyer of good health. His only stay in a hospital as a patient was the last two days of his life.

As a boy, cricket was at his shoulders temptingly. He began his education at a preparatory school overlooking Kennington Oval. Later he was a student at the City of London School. He joined Pardon's Cricket Reporting Agency in 1895 and was in active and faithful service for this same agency until 1951. In those days there was no radio to spread far and wide the latest cricket scores. The work of the Cricket Reporting Agency, responsible for the Press Association's sporting news, was comprehensive and exhaustive. But nothing could exhaust Hubert. He saw dynasty succeed unto dynasty at cricket – Grace and Shrewsbury, 'Ranji' and Trumper, right down the historic line, Abel, Hayward, Hobbs and Tyldesley, until the Bradman sunset. His life was full and happy. And he had the happy knowledge in his period of heavily accumulated years of knowing that his son was carrying on the good work of his life, as Editor of his beloved *Wisden*. He was loved as a man and a gentleman. And he was respected by his colleagues as a craftsman.

SIX GIANTS OF THE WISDEN CENTURY [1963]

In 1963 appeared the most exhaustive of all Cardus's contributions to the almanack. This was the centenary year, and the hundreth edition strained to be more elaborate than ever before. Among the essays was a history of Wisden, a review of international cricket, an account of the rise of Worcestershire and an amusing attempt to look through the crystal ball at the cricket of the future. But the main attraction was Cardus's 'Six Giants of the Wisden Century'. He selected his heroes without editorial assistance, and in a brief preamble explains the criterion of creativity which he used for his measuring rod. But the six virtually chose themselves. W. G. Grace and Bradman were foregone conclusions. So were Hobbs, Trumper and S. F. Barnes. A very faint element of doubt attaches only to Tom Richardson, an indisputably great bowler. Cardus must have been tempted to find a place for the minatory Tasmanian Ted Macdonald who spearheaded the Lancashire attack in the glorious days of Makepeace and the Professors. Was Richardson any more giantesque than Harold Larwood? Might not Constantine, George Hirst and Wilfred Rhodes have deserved entry as all-rounders? Should there have been one left-handed representative in Frank Woolley? The list of possibilities is endless, and choosing between them has indeed been for at least a century one of the most pleasurable of all cricketing parlour games. But in the end it is impossible to dispute Cardus's selections, so felicitously does he argue his case. The essay on Sydney Barnes is one of his best and contains one unforgettable phrase: 'A chill wind of antagonism blew from him on the sunniest day'. Yet even Cardus does not refer to the most beguiling of all unanswered questions about Barnes. Like all other historians and reporters, he never stops to wonder whether it occurred to anybody in 1921, when English cricket was being scattered to the four winds by the visiting Australians under that personification of obesity, Warwick Armstring, to approach Barnes, then languishing in the comfort of the leagues. Was he approached only to reject his suitors? Was he ignored because of his past record of intransigence? Had the selectors forgotten how to spell his name? If Cardus knew the answers to any of these questions, he gave no indication.

I HAVE been asked by the Editor of *Wisden* to write 'appreciations' of six great cricketers of the past hundred years. I am honoured by this invitation, but it puts me in an invidious position. Whichever player I choose for this representative little gallery I am bound to leave out an important name. My selection of immortal centenarians is as follows: – W. G. Grace, Sir Jack Hobbs, Sir Donald Bradman, Tom Richardson, S. F. Barnes and Victor Trumper. But where – I can already hear in my imagination a thousand protesting voices (including my own) – where are 'Ranji,' Spofforth, Rhodes, J. T. Tyldesley, who, in one rubber v. Australia, was the only professional batsman in England thought good enough to play for his country on the strength of his batting alone? Where are Macartney, Aubrey Faulkner, O'Reilly, Keith Miller, Woolley, Lindwall, Sir Leonard Hutton? And where are many other illustrious names, Australian and English?

I'll give reasons why my six have been picked. There have been, there still are, many cricketers who possess the gifts to bat brilliantly, skilfully and prosperously. There have been, there still are, many bowlers capable of wonderful and destructive arts. But there have been a few who have not only contributed handsome runs and taken worthy wickets by the hundred, but also have given to the technique and style of cricket a new twist, a new direction. These *creative* players have enriched the game by expanding in a fresh way some already established method. One or two of them have actually invented a technical trick of their own. Sadly for their posterity, they have often been the experimental unfulfilled pioneers, such as B. J. T. Bosanquet, who was the first bowler to baffle great batsmen in Test cricket by means of the 'googly.' J. B. King, a Philadelphian, demonstrated the potentialities of a swerving ball. My immortal six were at one and the same masters of the old and initiators of the new.

W. G. GRACE

In recent years his great bulk has seemed to recede. Others following long after him have left his performances statistically behind. In his career he scored 54,896 runs, average 39.55. He also took 2,876 wickets, average 17.92. He scored 126 hundreds in first-class matches, a number exceeded by Sir Jack Hobbs, Hendren, Hammond, Mead, Sutcliffe, Woolley and Sir Leonard Hutton. None of these, not even Sir Jack, dominated for decades all other players, none of them lasted so long, or wore a beard of his commanding growth. In the summer of 1871 his aggregate of runs was 2,739, average 78.25. The next best batsman that year was Richard Daft, average 37.

A Hobbs, a Bradman, a Hutton, a Compton might easily any year amass more than 2,000 runs, averaging round about the 70's. But some other batsmen will be running them close, as far as figures go, averaging 50, 60 and so on. Grace, in 1871, achieved an average which was proof that he stood alone in consistent skill, twice as skilful as the next best! His career ranged from the age of 17, in 1865, until 1908, when he was nearing sixty years. He had turned the fiftieth year of his life when for the Gentlemen v. the Players at Kennington Oval he scored 82 and one of the attack he coped with magisterially was none other than S. F. Barnes, approaching his best.

All these facts and figures tell us no more of the essential 'W. G.' than we are told of Johann Sebastian Bach if all his fugues, cantatas, suites, and even the B Minor Mass, are added up. In a way he *invented* what we now call 'modern' cricket. His national renown packed cricket grounds everywhere. He laid the foundations of county cricket economy. The sweep of his energy, his authority, and prowess, his personal presence, caused cricket to expand beyond a game. His bulk and stride carried cricket into the highways of our national life. He became a representative Victorian, a 'father figure.' People not particularly interested in cricket found the fact of 'W. G.'s' eminence looming into their social consciousness. The Royal family (in those days too) inquired from time to time about his health – a formal request, because 'W. G.' was seldom, if ever, unwell. We must not remember him as the 'Grand Old Man' of his closing years. He was an athlete, a champion thrower of the cricket ball, a jumper of hurdles. Yet, though I have seen portraits of him taken in early manhood, in his late teens in fact, I have never seen a portrait of a beardless 'W. G.' Is such a one in existence anywhere?

Ranjitsinhji wrote in his 'Jubilee' book (or C. B. Fry wrote it for him) that ' "W. G." transformed the single stringed instrument into the many

chorded lyre' which, translated, means that 'W. G.' elaborated batsmanship, combined back-and-forward play for the first time, and perfected the technique of 'placing' the ball. When he began to play cricket,
round-arm bowling had been the fashion for some thirty years. He
inherited a technique formed from an obsolete attack and soon he was
belabouring over-arm fast bowling at ease – often on rough wickets. He
'murdered' the fastest stuff right and left.

He kept his left leg so close to the ball when he played forward that
an old professional of the late 1900's told me (long after his retirement)
that 'W. G.' 'never let me see daylight between pads and bat. Ah used
to try mi best to get 'im out on a good wicket, then suddenly summat
"give" in me, and we all knew it were hopeless.' If 'W. G.' kept
religiously to a rigid right foot in his batting, we must take it for granted,
from the greatness he carved out of the game, that this principle suited
all the needs and circumstances of cricket as he had to meet them. It is
stupid to argue that he couldn't have scored heavily against bowlers of
1963. He mastered the bowling problems presented in *his* period. Logi-
cally, then, we can demonstrate that he would have mastered those of
today.

'W. G.'s' mastery over speed compelled bowlers to think again. Thus,
ironically, he was the cause of the first extensive developments of spin.
A. C. M. Croome played with Grace (later he became cricket correspondent of *The Times*, one of the most learned). 'The first season I saw
Grace play,' he wrote, 'was 1876. In August he scored 318 v. Yorkshire.
Earlier in the week he had made 177 v. Nottinghamshire, and on the
previous Friday and Saturday 344 at Canterbury v. Kent. He scored 1200
runs in first-class cricket during that month of August, yet he found time
before September came to run up to Grimsby and score 400 not out for
United South against twenty-two of the district. That would be a normal
month for him if he could begin again today, knowing that even bowlers
and wicket-keepers know now all about the "second line of defence,"
and enjoy the advantages of true wickets, longer overs and shorter
boundaries.'

He conquered the entire world and range of the game – 15 centuries
v. the Players, so that in 18 years of his reign the Players won only seven
times. He scored 1,000 runs in May 1895, within two months of his 47th
birthday, scored two hundreds in one match v. Kent; took 17 wickets in
one and the same match v. Notts; and took all ten wickets in an innings
v. Oxford University. He was cricket of his period personified; he was
one of the eminent Victorians; he had the large girth and humanity of
the foremost Englishmen of his epoch. Nobody before him, nobody
following greatly in his train, has loomed to his stature or so much stood
for cricket, or done as richly for it.

SIR J. B. HOBBS

Sir Jack is the only cricketer of whom we might fairly say that he directly
descended from 'W. G.' full-armed, like Jove. It was Hobbs who first

challenged the 'Old Master's' primacy as Centurion, passing his record of 126 hundreds, and going as far as 197 in first-class cricket. He commanded in his earliest years a technique inherited from 'W. G.' and his period, adding to it the strokes and protective method evolved from having to cope with the more or less 'modern' swinging and 'googly' attack. It is not generally realised that Hobbs learned to bat in an environment of technique and procedure very much like those in which 'W. G.' came to his high noon. The attack which Hobbs as a young man had to face day-by-day was more or less concentrated on the off-stump or just outside it. Bowlers were allowed to use only one ball through a team's innings; as a consequence they were obliged to make the best possible use of an old one by means of spin, variations of length, pace and direction, or by sheer pace. Only a few were developing back of the hand trickery in the early 1900's – Bosanquet, Vine of Sussex and Braund were three of these.

Yet in 1907 when South Africa sent a team to England containing at least four back-of-the-hand spinners – Vogler, Faulkner, Gordon White and Schwarz – Hobbs, then aged 24 and a half, was able to find the answer to the new 'witchery' (as the old cricketers called it then) and teach the remedy to others. Hobbs was, of course, not the only batsman to demonstrate how the 'googly' should be played. Johnny Tyldesley, Jessop, R. H. Spooner, Braund and George Gunn mastered it up to a point. But Hobbs gathered together in his method all the logical counters for the ball that 'turned the other way.' Moreover, on all sorts of pitches, fast, slow, 'sticky' or matting, here or in Australia or in South Africa, even on the horrible spitting and kicking pitches of Melbourne after rain and hot sun, he asserted his mastery. Confronted by every manner of attack so far conceived and rendered practical by the mortal skill of bowlers in every kind of circumstance, in fine weather or foul, Hobbs reigned supreme. He must be named the Complete Batsman, the Master of all, a later 'W. G.' in fact.

His cricket extended from 1905 to 1934. He opened an innings for England when he was within four months of his 48th birthday. In his career he scored 61,237 runs, average 50.65. Like 'W. G.' he added to the batsman's armour and so, by forcing the attack to resort to fresh ideas, he gave cricket a new twist. Pad play among the Victorians was not done. It was a 'caddish professional, don't you know, from Nottinghamshire, named Arthur Shrewsbury,' who began to exploit pads as a second line of defence. Hobbs seldom, until towards the end, used pads merely obstructively. He perfected footwork which brought the batsman not only to the line of the ball, spin or swerve, but behind it.

We can divide the reign of Hobbs, into two periods, each different in general method from the other. Before the war of 1914 he was quick on the attack on swift feet, strokes all over the field, killing but never brutal, with no strength wasted or strained, most of the strokes governed by the wrists, after the body's balance had provided the motive power. After the resumption of cricket in 1919, when he was moving towards his 37th birthday, he entered his second period, and cut out some of his most daring strokes. He ripened to a classic. His style became as serenely-poised as any ever witnessed on a cricket field, approached only by Hammond (another great player I have been obliged to omit from my Six!). The astonishing fact about Hobbs is that of the 130 centuries to his name in county cricket, 85 were scored after the war of 1914–18; that is, after he had entered 'middle-age.' From 1919 to 1928 his seasons' yields were as follows – the more his years increased, the more he harvested:

1919	2,594	runs	average	60.32
1920	2,827	,,	,,	58.89
1921	321	,,	,,	78.00
		(a season of illness)		
1922	2,552	,,	,,	62.24
1923	2,087	,,	,,	37.78
1924	2,098	,,	,,	58.16
1925	3,024	,,	,,	70.32
1926	2,949	,,	,,	77.60
1927	1,641	,,	,,	52.93
1928	2,542	,,	,,	82.00

From his 43rd to his 48th birthday Hobbs scored some 11,000 runs, averaging round about the sixties. Yet he once said that he would wish to be remembered for the way he batted before 1914. 'But, Jack,' his friends protested, 'you got bags of runs after 1919.' 'Maybe,' replied Hobbs, most modest of cricketers, 'but they were nearly all made off the back foot.'

His baptism to first-class cricket happened under the eye of and in the actual presence of 'W. G.' – on Easter Monday, 1905, at Kennington Oval in a match between Surrey and the Gentlemen of England. He made 18 in his first innings, tieing with Ernest Hayes for top-score. Next innings, his genius announced itself plainly: 88 in two hours. Next morning *The Times* ventured a prophecy: Hobbs had done well enough 'to justify the belief that he will prove a useful addition to the Surrey XI.'

The truth about his career cannot be emphasised too often. In every changing circumstance of the game, on every sort of pitch, against every form of bowling as it developed during the quarter of a century of his mastery, he went his way, calmly in control, never arrogant, full of the spring and pride of early manhood, then quietly enjoying the ripeness that is all. Twice he asserted his command on difficult turf, with the Australians hungry for a victory close at hand. Twice, with Herbert Sutcliffe, he frustrated them – at The Oval in 1926, and at Melbourne in 1928. At Melbourne, England needing 332 to win, were trapped on a Melbourne 'gluepot.' The general idea in the crowd and amongst cricketers was that England would do well to scrape or flash 80 or so all out. The score was 105 for one when Hobbs was leg-before. The match was won by England, Sutcliffe 135. And Hobbs was the architect.

We nearly lost him in 1921. He was attacked by acute appendicitis during the Test match v. Australia at Leeds. He was rushed to the operating table. The celebrated surgeon, Sir Berkeley (later Lord) Moynihan, told Hobbs afterwards, 'You couldn't have lived five hours.'

I never saw him make an uneducated stroke. When he misjudged the nature of a ball he could, naturally enough, make the wrong right stroke. He not only enlarged and subtilised the art of batmanship; he, like 'W. G.,' widened and strengthened cricket's appeal and history. He was in his 44th year, let us remember, when he passed 'W. G.'s' roll of 126 centuries. The game will retain the image of him in its Hall of Fame – the twiddle of his bat before he bent slightly, to face and look at the attack; the gentle accurate to-an-inch push for a single to get off the mark, the stroke so nicely timed that he could, had he wished, have walked it. The Trumperesque Hobbs of the pre–1914–19 days, lithe, but his slender physique, concentrated and yet graceful! Then the vintage Hobbs, the 'Master' of our time, biding his own, and often getting himself out as he reached his hundred.

Every honour that the game – and the nation – could bestow came to him, not the least of all, in lasting value, the pride and affection of cricketers the world over.

TOM RICHARDSON

I choose Richardson as one of my Six, not on the supposition that he was the greatest fast bowler of the century, though certainly he was in the running. I take him as the fully-realised personification of the fast bowler as every schoolboy dreams and hopes he might one day be himself. Richardson was, in his heyday, a handsome swarthy giant, lithe, muscular, broad of shoulder, and of apparently inexhaustible energy. He bowled fast, with a breakback obtained by body action and the swing of the upper part over the left leg at the moment of release, the right hand sweeping away nearly at a right angle to the line of flight. He could bring the ball back inches on Sam Apted's most heavily-rolled grassless stretch of turf. Herbert Strudwick loves to tell how when he first kept wicket for Surrey, Richardson pitched a very fast one rather outside the off-stump. Strudwick moved, naturally enough, towards the off, in antici-pation. But the ball, beating the bat, just missed the leg-stump and went for four byes – to Strudwick's excusable amazement.

Richardson didn't 'go in' for swing or seam refinements. In his period it wasn't possible for any fast bowler to do so. Only one and the same ball was at his service during the batting side's longest innings. Moreover, the seam of a cricket ball wasn't as pronounced in Richardson's day as it is in ours. We need to bear in mind this fact – that Richardson had to get through most of his thousand overs a season using an 'old ball.'

In the four summers of 1894–97 he bowled some five thousand eight hundred overs and – take your breath – took 1,005 wickets: –

	Overs	Runs	Wickets	Average
1894	936.3	2,024	196	10.32
1895	1690.1	4,170	290	14.37
1896	1656.2	4,015	246	16.32
1897	1603.4	3,945	273	14.45

Between the English seasons of 1894 and 1895 he bowled, in Australia, 3,554 balls, taking 69 wickets at 23.42 each; and after his haul of 273 wickets at home in 1897 (and his 1,600 overs), he went to Australia again and, bowled at last to his knees, took only 54 wickets, average 29.51.

Yet on his return to England the great giant achieved an herculean revival, his season's plunder amounting to 161 wickets, average 19.54, in more than twelve hundred overs. All done, remember, or nearly all, with a seamless ball.

In his career, extending from 1892 to 1905, his performances, in statistics, work out at 2,105 wickets, average 18.42, from nearly 16,000 overs. He, like most fast bowlers of the 1890's, was expected in dry weather to bowl all day, or the better part of it. Fast bowlers of the 1890's shared the White Man's burden in hot weather, and were given rest (now and again) when the rain swamped the ground so much that they couldn't stand up. Wickets were not covered in the 1900's. At Old Trafford, in 1902, when Victor Trumper scored a century before lunch, Lockwood was unable to bowl or get a foothold until mid-afternoon. He then came on and took six for 48.

Lockwood, of course, opened the Surrey county attack with Richardson. Ranjitsinhji maintained that Lockwood was the more dangerous fast bowler of the two. 'On a good wicket Tom's speed and breakback needed watching, but I knew what was coming. With Lockwood I had to keep awake for his slower ball.' Lockwood was temperamental, an artist, moody. One day his fires were sullen and slow. Batsmen played him with impunity – poor innocents, cultivating their gardens on the slopes of a Vesuvius, which next day erupted.

In Australia, Lockwood was a dead failure – his Test figures for his only rubber in Australia were 124.5 overs, 31 maidens, 340 runs, five wickets. But in Australia, under the hottest suns experienced there during the century, Richardson's labours were heroic, unparalleled. Today they would probably be considered servile. In the service of Stoddart's team of 1894–95, in five Test matches he bowled more than 300 five-ball overs for 849 runs and 26 wickets. At Sydney, December 1894, when Australia scored 586, Richardson sweated and toiled for 53 overs for five wickets and 181 runs.

The greatest of his lion-hearted endeavours was at Manchester in the Test Match there of 1896. He bowled 68 five-ball overs in Australia's first innings of 412. On the third and last day, Australia needed 125 to win – England having 'followed on.' Richardson nearly won the match. For three hours he attacked without an over's rest, taking six of the seven wickets which fell before Australia scraped home. A missed catch frustrated Richardson at the pinch. His devotion – and his will-power and stamina – is faintly indicated by his figures for the match:–

110 overs 3 balls, 39 maidens, 244 runs, 13 wickets.

The one favour granted to Richardson, but hardly a compensation for bondage to an 'old' ball – was the pace of the wickets he bowled on; they usually had a certain hardness and resilience. Strudwick, again, is witness; he tells that often he had to 'take' Richardson standing back to him, of course, and standing 'pretty well' high up, near his 'middle.' Richardson seldom, if ever, 'bounced' a ball deliberately. He was a good-natured soul, loving a pint of ale and a good laugh at the long day's end.

In Richardson's period, bowlers exploited off theory on hard, dry pitches, hardly a fieldsman on the other side of the wicket excepting mid-on. When I was a small boy I saw J. T. Tyldesley pull square a short ball from Richardson, the only loose one on a scorching sun-streamed afternoon. The stroke dropped short of the boundary, was retrieved an inch or two from the edge and thrown back to the middle by – believe it or not – Richardson. The Surrey mid-on had seen the ball pass him and was content to 'let it go.' Richardson who had been attacking with his long striding run for hours had thought differently.

He was indeed the ideal fast bowler, aiming at the stumps, always on the attack. His leap before the right arm wheeled over was superb in poise. Never did he send down a defensive ball. He would have been too proud.

'He tried,' A. C. MacLaren told me, 'to get a wicket every ball. Honest Tom!' Let us remember him by those two words of MacLaren's tribute – 'Honest Tom.'

VICTOR TRUMPER

It is futile to ask 'who was the greatest batsman?' There are different orders of greatness. Talent, even genius, is conditioned by the material circumstances in which it is developed. Victor Trumper was the embodiment of gallantry as he made his runs. He was a chivalrous batsman, nothing mean or discourteous in any of his movements or intentions at the wicket. 'He had no style,' wrote C. B. Fry of him, 'but he was all style.' But the most handsome compliment ever made to him, or to any other cricketer, was A. C. MacLaren's: 'I was supposed to be a batsman of the Grand Manner. Compared to Victor I was as a cab-horse to a Derby winner.'

His stance was relaxed, but watchful, a panther ready to spring. Yet this panther simile suggests a certain cruelty and hungriness. Trumper scored his runs generously, as though out of an abundance of them in his possession. He, so to say, *donated* runs over the field, bestowing them like precious jewels to us, to the crowd, to the bowlers even. He wasn't, as Bradman was, a 'killer.' His strokes didn't stun or insult a bowler. I have seen bowlers applaud the glory of Trumper's strokes; he put them, with the rest of us, under an enchantment. Do I exaggerate?

I confess that whenever I write about Trumper I am in danger of exhausting a store of superlatives. So I'll be content for the moment to quote from the formal and restrained prose of the 'M.C.C.'s Cricket Scores and Biographies':-

'For Trumper the English season of 1902 was a triumphal progress, and those who were fortunate to witness his amazing brilliance will never be able to forget the unrivalled skill and resource he displayed. On "sticky" wickets he hit with freedom, whilst everybody else were puddling about the crease, unable to make headway and content if they could keep up their wickets.'

The season of 1902 was the spin-bowler's dream of heaven. Rain and hot sun day by day. Wickets uncovered. When the pitch dried the ball whipped in, whipped away, reared and kept low, changing direction and pace, sometimes startling the bowlers themselves. And in 1902 Trumper had to cope with the greatest spinners the game had so far evolved – Rhodes, Blythe, Haigh, Wass (fast from leg stump to the off), Walter Mead, J. T. Hearne, S. F. Barnes, to name a few. In this year of 1902 Trumper scored 2,570 runs, average 48.49, with eleven centuries. His rate of scoring was round about 40 an hour, and 1902 was his first experience of vicious English wickets, for in 1899, his first visit to this country, the summer had been dry.

In the upstairs tea-room at Kennington Oval hangs a photo of Victor showing him jumping out to drive, yards from the crease, bat aloft behind him, the left leg prancing like a charger's in the Bayeux tapestry. A certain England batsman, vintage 1950, looked at this picture in my company and said, 'Was he really any good?' 'Why do you ask?' was my natural question. 'Well,' said this International, 'just look where he is – stumped by yards if he misses.'

This sceptical England batsman had never in his life been so far out of his crease. But Trumper was stumped only once in all the 89 Test innings of his career. And only five times was he lbw.

Like Hobbs, he led the way to the counter-attack of the 'googly' bowling, a new problem to harass batsmen of his period. In Australia, 1910–11, against the superb South African back-of-the-hand bowlers, such as Vogler, Schwarz, Pegler and Faulkner, his Test scores in the rubber were 27 (run out) 34, 159, 214 (not out), 28, 7, 87, 31 and 74 not out – 661 runs, average 94.42. Let me quote Jack Fingleton: 'He teased Percy Sherwell, the South African captain. When a fieldsman was shifted, Trumper deliberately hit the next ball where the man had been . . . Later, somebody commiserated with Sherwell at having his captaincy and his fieldsmen torn to tatters while Trumper made 214. Whereupon Sherwell said, "Ah, don't talk about it. We have seen batting today." '

For six balls apparently alike in pitch, or pace or spin, Trumper could produce six different strokes. His footwork was quick, graceful and effortless. With the easiest swing of the bat he could drive an extraordinary distance. His cutting and his leg glancing were performed by wrists of rare flexibility. 'He played a defensive stroke,' wrote C. B. Fry, 'as a last resort.'

At Old Trafford, in 1902, A. C. MacLaren lost the toss for England on a slow wicket which, he knew, would turn difficult by mid-afternoon. Lockwood was unable to get a sure foothold until shortly before lunch. So MacLaren's plan was, as he himself put it, 'to keep Victor quiet for an hour or two.' Then, with the pitch developing tantrums, Australia could be disposed of at ease. MacLaren's reserve bowlers were Rhodes, F. S. Jackson, Tate and Braund, and they were ordered to operate defensively. 'I set my field with the inner and outer ring,' said MacLaren. Some of the best cricket brains and skill in England concentrated to 'keep Victor quiet.' At lunch Australia's score was 173 for one, Trumper a century.

So easily did Trumper bat, though his rate of scoring frequently equalled Jessop's, never for a moment did he make an impression of violence or hurry. His every movement was lovely to see. Against Victoria for New South Wales at Sydney, in 1905, on a bowler's wicket, he scored 101 out of 139 in fifty-seven minutes. On a Melbourne 'gluepot,' in 1904, he scored 74 out of Australia's all out total of 122 v. England – England's bowlers being Rhodes (who took 15 wickets in the match for 124), Hirst, Relf and Braund. In 1913, playing in a match at Goulburn for the benefit of J. A. O'Connor, Australian Test cricketer, Victor scored 231 in ninety minutes. In 1899 he scored 300 not out v. Sussex in five hours. In 1902 he scored 62 out of 80 in fifty minutes v. England at Sheffield. His achievements in high-class 'Grade' cricket in Sydney have become historic. For his team, Paddington, in 1897 and 1898, he averaged 204, with 1,021 runs, when he was only twenty years old.

These statistics chosen at random, tell their tale. But not by counting Victor's runs, not by looking at any 'records,' will you get the slightest idea of Trumper's glorious cricket. You might as well count the notes of the music of Mozart.

He was sadly on his way to a fatal illness when he came to England in 1909, for the last time, but a flash of the dauntless Victor came out at The Oval in an innings for Australia of 73, scored against D. W. Carr (googly), Barnes, Woolley, Rhodes, and Sharp. And, as we have noted, his genius burnt in wonderful flame and colour against South Africa in Australia in 1910–11. But it was burning itself out. He died, only 37 years old, in June 1915; and the Sydney streets were packed with sorrowing crowds as the funeral passed by.

He was good-looking, clean-shaven (a rare and boyish thing in those days), weighing 12 stones, and 5 feet 10 inches of height. He was, as everybody vowed who came his way, even the bowlers, a quiet but delightful companion. The gods of cricket loved him, so he died young.

S. F. BARNES

Most cricketers and students of the game belonging to the period in which S. F. Barnes played were agreed that he was the bowler of the century. Australians as well as English voted him unanimously the greatest. Clem Hill, the famous Australian left-handed batsman, who in successive Test innings scored 99, 98, 97 v. A. C. MacLaren's England team of 1901–2, told me that on a perfect wicket Barnes could swing the new ball in and out 'very late,' could spin from the ground, pitch on the leg stump and miss the off. At Melbourne, in December 1911, Barnes in five overs overwhelmed Kellaway, Bardsley, Hill and Armstrong for a single. Hill was clean bowled by him. 'The ball pitched outside my leg-stump, safe to the push of my pads, I thought. Before I could "pick up" my bat, my off-stump was knocked silly.'

Barnes was creative, one of the first bowlers really to use the seam of a new ball and combine 'swing' so subtly with spin that few batsmen could distinguish one from the other. He made a name before a new ball was available to an attack every so many runs or overs. He entered first-class cricket at a time when one ball had to suffice for the whole duration of the batting side's innings.

He was professional in the Lancashire league when A. C. MacLaren, hearing of his skill, invited him to the nets at Old Trafford. 'He thumped me on the left thigh. He hit my gloves from a length. He actually said, "Sorry, sir!" and I said, "Don't be sorry, Barnes. You're coming to Australia with me." ' MacLaren on the strength of a net practice with Barnes chose him for his England team in Australia of 1901–2. In the first Test of that rubber, Barnes took five for 65 in 35 overs, 1 ball, and one for 74 in 16 overs. In the second Test he took six for 42 and seven for 121 and he bowled 80 six-ball overs in this game. He broke down, leg strain, in the third Test and could bowl no more for MacLaren, who winning the first Test, lost the next four of the rubber.

Barnes bowled regularly for Lancashire in 1902, taking more than a hundred wickets in the season, averaging around 20. *Wisden* actually found fault with his attack this year, stating that he needed to cultivate an 'off break.' In the late nineties he had appeared almost anonymously in the Warwickshire XI.

Throughout his career he remained mysteriously aloof, appearing in the full sky of first-class cricket like a meteor – declaring the death of the most princely of batsmen! He preferred the reward and comparative indolence of Saturday league matches to the daily toil of the county tourney. Here is one of the reasons of his absence from the England XI between 1902 and 1907. He didn't go to Australia as one of P. F. Warner's team of 1903–4 and took no part of the 1905 England v. Australia rubber. The future historian of cricket may well gape and wonder why, in the crucial Test of 1902, Barnes didn't play for England at Manchester, where the rubber went to Australia by three runs only.

Barnes had bowled for England at Sheffield in the third and previous Test, taking six for 49 and one for 50. It is as likely as conjecture about cricket ever can be likely that had Barnes taken part in the famous Manchester Test of 1902 England wouldn't have lost the rubber by a hair's breadth.

He was in those days not an easy man to handle on the field of play. There was a Mephistophelian aspect about him. He didn't play cricket out of any 'green field' starry-eyed realism. He rightly considered that his talents were worth estimating in cash values. In his old age he mellowed, yet remained humorously cynical. Sir Donald Bradman argued that W. J. O'Reilly must have been a greater bowler than Barnes because he commanded every ball developed in Barnes's day – plus the 'googly.' I told Barnes of Bradman's remark. 'It's quite true,' he said, 'I never bowled the "googly."' Then with a glint in his eye, he added, 'I never needed it.'

Against Australia he took 106 wickets, average 21.58. Only Trumble and Peel have improved on these figures in Tests between England and Australia (I won't count Turner's 101 wickets at 16.53 because he bowled in conditions not known to Barnes and Trumble). Barnes had no opportunities to pick up easy victims. He played only against Australia and South Africa and, in all Test matches, his haul was 189 at 16.43 each. On matting in South Africa when South Africa's batsmanship, at its greatest, was represented by H. W. Taylor, A. D. Nourse, L. J. Tancred, J. W. Zulch, in 1913–14, he was unplayable, with 49 wickets in Tests at 10.93 each.

Yet against this fantastically swinging, bouncing, late-turning attack, 'Herbie' Taylor scored 508 runs, average 50.80, perhaps the most skilful of all Test performances by a batsman. He was a man of character (and still is). At Sydney on the 1911–12 tour, J. W. H. T. Douglas opened the England attack using the new ball with Frank Foster. Barnes was furious. He sulked as he sent down 35 overs for three wickets and 107 runs (in the match he took only four for 179). England lost by 146 runs.

At Melbourne, Australia batted first and Barnes this time had the new ball. We all know with what results. Australia suffered defeat – and also in the ensuing three games. The destruction wreaked by Barnes, and on all great days, was mostly done by the ball which, bowled from a splendid height, seemed to swing in to the leg stump then spin away from the pitch, threatening the off-stump. Barnes has assured me that he actually turned the ball by 'finger twist.' The wonder of his career is that he took 77 of his 106 Australian Test wickets on the wickets of Australia when they were flawless and the scourge of all ordinarily good bowlers. He clean bowled Victor Trumper for 0 at Sydney in the 1907–8 rubber, then Fielder and J. N. Crawford in the following Test, dismissed Trumper for a 'pair,' so Trumper was out for 0 in three successive Test innings.

Barnes remained a deadly bowler long after he went out of first-class cricket. So shrewdly did he conserve his energy that in 1928 when he was in his mid-fifties, the West Indies team of that year faced him in a club match and unanimously agreed he was the best they had encountered in the season.

For Staffordshire, in his fifty-sixth year, he took 76 wickets at 8.21 each. Round about this period a young player, later to become famous in international company, was one of the Lancashire Second XI playing against Staffordshire. His captain won the toss and the Lancashire lads went forth to open the innings against Barnes. As this colt was No. 6 in the batting order he put on his blazer and was about to leave the pavilion to watch Barnes 'from behind.' But his captain told him to go back to the dressing room and 'get on his pads.' 'But,' said the colt, 'I'm not in until number six and I'd like to look at Barnes.' His captain insisted. The young colt returned to the dressing room. 'And there,' he said 'there were four of us all padded up waiting. And we were all out in the middle and back again in half an hour.'

Barnes had a splendid upright action, right arm straight over. He ran on easy strides, not a penn'orth of energy wasted. He fingered a cricket ball sensitively, like a violinist his fiddle. He always attacked. 'Why do these bowlers to-day send down so many balls the batsman needn't play?' he asked while watching a Test match a few years ago. 'I didn't. I never gave 'em any rest.' His hatchet face and his suggestion of physical and mental leanness and keenness were part of Barnes's cricket and outlook on the game. He was relentless, a chill wind of antagonism blew from him on the sunniest day. As I say, he mellowed in full age and retirement. He came to Lord's for Test matches heading for his ninetieth year, leading blind Wilfred Rhodes about.

As we think of the unsmiling destroyer of all the batsmen that came his way, let us also remember Barnes immortalised in that lovely verse of Alan Ross:

'Then, elbows linked, but straight as sailors
On a tilting deck, they move. One, square-shouldered as a tailor's
Model, leans over whispering in the other's ear;
"Go easy, Steps here. This end bowling"
Turning, I watch Barnes guide Rhodes into fresher air,
As if to continue an innings, though Rhodes may only play by ear.'

SIR DONALD BRADMAN

Sir Donald Bradman (hereinafter to be named Bradman, or 'The Don'), must be called the most masterful and prolific maker of runs the game has so far known. He was, in short, a great batsman. Critics have argued that he was mechanical. So is a majestically flying aeroplane. The difference between Bradman and, say, Victor Trumper as batsmen, was in fact the difference between an aeroplane and a swallow in flight. But it is nonsense to say that Bradman's batsmanship was without personality or character, or nature, or that it was in the slightest anonymous. He had a terrifically dynamic style. It was thrilling to see him gathering together his energy at the last second to hook, a stroke somehow reminding me of a boxer's swinging stunning 'right.'

Like all great players, he made his strokes very late. He didn't move at all until the ball was on him; then the brilliant technique shot forth concentrated energy – and the axe fell. All the strokes were at his command. After he had appeared almost for the first time in an Austra-

Cardus in 1970, bridging
the gulf between music
and cricket. Yehudi
Menuhin and Len
Hutton, a couple of old
masters

Lord's, 1944. For
Hammond it is too late in
the day, but the majesty
of the strokeplay remains
as rich as ever

Wilfred Rhodes, the most prolific wicket-taker of all time, seen here in the frozen photographic postures of his youth, complete with the carboard ramparts of nobility thoughtfully included by the camera eye

lian State match, J. V. Ryder, Australian captain, was asked, 'How does this young Bradman bat?' and Ryder, a man of few but eloquent words, replied: 'He belts the hell out of everything he can reach.'

Bradman's achievements stagger the imagination. No writer of boy's fiction would dare to invent a 'hero' who performed with Bradman's continual consistency. Nobody would even suspend disbelief as he read such fiction. Between 1927 and 1948 he scored 28,067 runs. (The war interrupted his genius at its high noon.) In his career as cricketer he scored these 28,067 runs with an average of 95.14, an average 'for life' twice as high as that of most other master batsmen. He made 117 centuries in 338 innings, forty-three times not out – a century every third time he walked to the wicket. He scored 6,996 runs in Test matches, average 99.94. He scored 1,000 runs between April 30 and May 31 in an English season. He scored 1,000 runs in a season sixteen times. He scored 974 runs in one and the same rubber v. England. He scored a triple Test match century – 309 – in a day. He scored 13 centuries in the English season of 1938. He scored six centuries in consecutive innings. He hit thirty runs in one over. He scored two centuries in the same Test match, v. India.

Moreover, I think he knew at the time that he was about to do these extraordinary things; for he planned everything. No cricketer has had a quicker, shrewder brain than Bradman's. At Leeds in 1934, Australia bowled England out on a beautiful turf for 200. Then, at the afternoon's fall, Australia lost three wickets for 39. That evening Bradman cancelled dinner with me, saying he was going to bed early as, next day, it would be necessary for him to score 200 'at least!' I reminded him that on his previous Test appearance at Leeds, in 1930, he had scored 334. 'The law of averages is against you pulling-off another big score here tomorrow in a Test,' I said. He replied: 'I don't believe in the law of averages.' Next day he set about scoring 304.

The extraordinary point of this innings is that until this Leeds Test, Bradman had battled in the rubber with a certain lack of concentration, as though the effects of the Jardine-Larwood 'body-line' assaults on him of 1932–33 were still shaking him. At Nottingham and Lord's, he played fast bowling with a rhetorical slash, a quite wild impetuosity. Now, at Leeds, in a serious hour for Australia, he could summon back at one call the old cool, premeditated craft and foresight.

I asked him once, in Melbourne, to give me some idea of how he did it all. 'Every ball for me is the first ball,' then, he added, taking away my breath, 'and I never think there's a possibility of anybody getting me out.'

The critics say he couldn't bat on a turning pitch. Hedley Verity held the opposite opinion – from experience. It is a fact, though, that 'The Don' seemed occasionally not to face up to a 'sticky' pitch, *on principle*. He argued that wickets should be covered from rain, especially in his own country. It wasn't fair that a side should bat in perfect run-getting conditions one day. Then next day, the other side could be trapped on a spitting pitch.

Bradman had all the attributes needed to cope with the spinning, kicking ball – swift feet, and an eye rapid and comprehensive. Against Larwood's devastating 'body-line' attack, dangerous to breastbone and skull, Bradman in the Tests scored 396 runs, average 56.57. Jardine reduced his powers temporarily by half; but no other mortal batsman could have coped with Larwood as Bradman coped with him. In spite of Larwood's velocity and menace – seven fieldsmen on the leg- or on-side – Bradman was driving or punching to the vacant off-side bowling coming like lightning from a spot on or outside the leg stump, often rising shoulder high.

He first came to England in 1930, twenty-one years old. He began at Worcester with 236 in four and a half hours, twenty-eight boundaries. To Leicester he proceeded, to score 185 not out. Then, on the soft wicket v. Yorkshire, he scored 78. And a newspaper placard announced, 'Bradman fails.' It was in 1930 that he exhibited, I think, the most wonderful batsmanship of his life, when during the Lord's Test match he came to the wicket after Ponsford had got out. In two hours and forty minutes before half-past six, he cut, drove and hooked the England attack, to the tune of 155. J. C. White, the untouchable, was brought on immediately to keep 'The Don' quiet. White's first ball, a good length, was slapped to the on-boundary, near the clock at the Nursery. Bradman leaped yards out of his crease; and the crack of his bat sent the Lord's pigeons flying in affrighted circles.

It was at Lord's in 1938, during the M.C.C. v. Australians match that the effervescent J. W. A. Stephenson, a splendid opening bowler, appealed for lbw against Bradman, and Bradman had not yet got into double figures. Stephenson leapt skywards as he appealed. The 'near thing' was negatived. If the reply had been in the affirmative, I imagine Stephenson would have been the first into and beyond the 'barrier.' Bradman went on to amass 278. He was ruthless. None the less, he didn't ever fail to respond to a bowler's challenge.

Nobody ever saw Bradman show mercy to a loose ball. If he went on the defensive, there was good reason. At Trent Bridge, in 1938, Australia followed-on after they had scored 411 in response to England's 658 for eight (declared). McCabe made history with a marvellous and gallant 232. But the pitch grew dusty and the closing day had a severe ordeal waiting for Bradman. Early that day Bradman wrote home to the young lady he was later to marry, telling her that a job of work had to be done, but, he guessed, all would have turned out well for Australia long before his letter reached her. Bradman then set forth to Trent Bridge and saved the day by batting nearly six hours.

Never, as I say, did he play with sterile negation. He was a Test cricketer of our contemporary temper, realistic and without cant. He reacted to the environment in which he found himself. He hadn't to play, as Trumper was obliged to play, in this country, in games limited to three days. If he didn't throw his wicket away as Trumper frequently did on reaching his hundred, the reason was that he played in a different economy of the game than Trumper ever knew. If and when Bradman stayed at the wicket all day he not only put his team in a position pretty secure from defeat but into a position from which the Australian bowlers could attack, with time to bring in victory; also he was holding the crowd in thrall.

He was a born batsman, out of a remote part of his beloved Australia, never coached academically; consequently he was free to give rein to his innate and rare gifts. He was born, too, with a good brain. Nobody has excelled Bradman's 'cricket sense,' his intuitions and understanding. He must be counted among Australia's cleverest, most closely calculating cricket captains.

After he had scored a triple century on a warm day at Leeds in 1930, he came from the field apparently cool, no sign of perspiration, not a buckle out of place, flannels immaculate, and, as the crowd roared him home, he seemed withdrawn and impersonal. People said that he lacked emotion. Maybe he was content to be the cause of 'emotion' in others – in bowlers, for example. 'Stripped to the truth,' wrote Robertson-Glasgow, in a brilliant appreciation of Bradman in *Wisden*, 'he was a solitary man with a solitary aim.' Personally I have found in Sir Donald plenty of friendliness and humour. But, then, I was never called on to bowl or play cricket against him! Discussing him entirely from the point of view of a writer on the game, I am happy to say that he was for me a constant spur to ideas. A newspaper column couldn't contain him. He was, as far as a cricketer can be, a genius.

OBITUARIES [1963]

Although his only apparent billing in the 1963 edition was for 'Six Giants of the Wisden Century', Cardus does appear elsewhere in the same edition. On more than one occasion when a great cricketer died, the editors of the almanack, rather than commission an obituary, chose instead to reprint Cardus's essay on the subject from the pages of 'The Guardian'. Apart from being an excellent idea, it was also a remarkable tribute to the primacy of Cardus's opinions on great players, the implication being that since he had covered the subject, there was nobody anywhere who might be able to add anything worth reading to what he had said.

Tucked away in the small print of the 1963 edition, among the obituaries, following Subbaroyan, Dr. P. of Madras, and preceding Webber, Roy, cricket statistician, was a notice by Cardus on Ernest Tyldesley, younger brother of J. T. and a leading star of the great Makepeace elevens of the 1920s. When Cardus had returned to Old Trafford after his self-imposed exile in the intellectual wilderness, Ernest Tyldesley had been one of the men who opened his eyes to what he had been missing. After making an amusing indirect reference to Thomas Gray's 'Elegy in a Country Churchyard' at the expense of Arthur Milton, Cardus goes on to his grand finale, one of those conversational exchanges between cricketers which has so vexed students of his work. Did they say it or did they not? Who cares?

TYLDESLEY, ERNEST, of Lancashire and England, died at his home at Rhos-on-Sea on May 5, aged 73.

Neville Cardus wrote in *The Guardian*:

Ernest Tyldesley, one of the most accomplished batsmen ever to play for Lancashire, was born in Lancashire, brother of one of the three greatest professional batsmen in the game's history. As a boy he played for Roe Green, which in a way was a Tyldesley club; for the famous 'J. T. T.' learned his cricket on the same village green. J. T. Tyldesley kept a more than brotherly eye on Ernest but turned the other way when he saw the youngster's cross-bat. 'J. T. T.' also tended to bring his bat along a line beginning at third man. 'A straight bat's all right to a straight ball,' said 'J. T. T.' one day, 'but there are not many runs to be made by straight pushing.' 'J. T. T.' never pushed; but Ernest seldom began an innings without one or two anxious or tentative thrusts. Once he had 'seen' the ball he could be as brilliant and as punitive as he was defensively sound.

'J. T. T.' was a genius, and it is to Ernest's credit that, though on his entrance into Lancashire cricket he had to survive a disheartening comparison, he never lost faith. 'J. T. T.' of course, constantly encouraged him. 'Some day,' he said, 'he'll be a better bat than ever I was.' Ernest certainly scored a few more runs in his career than came from the broadsword of his brother. Between 1909 and 1936 Ernest scored 38,974, average 45.46; 'J. T. T.'s' portion was, between 1895 and 1932, 37,809, average 40.69.

In style they were more than different. Ernest's batting was always courteous; in his most aggressive moods, when he would hook fast bowling vividly, he rarely suggested militancy or the ruthless slayer of bowling. 'Johnny' was usually on the kill. . . . If a maiden over were bowled at him, 'J. T. T.' would gnaw a glove at the end of it. He had, with Macartney, no patience with a good attack; he felt the necessity of falling on it and demolishing it without delay. Ernest was more patient. But when the situation called for valiance Ernest could go into battle with chivalric manners concealing ruthless and belligerent purpose.

In the Test match of 1921 at Old Trafford he was the first England cricketer that year really to treat the conquering attack of Armstrong with contumely. In 1925 at Kennington Oval he played one of the most tremendously incisive, powerful, merciless, and gallant innings I have ever seen. At close of play on the second day Lancashire were apparently at Surrey's mercy. Four wickets had fallen, with 117 still needed to escape defeat by an innings. Hitch began the Surrey attack next morning at a hair-raising pace. He employed five slips. In a quarter of an hour four of those slips had been moved to the leg and on sides – defensively. Tyldesley's hooking was savage and daring: he hooked from his eyebrow. His hits to the off were no less swift and exacting. In five hours he scored 236 without a shadow of error. Lancashire saved the game easily.

Ernest's experiences in Test cricket were peculiar, making strange reading these days when all manner of inglorious Miltons are asked, almost on bended knees, to bat for England. In 1921 Tyldesley played for England at Nottingham against the ferocious McDonald and Gregory attack. He made 0 and 7, knocked out second innings by Gregory, bowled off his cheek-bone. He was recalled for the Old Trafford Test, when he scored 78 not out, and for the fifth Test at Kennington Oval where he made a pleasant 39. Not until 1926 was he again asked to play for England against Australia at Old Trafford in the fourth Test of the rubber. He scored 81; and was dropped for the concluding game of the same rubber.

He was taken to Australia, one of Chapman's team of 1928–29, but was entrusted with only one Test, in which he made 31 and 21. He was never again chosen for the England eleven against Australia. So, in five opportunities against the strongest cricket power, his record was, and remains, 0, 7, 78 not out, 39, 81, 31, and 21. In South Africa, in the Test matches there of the 1927–28 rubber, he headed England's average – 65 an innings for 520 runs, with these scores: 122, 0, 87, 78, 62 not out, 42, 8, 100, and 21. And South Africa's attack was then composed of Nupen, Morkel, Vincent, Bissett, and Hall.

In 1928 Tyldesley amassed 3,024 runs in the season, average 79.57. In 1926, when he was only once picked for the England eleven (and scored his 81), he made four centuries in successive innings, with a season's aggregate of 2,826, average 62.22, only Hobbs and Sutcliffe his statistical peers. Yet he could not hold a place in the England side. In his career he reached the century 102 times, and twice he scored two centuries in the same match.

Figures alone will give some idea to posterity of his quality. Like his brother, he had the answer to unpleasant wickets. His great cricket in South Africa was achieved on matting, against Nupen spinning viciously. In fact, he preferred a turning ball to the one that came straight through quickly enough to find a slight chink in the armour – the bat just a little out of the straight. But those of us who saw him play and knew him off the field as a friend will remember his batsmanship not only for its skill, resource, and plenty, but mainly because it was so like the man himself – modest yet firm of character, civilised in all its called-for action. He was, in a word, a gentlemanly babuean who, when he needed to assert his authority, never exceeded the privileges of class and manners.

His cricket was part and parcel of a Lancastrian of quiet charm, having a modesty that concealed the tough fibre in him of Lancashire. A year or two ago, at a painful stage of his broken health, George Duckworth went to visit him at his home. 'And how are you Ernest?' 'Well, George I was at the specialist's yesterday, and he says my eyes are in a bad way. And I've had awful pains in my thighs, and my chest's been giving me jip.' Then he paused, before adding, 'But, mind you, George, there's nothin' the matter with me!'

That's the Lancashire man for you, all over. We'll not forget him.

SIR JOHN BERRY HOBBS
[1964]

Born at Cambridge December 16, 1882
Died at his home, at Hove, December 21, 1963
Knighted for his Services to Cricket 1953

Having apotheosised Jack Hobbs at some length in 1963, Cardus was obliged to perform the deed all over again, even more exhaustively, for a much sadder reason. Sir Jack, as he now was, had always been acknowledged as the most complete batting master of any age on any wicket. His death shortly after his 81st birthday was a further grim reminder that the golden age was receding at a terrifying pace. Hobbs was the epitome of the professional sporting hero as he ought to be but almost never is. A churchgoer, teetotal, non-smoker, a man who sincerely believed that home is the best place for a man to be, a modest gentle citizen to whom no vestige of scandal ever clung, Hobbs was perhaps the most loveable of all the great sporting virtuosi of the postwar world. Not so prolific a run-maker as Bradman, but superior to him on the sticky dogs of the English summers, a man who, by making his debut in one era and scoring his last century in quite another, was obliged to master new bowling innovations as they arose and who never failed in his quest, Hobbs scored more runs and more centuries than any other cricketer, and scored more centuries against Australia than any other Englishman. None of these records is ever likely to be surpassed, although it is theoretically possible that one day someone will break his record for the highest individual score ever made at Lord's – 316 not out for Surrey against Middlesex in 1926. Like all cricket writers, Cardus revered Hobbs, and he makes the point which a later age tends to forget – that before the Great War there was great brilliance in Hobbs' batting style; only after the war did he graduate to the classical calm of his years as the leader of English batsmanship.

JOHN BERRY HOBBS, the great batsman whose first-class cricket career spanned thirty years and brought him fame everywhere as a player second to none, was born in humble surroundings at No. 4 Rivar Place, Cambridge, quite close to Fenner's, Parker's Piece and Jesus College.

Christened John Berry Hobbs because his father's name was John and his mother's maiden name Berry, John – or Jack as he was always known – was the eldest of twelve children, six boys and six girls. His father was on the staff at Fenner's and also acted as a professional umpire. When Hobbs senior became groundsman and umpire to Jesus College, young Hobbs took immense delight in watching cricket there. During the school holidays he used to field at the nets and play his own version of cricket with the College servants, using a tennis ball, a cricket stump for a bat and a tennis post for a wicket on a gravel pitch. This primitive form of practice laid the foundations of his skill. Little more than ten years old at the time, young Jack tried to produce the strokes which he had seen players employ in college matches. The narrow straight stump helped him to appreciate the importance of a straight bat, and with the natural assets of a keen eye and flexible wrists he learned to hit the ball surely and with widely varied strokes. Hobbs was self-taught and never coached, but he remembered all his life a piece of advice which his father gave him the only time the pair practised together, on Jesus College Close. Jack, facing spin bowling from his father, was inclined to stand clear of his stumps. 'Don't draw away,' his father told him. 'Standing up to the wicket is all important. If you draw away, you cannot play with a straight bat and the movement may cause you to be bowled off your pads.'

When 12, Jack joined his first cricket team, the Church Choir Eleven at St Matthew's, Cambridge, where he was in the choir of Jesus College who borrowed him, on their ground. He helped to form the Ivy Boys Club and they played both cricket and football on Parker's Piece.

Ranjitsinhji practised there, and Hobbs watched his beautiful wrist-play wonderingly, but the hero of Jack's boyhood was Tom Hayward, son of Dan Hayward who looked after the nets and marquees on Parker's Piece. Cricket became Jack's passion and his supreme ambition was to be good enough to play for one of the leading counties, preferably Surrey, the county of his idol, Tom Hayward. Hobbs practised morning, noon and night, and when he knew that he would be busy during the day he rose at six and practised before he went to work.

Tom Hayward first saw him bat when the noted Surrey player took a team to Parker's Piece for the last match of the summer in 1901, the season in which Jack played a few times for Cambridgeshire as an amateur.

In 1902, Hobbs obtained his first post as a professional – second coach and second umpire to Bedford Grammar School – and in the August of that year he helped Royston, receiving a fee of half a guinea for each appearance. He hit a fine century against Herts Club & Ground, so bringing immense joy to his father, but Mr. Hobbs was not destined to see further progress by his son, for he died soon afterwards.

Tom Hayward was instrumental in Jack going to Surrey. A generous man, Hayward arranged a benefit for the widow Hobbs, and another friend of the family, a Mr. F. C. Hutt, asked Hayward to take a good look at Jack. Hobbs was set to bat for twenty minutes on Parker's Piece against William Reeves, the Essex bowler, and Hayward was so impressed that he promised to get Jack a trial at the Oval the following spring. Mr. Hutt thought that Hobbs should also try his luck with Essex, but they declined to grant him a trial, and so, in April 1903, Hobbs went to Surrey. Immediately they recognised his budding talent and engaged him. A two years' qualifying period had its ups-and-downs for Hobbs – he began with a duck when going in first for Surrey Colts at the Oval against Battersea – but soon his promise was clear for all to see. In his first Surrey Club & Ground match he made 86 against Guy's Hospital, and in his second qualifying year – 1904 – when he played several matches as a professional for Cambridgeshire, he scored 195 in brilliant style against Hertfordshire. His apprenticeship over, Hobbs commenced in 1905 the long and illustrious career with Surrey in first-class company which was to make his name known the world over and earn him a knighthood from the Queen – the first professional cricketer to receive the honour.

From the time he was awarded his county cap by Lord Dalmeny, afterwards Lord Rosebery, following a score of 155 in his first Championship match against Essex, Hobbs built up the reputation of the 'Master' cricketer – a reputation perpetuated by the Hobbs Gates at the Oval and by his other permanent memorial, the Jack Hobbs Pavilion, at Parker's Piece. The tables of his achievements tell eloquently how thoroughly he deserves remembrance by cricket enthusiasts, but comparisons with 'W. G.' will still be made.

From this point of view, Hobbs was, without argument, the most accomplished batsman known to cricket since W. G. Grace. In his career, Hobbs scored 61,237 runs with an average of 50.65 and scored 197 centuries. He played in 61 Test Matches. Other players have challenged the statistical values of Hobb's cricket. None has, since Grace, had his creative influence.

Like 'W. G.', he gave a new twist or direction to the game. Grace was the first to cope with overarm fast bowling, the first to mingle forward and back play. Hobbs was brought up on principles more or less laid down by 'W. G.' and his contemporaries – left leg forward to the length ball. Right foot back to the ball a shade short, but the leg hadn't to be moved over the wicket to the off. Pad-play among the Victorians was not done. It was caddish – until a low fellow, a professional from Nottingham, named Arthur Shrewsbury, began to exploit the pad as a second line of defence – sometimes, in extremity, a first.

When Hobbs played his first first-class match for Surrey on a bitterly cold Easter Monday (April 24) in 1905, the other side, captained by 'W. G.' was called 'The Gentlemen of England'. Hobbs, then 22 years and 4 months old, scored 18 and 88 – taking only two hours making the 88. Grace contemplated the unshaven youth from his position of 'point'. He stroked the beard and said: 'He's goin' to be a good 'un.' He could not have dreamed that 20 years later Hobbs would beat his own record of 126 centuries in a lifetime – and go on to amass 197 before retiring, and receive a knighthood for services rendered.

Hobbs learned to bat in circumstances of technique and environment much the same as those in which Grace came to his high noon. The attack of bowlers concentrated, by and large, on the off stump. Pace and length on good pitches, with varied flight. On 'sticky' pitches the fast bowlers were often 'rested', the damage done by slow left-hand spin or right-hand breaks. Leg breaks were called on but rarely, then as a last resort, though already Braund, Vine and Bosanquet were developing 'back-of-the-hand' trickery. Swerve was not unknown in 1905; there were Hirst, Arnold, Relf, Trott, and J. B. King 'swinging' terrifically. But in those days only one and the same ball was used throughout the longest of a team's innings. And the seam was not raised as prominently as on balls made at the present time.

In 1907, two summers after Hobbs's baptism of first-class cricket, the South Africans came to this country, bringing a company of 'googly' bowlers as clever as any seen since – Vogler (quick), Gordon White, Faulkner and Schwarz. Hobbs faced them only twice, scoring 18 and 41 for Surrey and 78 and 5 for C. I. Thornton's XI at Scarborough. J. T. Tyldesley, Braund, Jessop and Spooner also coped with the new witch-craft, so did George Gunn, who could cope with anything. Partly on the strength of his showing against the South Africans, Hobbs was chosen for his first overseas tour: 1907–1908 in Australia.

But it was two years later, when the M.C.C. visited South Africa, that Hobbs demonstrated quite positively that he had found the answer to the problems of the back-of-the-hand spinners. The amazing fact is that he made his demonstration on the matting wickets then used in South Africa. What is more, it was Hobbs's first taste of the mat, on which the South African spinners were at their most viciously angular. South Africa won this rubber of 1909–1910 by three wins to two. In the Tests Hobbs scored 539 runs, average 67.37; double the averages of England's next best three run-makers: – Thompson (33.77), Woolley (32.00), Denton (26.66) and Rhodes (25.11). It was Hobbs who first assembled into his methods all the rational counters against the ball which turned the other way. Moreover, on all kinds of pitches, hard and dry, in this country or in Australia, on sticky pitches here and anywhere else, even on the 'gluepot' of Melbourne, on the matting of South Africa, against pace, spin, swing, and every conceivable device of bowlers Hobbs reigned supreme.

His career was divided into two periods, each different from the other in style and tempo. Before the war of 1914–1918 he was Trumperesque, quick to the attack on springing feet, strokes all over the field, killing but never brutal, all executed at the wrists, after the preliminary getting together of the general muscular motive power. When cricket was resumed in 1919, Hobbs, who served in the Royal Flying Corps as an Air Mechanic after a short spell in a munition factory, was heading towards his thirty-seventh birthday, and a man was regarded as a cricket veteran in 1919 if he was nearing the forties. Hobbs entering his second period, dispensed with some of the daring punitive strokes of his youthful raptures. He ripened into a classic. His style became as serenely poised as any ever witnessed on a cricket field, approached only by Hammond. He scored centuries effortlessly now; we hardly noted the making of them. They came as the hours passed on a summer day, as natural as a summer growth. An astonishing statistical fact about 'The Master' is that of the 130 centuries to his name in county cricket, 85 were scored after the war of 1914–1918; that is, after he had entered 'middle age'. The more his years increased the riper his harvests. From 1919 to 1928 his season's yields were as follows:

1919	2,594	runs	average	60.32
1920	2,827	runs	average	58.89
1921	3,120	runs	average	78.00
	(a season of illness)			
1922	2,552	runs	average	62.24
1923	2,087	runs	average	37.94
1924	2,094	runs	average	58.16
1925	3,024	runs	average	70.32
1926	2,949	runs	average	77.60
1927	1,641	runs	average	52.93
1928	2,542	runs	average	82.00

From the time of his forty-third to his forty-sixth birthday, Hobbs scored some 11,000 runs, averaging round about the sixties. Yet he once said that he would wish to be remembered for the way he batted before 1914. 'But, Jack,' his friends protested, 'you got bags of runs after 1919!' 'Maybe,' replied Hobbs, 'but they were nearly all made off the back foot.' Modest and true to a point. 'The Master' knows how to perform within limitations. Hobbs burgeoned to an effortless control not seen on a cricket field since his departure. The old easy footwork remained to the end. At Old Trafford a Lancashire 'colt' made his first appearance against Surrey. He fielded at mid-off as McDonald, with a new ball, opened the attack on Hobbs. After a few overs, the 'colt' allowed a forward stroke from Hobbs to pass through his legs to the boundary. His colleagues, notably burly, redfaced Dick Tyldesley, expostulated to him – 'What's matter? Wer't sleepin'?' – with stronger accessories. The 'colt' explained, or excused his lapse. He had been so much 'mesmerised' watching Hobbs's footwork as he played the ferocious speed of McDonald that he could not move.

It is sometimes said that Hobbs in his harvest years took advantage of the existing leg-before-wicket rule which permitted batsmen to cover their wickets with their pads against off-spin pitched outside the off-stump. True it is that Hobbs and Sutcliffe brought 'the second line of defence' to a fine art. By means of it they achieved the two wonderful first-wicket stands at Kennington Oval in 1926 and at Melbourne two years later, v. Australia, each time on vicious turf. But, as I have pointed out, Hobbs's technique was grounded in the classic age, when the bat was the main instrument in defence. Always was the bat of Hobbs the sceptre by which he ruled his bowlers. In his last summers his rate of scoring inevitably had to slacken – from 40 runs an hour, the tempo of his youth, to approximately 30 or 25 an hour. In 1926, at Lord's for Surrey v. Middlesex, he scored 316 not out in six hours 55 minutes with 41 boundaries – a rate of more than forty an hour, not exceeded greatly these days by two batsmen together. And he was in his forty-fourth year in 1926, remember. It was in his wonderful year of 1925 that he beat 'W. G.'s' record of 126 centuries, and before the summer's end gathered at his sweet will 3,024 runs, with 16 hundreds, average 70.32. He was now fulfilled. He often got himself out after reaching his century. He abdicated.

Those of us who saw him at the beginning and end of his career will cherish memories of the leaping young gallant, bat on high, pouncing at the sight of a ball a shade loose, driving and hooking; then, as the bowler desperately shortened his length, cutting square, the blow of the axe – a Tower Hill stroke. Then we will remember the coming of the regal control, the ripeness and readiness, the twiddle of the bat before he bent slightly to face the attack, the beautifully timed push to the off to open his score – the push was not hurried, did not send the ball too quickly to the fieldsman, so that Hobbs could walk his first run. I never saw him make a bad or a hasty stroke. Sometimes, of course, he made the wrong good stroke, technically right but applied to the wrong ball. An error of judgment, not of technique. He extended the scope of batsmanship, added to the store of cricket that will be cherished, played the game with modesty, for all his mastery and produce, and so won fame and affection, here and at the other side of the world. A famous fast bowler once paid the best of all compliments to him – 'It wer' 'ard work bowlin' at 'im, but it wer' something you wouldn't 'ave missed for nothing.' Let Sir Jack go at that.

Other tributes:

Andrew Sandham: Jack was the finest batsman in my experience on all sorts of wickets, especially the bad ones, for in our day there were more bad wickets and more spin bowlers than there are to-day. He soon knocked the shine off the ball and he was so great that he really collared the bowling. He could knock up fifty in no time at all and the bowlers would often turn to me as if to say 'Did you see that?' He was brilliant. Despite all the fuss and adulation made of him he was surprisingly modest and had a great sense of humour.

Herbert Strudwick: On any type of wicket, he was the best batsman in my experience, a first-class bowler if given the chance, and the finest cover point I ever saw. He never looked like getting out and he was just the same whether he made 100 or 0. I remember G. A. Faulkner after an England tour in South Africa, saying to Jack: 'I only bowled you one googly.' 'Why,' said Jack, 'I did not know you bowled one.' Faulkner said, 'You hit the first one I bowled for 4. If you did not know it how did you know it would turn from the off?' 'I didn't,' answered Jack. 'I watched it off the pitch.'

Herbert Sutcliffe: I was his partner on many occasions on extremely bad wickets, and I can say this without any doubt whatever that he was the most brilliant exponent of all time, and quite the best batsman of my generation on all types of wickets. On good wickets I do believe that pride of place should be given to Sir Don Bradman. I had a long and happy association with Sir Jack and can testify to his fine character. A regular church-goer, he seldom missed the opportunity to attend church service on Sunday mornings both in England and abroad. He was a man of the highest integrity who believed in sportsmanship in the highest sense, teamwork, fair-play and clean-living. His life was full of everything noble and true.

Percy Fender: Jack was the greatest batsman the world has ever known, not merely in his generation but any generation and he was the most charming and modest man that anyone could meet. No-one who saw him or met him will ever forget him and his legend will last as long as the game is played – perhaps longer.

George Duckworth: My first trip to Australia in 1928 was Jack's last and I remember with gratitude how he acted as a sort of father and mother to the young players like myself. Always a boyish chap at heart, he remained a great leg-puller. When 51 he promised to come up and play in my benefit match in 1934 and despite bitterly cold weather he hit the last first-class century of his career. He told me he got it to keep warm!

Frank Woolley: Jack was one of the greatest sportsmen England ever had, a perfect gentleman and a good living fellow respected by everyone he met. I travelled abroad with him many times to Australia and South Africa, and I always looked upon him as the finest right-handed batsman I saw in the 30 years I played with and against him.

Wilfred Rhodes: He was the greatest batsman of my time. I learned a lot from him when we went in first together for England. He had a cricket brain and the position of his feet as he met the ball was always perfect. He could have scored thousands more runs, but often he was content to throw his wicket away when he had reached his hundred and give someone else a chance. He knew the Oval inside out and I know that A. P. F. Chapman was thankful for his advice when we regained the Ashes from Australia in 1926.

TOM GRAVENEY – A CENTURY OF CENTURIES [1965]

In mid-May, 1895, there was a county cricket match at Bristol between the two champions of the West Country, Gloucestershire and Somerset. Britain at that time was convulsed by two developments in national life, one of genuine significance, the other comically piddling. In the palaces of Westminster there was some confusion as to whether the Prime Minister should be Lord Salisbury, the one with the beard, or Lord Rosebery, the one with the racehorses. This was an issue of great moment, especially to Lord Salisbury and Lord Rosebery, but the perspectives of history have shrunk the importance of the outcome to a speck on the landscape. Of far greater importance was the fate of a far more gifted man than both of their lordships put together, William Gilbert Grace, of Downend, Gloucestershire, The Gentlemen, M.C.C. and England, not simply the greatest batsman the world had ever seen, but an authentically Eminent Victorian omitted from that pantheon only because of Mr. Strachey's blanket ignorance of outdoor sports. Dr. Grace had been playing first-class cricket ever since, as a teenager in June 1865 he had made his debut for Gentlemen of the South versus Players of the South at the Oval. Since then runs had accrued to him like barnacles to a hulk. Still an adolescent, he registered his first first-class century, 224 not out, for England against Surrey at the Oval. Thirty nine seasons later he arrived at the ground at Bristol to lead his county against Somerset, knowing that his tally of hundreds had reached 99 and that the whole of England was holding its breath until he duly crowned his career with the hundredth.

It should be remembered that no cricketer before him had ever come even remotely close to this mark and that the Doctor was approaching his 47th birthday and was thought to be getting a bit too old for this sort of thing. In addition, May, 1895 was a cold, discouraging month for a batsman. At the end of the first day, Somerset were all out for around 300 and Gloucestershire in reply had lost two wickets, with their captain 38 not out.

On the Friday morning, in freezing weather, W. G. resumed his innings, partnered by a local schoolboy called Charles Townsend. As the morning proceeded and the stand between the old man and the schoolboy flourished, word spread through the county. The local population began to converge on the cricket ground, aware that history was about to be made. At last, after a flurry of snowflakes had dappled the Doctor's beard, his score reached 98. The opposing captain, Sammy Woods, obligingly sent down a long hop on the leg side, W. G. thumped it to the ropes, and the deed was done. A century of centuries. W. G. then went on to his double hundred, while the schoolboy was finally dismissed in the nineties. A tray of champagne and glasses was carried on to the field and play paused for

*a few moments while the bubbly was quaffed, as Mr. Sherlock Holmes
would say, for strictly remedial purposes. The libation was perfectly justified, for a century of centuries seemed beyond the bounds of the rational.
Who would ever equal Grace's feat?*

*The answer is that in time, a great deal of time, twenty other batsmen
achieved their hundredth hundred. The fourteenth of these was Tom
Graveney and, when in 1964 he reached the mystical mark, it was a
foregone conclusion that he would be the subject of a tribute in Wisden.
Unlike most prolific scorers, Graveney was considered by some, including
at times the England selectors, to lack the mysterious quality called 'temperament', which was another way of acknowledging that he was a pure
stylist who gave pleasure every time he played the ball. Cardus hits him
off to perfection when he measures Graveney's exquisite balance against
Dexter's rhetoric and Roy Marshall's virtuosity. But how does a batsman
without temperament score 122 hundreds, as Graveney went on to do?
How does a player without the right spirit make nearly fifty thousand
runs? Cardus lets the detractors have it straight between the eyes.*

THOMAS WILLIAM GRAVENEY who in the summer of 1964 made his
hundredth hundred in first class cricket, is one of the few batsmen
today worth while our inspection if it is style and fluent strokes we are
wishing to see, irrespective of the scoreboard's estimate of an innings by
him. His accumulated runs, up to the moment I write this article, amount
to no fewer than 38,094, averaging a little above 45. Yet he has seldom
been regarded as a permanent member of the England XI; he has been
for more than a decade on 'trial'. Nobody in his senses with half-a-notion
of what constitutes a thoroughbred batsman would deny Graveney's
class, his pedigree.

He came out of the Gloucestershire stable following the glamorous
period of Hammond and Barnett, while the influence still pervaded the
atmosphere of the County. Eleven years ago *Wisden* wrote of him in
this eloquent way: 'Undoubtedly no brighter star has appeared in the
Gloucestershire cricket firmament since the early days of Hammond
himself; some who have played with both believe that with a comparable
intensity, almost ruthlessness, Graveney in time could emulate
Hammond's remarkable achievements'. Hammond as he matured and
compiled his seven hour double-century certainly developed in mental
determination. We who had seen him in his younger years realised the
price we were paying for his solid durable contributions to the cause of
England in Test matches – we knew that we wouldn't, except occasionally, see again the dauntless Hammond of his first raptures.

Since Hammond's glorious reign the character and economy have
become tougher and tighter. Cricket everywhere, reflecting character
and economy in the world at large, has tended to change from a sport and
artistic spectacle to a competitive materialistic encounter, each contestant
mainly setting his teeth not to lose. Batsmen not fit to tie Graveney's
bootlaces, considered from the point of view of handsome stroke-

embedded play, have been encouraged to oust Graveney from Test matches, stern and generally unbeautiful. 'Style' has become a 'corny' word everywhere, so it is natural enough that we have lived to see and extol an honest artisan such as Boycott building his brick wall of an innings, what time Graveney must needs content himself scoring felicitous runs for his adopted county (incidentally going far towards winning the championship for Worcestershire).

Were I myself Tom Graveney I shouldn't deplore my fate; I'd much rather remain a cricketer on the side of those who add to the aesthetic values and delight those lovers of the game who find it difficult to count and work out percentages and hours of labour at the crease endured by the unblessed toilers under the sun whose presence at the wicket might not be closely observed if the scoreboard didn't dutifully and mechanically draw our attention to them.

It is true – and not to be questioned – that in Test matches against Australia Graveney has seldom done his talents justice. In some 24 innings v. Australia he has failed to reach 20 twelve times and only six times gone beyond 40, with a single century put calmly together at Sydney, during the Hutton tour of 1954–55, when the rubber had already been decided in England's favour. At Lord's in 1953, he played a royal innings with Hutton, in the face of Australia's first-innings total of 346. He was not out 78, and Hutton still in possession, when stumps were drawn on the second day with England 177 for one. Next morning in bounteous sunshine Lindwall clean bowled Graveney before another run had accrued. 'Ah,' said the wise heads of short memories, 'he's no temperament this Graveney', forgetting at once that only a few hours since they had seen from Graveney batsmanship of the highest blood. As a fact Graveney was bowled on that morning of promise at Lord's by one of the finest balls bowled by Lindwall in his lifetime – a fast swinging yorker. 'I never bowled a better', he vowed.

We should in fairness judge a man at his best. No batsman not truly accomplished is able to play a characteristic Graveney innings. Today he has no equal as a complete and stylish strokeplayer. Dexter can outshine him in rhetoric, so to say; Marshall in virtuosity of execution. But neither Dexter nor Marshall is Graveney's superior in point of effortless balance. When he is in form Graveney makes batsmanship look the easiest and most natural thing in the world. I have no rational explanation to account for his in-and-out form in Test matches – which, by the way, has not persistently been too bad. Against the West Indies in England in 1957, he scored 258 at Nottingham and 164 at Trent Bridge. No 'Test match temperament'? Once on a time it was said of Hendren and W. J. Edrich that they hadn't any.

I decline to keep out of the highest class a fine batsman simply on the evidence of his half success in Test matches. Indeed I'm not too sure nowadays that success in Test cricket most times is not an indication of dreary efficiency. It is a modern notion that anybody's talents need be measured by utility value in the 'top' places of publicity. Some of the rarest artist-batsmen the game has ever nurtured have figured unobtrusively in Test matches; some of them have not appeared in Test matches at all. None the less they have adorned cricket, contributed to its memorable art, added to its summer-time appeal and delights.

Amongst these cricketers of style and pleasure can be counted L. C. H. Palairet, H. K. Foster, A. P. Day, Alan Marshal, Andy Ducat, Laurie Fishlock, George Emmett (superb stroke-playing colleague for a time of Graveney), the Hon. C. N. Bruce (as he was named), Jack Robertson – I could extend the list beginning from the days of W. G. Grace and continuing to Graveney himself and his Worcestershire captain, Donald Kenyon.

Consider cricket as a game of skill handsomely exhibited and who in the name of truth and common sense will argue that so and so's century in five hours in a Test match necessarily ranks him above, as a cricketer, Tom Graveney. Endurance and concentration, admirable factors in human nature in their proper place, don't inevitably add to the graces and allurements of any game, not even to its highly specialised technique. If some destructive process were to eliminate all that we know about cricket, only Graveney surviving, we could reconstruct from him, from his way of batting and from the man himself, every outline of the game, every essential character and flavour which have contributed to cricket, the form of it and its soul, and its power to inspire a wide and sometimes great literature. Of how many living Test match cricketers could you say as much as this? Could you imagine Bloggs of Blankshire reminding you of the soul of cricket as he plods his computing way to a century in six hours and a half?

Graveney is one of the few batsmen today ornamenting the game, who not out at lunch, pack a ground in the afternoon. Bloggs of Blankshire sometimes empties it or keeps people away – the truth of his performances may copiously be found out from the subsequent published statistics. An innings of Graveney remains in the memory. Simply by closing our eyes we can still see, in deep winter as we browse by the fire in the twilight, a stroke by Graveney; we can see and delight in, retrospectively, the free uplift of his bat, the straight lissome poise and the rhythm of his swinging drives.

In form he hasn't need to labour; he knows the secret of artistic independence of effort. He can cut late from flexible wrists – whenever the miser of a bowler isn't pegging away on the leg stump. A fair-weather cricketer? Is it possible that any batsman not strong in mental and technical fibre could play most of his 955 innings in England, scoring more than 38,000 runs, averaging 45? No cricketer not fairly complete in character and skill could hope to score a hundred hundreds in first-class cricket.

Moreover, Graveney has often enough proved that he is capable of facing stiff problems presented by the turning ball on a nasty wicket. Not really a 'Test' cricketer? – still the parrot question about him persists. Yet in Test matches Graveney has scored 3,107 runs, average 41.98.

This sop I toss to the statisticians. In a world of ideal cricket, a world in which the game could freely show its class, allurement and fine subtle technique unburdened by parsimonious competitive considerations, Graveney would be a first-choice in any England XI. Really, there should for the purposes of all representative games be a certain style insisted on. Here I am an unrepentant snob; I want to see breeding in an England XI. I'd rather lose a rubber than win it by playing against the game's spirit and pride, its tradition of style and summer-time spectacle, charm and glorious change and variety.

Critics who think of Test matches as though they were of dire consequence to the nation politically, economically and what have you, have maintained that Graveney had on occasion 'let England down'. But nobody has claimed that Tom Graveney has ever 'let cricket down'. In form or out of form he has rendered tribute to the graces of cricket.

NEVILLE CARDUS [1965]

BY JOHN ARLOTT

When in 1967 Neville Cardus became Sir Neville, his biographer described the honour in terms calculated to strike the cricketing world as perverse: 'Neville was, and remains, the only music critic to have been knighted this century'. The statement was just as true, and just as misleading, as the claim that Bernard Shaw was the only music critic to have refused a knighthood this century. Whatever the cause of Cardus's ennoblement, it is a fact that he is the only cricket journalist to be ennobled. His acceptance of the honour was tinged with ambivalence. In describing his experience of the investiture, he told a friend, 'You stand in a long queue, frozen cold, and very nervous; you can't joke, can't sit down, and can't pee'. Reduced by the bladder of an old man, he was obliged to ask a footman for the nearest lavatory and, on following his directions, ended up in a broom cupboard. Still, there were advantages. As Beecham always advised him, 'In the unlikely event of you being offered a knighthood, Neville, take it. It makes tables at the Savoy so much easier to come by'.

Cardus would have been aware that the most famous writers of the generation before his own had not only not been knighted, but would have regarded acceptance of the offer as a slur on their independence and even a tacit approval of a philistine society. As an omnivorous reader, Cardus, who had once drawn close parallels between Cecil Parkin and Henry Machin, would have known Arnold Bennett's views on knighthoods for writers. Far more deeply cherished by him were two other gestures which, unlike the flummery of knighthood, brought him closer to Summer

*Place and the aspirations of a fatherless boy. The Hallé Orchestra gave a
concert in his honour at the Free Trade Hall and in 1971 he was invited
to become President of the Lancashire County Cricket Club. In 'The
Guardian' for May 29th, 1971, he wrote warmly of this honour, describing
himself when young as 'the small, frail urchin who, for the first time,
pushed his way through the Old Trafford turnstiles':*

> The small schoolboy, aged ten, was, curiously enough, the President
> himself. He was not yet qualified to count among the 'working classes'
> but soon he would be, for the school-leaving age, at the turn of the
> century, was thirteen, with no 'O' level certificates and whatever was
> needed to get a job pushing a handcart from Oldham Street to the
> joiner's shop of E. Moss, in Upper Brook Street, Manchester.

*Cardus's elevation was marked by an essay in Wisden written by the man
best qualified for the job, his successor on the Cricket page of 'The
Guardian', John Arlott.*

THE BIRTHDAY HONOURS list of 1964 included the award of the C.B.E.
to Mr. Neville Cardus "for services to music and cricket". It was the
first – and, some may feel, belated – official recognition of the modest
man who, for almost fifty years, has written with sympathy and integrity
about the two chief interests – indeed, enthusiasms – of his life. Throughout that time his work has never become jaded, but has unfailingly
reflected the happiness of one who always felt privileged, even grateful,
to earn his living from his pleasures.

The honour was acclaimed in the two spheres where he has long been
accorded affection as a man, and respect as a writer. It would be shortsighted for cricketers to overlook Mr. Cardus's work on music. Few are
qualified to compare his writings on the two subjects: in any case, the
comparison would be pointless. It may be said, however, that while his
standing in the world of music is high, in the field of cricket it is unique.

The form of musical criticism had already been shaped, by such men
as Shaw, Newman, Langford, Hanslick and Professor Dent, before Mr.
Cardus came to it. On the other hand, by innovation and influence, he
virtually created modern cricket-writing. In doing so, he led thousands
of people to greater enjoyment of the game.

Today he may be regarded as just one of a number of imaginative
cricket-writers; but he appears so only to those who do not recall the
immense novelty and impact of his writing when it first reached the
public in the nineteen-twenties. Before then there had been much competent cricket-reporting, informed, sound in judgment, pleasant in
manner. But the Cardus of the years shortly after the First World War
first brought to it the qualities of personalization, literary allusion and
imagery. By such methods as presenting the contest between bowler and
batsman as a clash not only of skills but of characters, he created something near to a mythology of the game. His early writing has been
described, not always with complimentary intent, as romantic. That is

the essence of his appeal. To the enthusiast, cricket *is* romantic: and in Mr. Cardus's reports, the ordinary spectator saw his romantic and heroic feelings put into words for the first time.

Every modern cricket-writer with any pretensions to style owed half that he is to Neville Cardus, if only in the stern realism of making such an approach acceptable to editors. The consciously literary method can lead to lush and imprecise writing and, in the cases of some of Mr. Cardus's imitators, that has happened. His own work, however, always has a ballast of practicality, humanity and humour.

There was no cricket at his Board School, but on strips of waste land near his childhood home in the Rusholme suburb of Manchester, he learnt enough of the game to become assistant coach at Shrewsbury School. Though he does not labour technical points, he never loses sight of the basic principles. He is, too, sufficiently self-critical to relish the reaction to one of his high-flown passages of that earthy Lancashire cricketer and character, Richard Tyldesley: 'Ah'd like to bowl at bugger soom da-ay'. Thus, his unerring touch constantly saved him from the pitfall of extravagance, by balancing rich imagery with the earthiness of the genuine common tongue.

No cricketer of whom he ever wrote trod a more remarkable path from a humble upbringing to success than this man who achieved more than he would have dared to regard as ambition, but which must have seemed to him so remote as to be beyond dreams.

Nothing in his wide-ranging and relishable *Autobiography* is more vivid than the description of his childhood in the house of his grandfather who retired from the police force as a result of a series of blows – the bumps from which gleamed ever afterwards on his scalp – from the jemmy of no less a celebrity than Charles Peace. The grandmother took in washing: her three buxom daughters, one of them Neville Cardus's mother, laundered and ironed: the grandfather delivered the wash by pony-cart, except in the case of 'rush-orders', which the young Cardus took in a perambulator.

Once, as music critic of *The Manchester Guardian*, he was given dinner by the Chairman of the Hallé Concerts Society and, as he leant back and drew on one of his host's cigars, he could think: 'What a world! I have delivered his washing.'

He was ten years old when he earned his first money – as a pavement artist. He left school at thirteen with little more education than the ability to read and write: but he had discovered Dickens – and the urge to read. 'I went alone on Saturday evenings to the Free Library, not in the spirit of a good boy stirred upward and on by visions of an improving kind: I revelled in it all.'

By the time he was fourteen he had sold newspapers, pushed a builder's hand-cart, boiled type in a printing works and sold chocolate (and avidly watched the performance) in a Manchester theatre. But already Cardus the writer was beginning to take shape. He had been to Old Trafford and seen A. C. MacLaren and R. H. Spooner, two of the players from whom he gained so much pleasure, and whom he repaid with a measure of immortality in his writing. In his own words: 'I spent sixteen years of my youth mainly in books and music and in the sixpenny galleries of theatres. The men on the cricket field were mixed up with the heroes of books and plays.' This is why a Cardus quotation is always unforced: it springs from a mind not stocked by formal education but by enthusiastic reading.

He settled as a clerk in an insurance office, living in a lodging house, reading voraciously and attending free lectures at the University, until he reached the age of twenty-one and a salary of a pound a week. In 1912 he applied for a post at Shrewsbury school ('Shastbury' of some of his most charming essays) as assistant to the cricket professional, Attewell ('William' of *The Summer Game*). To his surprise he was engaged. He bowled *just* well enough – once, in desperation, *just* fast enough – to keep his job until the day the headmaster, Dr. C. A. Alington, finding his unlikely-looking young cricket pro reading *Euripides*, made him his secretary. During this time Cardus's first musical criticism was published – in the old *Daily Citizen*. When Alington left Shrewsbury, Cardus went back to Manchester – his poor eyesight alone precluded him from war service – and wrote, with slight hope, to ask for work as a clerk in *The Guardian* office. That remarkable man and editor, C. P. Scott saw the letter and took Cardus as his secretary. A year later he was put on the staff of the paper as a reporter and, by 1917, had worked his way up to edit the Miscellany and to be number two to C. E. Montague, the paper's dramatic critic.

By yet another odd circumstance, he fell ill in 1919; and afterwards the News Editor, W. P. Crozier, suggested he might be amused to combine convalescence with cricket reporting at old Trafford. The outcome was instantly successful. By the beginning of the next season he was *The Manchester Guardian*'s cricket correspondent, under the penname 'Cricketer', which, during the next twenty years, he made increasingly famous.

To his added delight he was also made assistant, and eventually successor, to Samuel Langford, the paper's music critic. *The Guardian*'s circulation and payment rates were small by comparison with those of the London papers. There was no doubt, however, that Neville Cardus was one of the rare cricket writers who positively *sold* newspapers: and he might have multiplied both his salary and his circulation considerably if he had accepted any of the offers to join a larger paper. He refused them for the reason which distinguished him both as man and writer – he was completely happy with his work and with the traditions and atmosphere of *The Guardian:* and, granted the variety afforded by a summer touring the cricket grounds, happy with Manchester, too.

He could not help but realise the impact of his work: he observed the opportunity to publish in book form and he knew the book world well enough to approach, quite astutely, Grant Richards, whose open-minded attitude to fresh types of writing made him one of the most successful publishers of new work and rising writers of the period. Yet Cardus's letters to him were so deferential as to suggest a complete lack of self-confidence in his own work.

Richards, however, was enthusiastic. The result was *A Cricketer's Book*, published in 1922. It began with 'The Greatest Test Match' an account of the last day of England-Australia at The Oval in 1882, still the most vivid reconstruction of a cricket match ever written. There followed a series of those evocative essays in which great players were presented larger, but credibly so, than life, and closed with accounts of the Test series of 1921 and some thoughts on Australian cricket. This book was a landmark in cricket-writing.

Over the next eight years he published *Days in the Sun, The Summer Game and Cricket*, in the 'English Heritage' series, and established his reputation widely and firmly. The last of these is slight in size but it is wide – almost majestic – in scope, and posterity could yet esteem it as the finest of his cricket books. It completed his reputation as the most widely accepted writer the game had known. His achievement could be defined as giving cricket the first sustained writing it had known of the type usually described as 'appreciation'.

By now he had many imitators but no peer, if only for the reason that, driven by the urge that possesses every worthwhile writer, he never stood still. He broke fresh ground with *Australian Summer*, a book-length account of the 1936–37 M.C.C. tour of Australia. Then, in 1940, he left *The Guardian* for Australia, attracted by a fresh challenge, to deliver an hour-long broadcast each week on music, which he did for the remarkable period of seven years. He also covered music for *The Sydney Morning Herald* and addressed himself to writing his autobiography by hand. This was one more successful departure: the *Autobiography* is expansive, richly human, poignant and humorous: but for the fact that its cricket content was not acceptable to the American reading public, it would have been a world best-seller.

A selection of his work was made by Rupert Hart-Davis under the title *The Essential Neville Cardus* in a series which, with Hemingway, Mary Webb, Joyce and Jefferies, reached a literary level never before attained by a cricket writer.

Although he had contentedly devoted himself to music for some years, the sailing of the Australian side for England in 1948 proved irresistible. He returned to report that tour and to become *The Guardian*'s London music critic. Meanwhile he wrote for *The Sunday Times* for a year, over a considerable period for *World Sports* and, from May, 1960, he has written a monthly essay for *The Playfair Cricket Magazine*. Still, too, usually on the occasion of the death of one of the players of earlier days, he contributes on cricket to *The Guardian*.

Of recent years, too, he has written regularly in *Wisden* – with mellow and dignified nostalgia about old comrades like George Gunn, Charlie Macartney and Hubert Preston: with genuine appreciation of what is for him the younger generation in Sir Leonard Hutton, Godfrey Evans,

Cyril Washbrook; of current influences; and with genuine historic sweep, of Lancashire cricket and 'Six Giants of the Wisden Century'.

In the post-war period he produced a series of books on music – *Ten Composers, Talking of Music*, studies of Sir Thomas Beecham and Mahler, and edited a book about Kathleen Ferrier.

Nowadays, rising seventy-seven, he covers chosen events in European music and watches cricket for pleasure. Though his last collection of cricket essays, *The Playfair Cardus*, revealed fresh facets of style, he probably is content to be judged on his already published work.

Some critics, though amiably disposed, have, nevertheless, done him the injustice of failing to observe his development. There are times when he blushes for what he regards as the excesses of his youth. His essential qualities, as a man, observer and recorder are, of course, constant: but his genuine artistic sensibility, if only that, dictated change in his style. The later Cardus is not to be categorised as better or worse than the early Cardus: but it does him less than justice not to recognise it as different.

Let us take two examples of the change: thirty years ago, in *Good Days*, which some critics regard as his best book, he concluded a study of A. C. MacLaren with this paragraph: 'He was the noblest Roman of them all. The last impression in my memory of him is the best. I saw him batting in a match just before the (1914) war; he was coming to the end of his sway as a great batsman. And on a bad wicket he was knocked about by a vile fast bowler, hit all over the body. Yet every now and then one of the old imperious strokes shot grandeur over the field. There he stood, a fallible MacLaren, riddled through and through, but glorious still. I thought of Turner's 'The Fighting Temaraire' as MacLaren batted a scarred innings that day, and at last returned to the pavilion with the sky of his career red with a sun that was going down.'

Lately his essay on Sir Leonard Hutton in *The Playfair Cardus* contained: 'Technically his batsmanship was as soundly based and studied as any since Jack Hobbs. He played very close to the line of the ball, so much over it that he sometimes suggested, by the slope of his shoulders, the concentration of the student. Even in his beautiful cover drives – and none have been more beautifully poised than his – his head and eyes were inclined downward, and the bat's swings seldom went beyond the front leg before the ball was struck. Like every master he played 'late', so late that he could check the movement of any stroke at the last split second, if the ball suddenly "did" something contrary to the eyes' and instinct's first promptings.'

Comparisons would be pointless: not better, nor worse, but different – with the difference that thirty years make in any man's mind. There was a period when he felt his writings on music were more important than those on cricket. Perhaps he was temporarily, if understandably, disenchanted. Mozart and Beethoven do not change: cricket does. Few cricket-followers past middle age have ever been content that the players they watch then are so good as those of thirty years earlier. Perhaps indeed, Mr Cardus was right: perhaps cricket is not what it was in 1930, or 1920 or 1900. But he has written as felicitously of Denis Compton, Richie Benaud, Neil Harvey, Sir Leonard Hutton and Keith Miller as he once did of Frank Woolley, Ted McDonald, Archie MacLaren or Reggie Spooner – or nearly so.

Moreover, without professional compulsion, he has returned to watching cricket. Much of his erstwhile diffidence has evaporated: indeed, he has developed into a conversationalist and a salty raconteur, irresistible on such of his old theme characters as George Gunn, Walter Brearley, Harry Makepeace and Maurice Tate. He may be found taking coffee and talk at Lord's or The Oval half an hour or so before play begins: and he occasionally holds modest court on the little triangle of grass behind the Warner Stand.

He has many friends and still not a few imitators. He is courteous to them all: and, apparently effortlessly, he can observe a cricket match and turn a phrase with any of them. He has made a contribution to cricket which no one can ever duplicate. It may be true that cricket was always an art, but no one until Neville Cardus presented it as an art with all an artist's perception. Because of him, thousands of people enjoy watching the game more than they would have done if he had not lived and written. He has said that his recipe was laid down by C. E. Montague: 'To bring to the day's diet of sights and sounds the wine of your own temperament.'

BOOKS BY NEVILLE CARDUS

1. A CRICKETER'S BOOK: Grant Richards, 1922. 256 pp.
2. THE CLUB CRICKETER [by 'Cricketer' of *The Manchester Guardian*]: Manchester Guardian: N. D., 1922. 54 pp.
3. DAYS IN THE SUN: Grant Richards, 1924. 263 pp.
4. LANCASHIRE COUNTY CRICKET CLUB SOUVENIR [by 'Cricketer']: Manchester Guardian and Lancashire C.C.C.: 1924. 40 pp.
5. AUSTRALIA v. ENGLAND 1877–1926 [by 'Cricketer'] Manchester Guardian: 1926. 48 pp.
6. THE SUMMER GAME: Grant Richards and Humphrey Toulmin: 1929. 255 pp.
7. DAYS IN THE SUN: Cape ('Travellers' Library') 1929. Selection from *A Cricketer's Book and Days in the Sun*, revised.
8. CRICKET: Longmans, Green: 1930. 177 pp.
9. IDLE THOUGHTS ON CRICKET: A Broadcast Talk Printed for the Members of the Ditchling Cricket Club by G. T. Meynell: 1934. 6 pp.
10. GOOD DAYS: Cape, 1934, 288 pp.
11. THE AUSTRALIANS IN ENGLAND 1934 [by 'Cricketer'] Manchester Guardian: 20 pp.
12. AUSTRALIAN SUMMER: Cape, 1937. 250 pp.
13. THE AUSTRALIANS IN ENGLAND 1938: Manchester Guardian. 32pp.
14. ENGLISH CRICKET: Collins, 1945, 48 pp. 'Britain in Pictures' series.
15. TEN COMPOSERS: Cape, 1945. 166 pp.
16. AUTOBIOGRAPHY: Collins, 1947. 288 pp.
17. THE ASHES: Sporting Record, 1948. 49 pp.
18. THE ESSENTIAL NEVILLE CARDUS: selected with an introduction by Rupert Hart-Davis: Cape, 1949. 316 pp. (contains accounts of Test Matches of

1938 reprinted from *The Manchester Guardian* and not elsewhere published in book form).
19. SECOND INNINGS: Collins, 1950. 250 pp.
20. CRICKET ALL THE YEAR: Collins, 1925. 222 pp.
21. KATHLEEN FERRIER: Hamish Hamilton, 1954. 128 pp. A symposium edited and introduced by Neville Cardus.
22. CLOSE OF PLAY: Collins, 1956. 192 pp.
23. TALKING OF MUSIC: Collins, 1959. 320 pp.
24. SIR THOMAS BEECHAM: Collins, 1962. 128 pp.
25. THE PLAYFAIR CARDUS: Dickens Press, 1963. 160 pp.
26. MAHLER: THE MAN AND HIS MUSIC: Gollancz, 1965. Vol. 1, 192 pp.

WALTER REGINALD HAMMOND
[1966]

Born at Dover, June 19, 1903
Died at his home at Durban, South Africa, July 2, 1965

The death of Walter Hammond was precisely the sort of trumpet call to duty to which Cardus, of all his generation, was best fitted to respond. In a sense his cricketing career and Hammond's had run concurrently, for Cardus had not long become 'Cricketer' before young Hammond made his first-class debut. It was Cardus who had been first to recognise the limitless potential of this athlete of genius. There are one or two revelations in his obituary without which no obituary is worth reading, and one omission which might have made Hammond's even more readable. Delighting in the intimate knowledge of the insider, Cardus describes one of Hammond's most audacious innings in terms of the failure of Ted Macdonald and Richard Tyldesley to get to Manchester Races in time to lose their money. And he reminds posterity of the long-forgotten incident in a Gloucestershire match against Lancashire at Bristol when Hammond showed his distaste for the spoiling tactics of the visiting batsmen by bowling a full over of underarm deliveries, all along the ground.

The omission concerns the sensational sequence of events in 1922 when Lord Harris took umbrage at Hammond, who was born in Dover, repre-senting Gloucestershire. Wielding his influence like a flail, Harris had Hammond removed from the Championship for the rest of the season, an act of such comic blackguardism that uproar followed. In his own defence Harris said that Hammond's attempt to pass himself off as a member of the Gloucestershire side was a graphic example of the advance into English life of Bolshevism. Harris's dementia on this point is hardly mitigated by the fact that he had, on his own admission, condoned the appearance for Lancashire of one Schultz, who had been born elsewhere. Schultz, how-ever, had been a fellow gentleman which presumably altered the case. It would have taken a resolute non-Gentleman to draw attention to the possibility that Harris's dotty spitefulness in the Hammond affair may have had something to do with the fact that Harris was president of the Kent club and that, had his committee been a little more alert, Hammond would have been playing for them. The affair is central to Hammond's career, and the reader assumes that the reason for Cardus's reticence has something to do with his respect for the oldtime grandees of the game. He is tactful too on the question of the sad decline of Hammond in his later years. He does hint at 'some strain in his life', but does not refer to the bewilderment of the rest of the 1946–47 tourists to Australia at the extent to which Hammond, their captain, kept his own company. For Hammond that tour was a bridge too far; Cardus prefers to celebrate the long years of brilliance and virtuosity, which is only fair to the memory of one of the greatest cricketers of the century. But the obituary is partial in more senses than one. Perhaps Lord Harris should have written it.

WHEN the news came in early July of the death of W. R. Hammond, cricketers everywhere mourned a loss and adornment to the game. He had just passed his 62nd birthday and had not played in the public eye for nearly a couple of decades, yet with his end a light and a glow on cricket seemed to go out. Boys who had never seen him said, 'Poor Wally'; they had heard of his prowess and personality and, for once in a while, youth of the present was not sceptical of the doings of a past master.

'Wally' indeed was cricket in excelsis. You had merely to see him walk from the pavilion on the way to the wicket to bat, a blue handkerchief peeping out of his right hip pocket. Square of shoulder, arms of obvious strength, a beautifully balanced physique, though often he looked so weighty that his sudden agility in the slips always stirred onlookers and the batsmen to surprise. At Lord's in 1938, England won the toss v. Australia. In next to no time the fierce fast bowling of McCormick overwhelmed Hutton, Barnett and Edrich for 31. Then we saw the most memorable of all Wally's walks from the pavilion to the crease, a calm unhurried progress, with his jaw so firmly set that somebody in the Long Room whispered, 'My God, he's going to score a century.' Hammond at once took royal charge of McCormick, bouncers and all. He hammered the fast attack at will. One cover drive, off the backfoot, hit the palings under the Grandstand so powerfully that the ball rebounded half-way back. His punches, levered by the right forearm, were strong, leonine and irresistible, yet there was no palpable effort, no undignified outbursts of violence. It was a majestic innings, all the red-carpeted way to 240 in six hours, punctuated by thirty-two 4's.

I saw much of Hammond in England and in Australia, playing for Gloucestershire on quiet west country afternoons at Bristol, or in front of a roaring multitude at Sydney. He was always the same; composed, self-contained, sometimes as though withdrawn to some communion within himself. He could be changeable of mood as a man; as a cricketer he was seldom disturbed from his balance of skill and poise. His cricket was, I think, his only way of self-realization. On the field of play he became a free agent, trusting fully to his rare talents.

His career as a batsman can be divided into two contrasted periods. To begin with, when he was in his twenties, he was an audacious stroke-player, as daring and unorthodox as Trumper or Compton. Round about 1924 I recommended Hammond to an England selector as a likely investment. 'Too much of a "dasher" ', was the reply. In May 1927, in his 24th year, Hammond descended with the Gloucestershire XI on Old Trafford. At close of play on the second day Lancashire were so cocksure of a victory early tomorrow (Whit Friday) that the Lancashire bowlers Macdonald, Richard Tyldesley and company, arranged for taxis to be in readiness to take them to the Manchester races.

Macdonald opened his attack at half-past eleven in glorious sunshine. He bowled his fastest, eager to be quick on the spot at Castle Irwell to get a good price on a 'certainty'. Hammond not out overnight, actually drove the first five balls, sent at him from Macdonald's superbly rhythmical arm, to the boundary. The sixth, also would have counted – but it was stopped by a fieldsman sent out to defend the edge of the field, in front of the sight-screen – a straight deep for the greatest fast bowler of the period, bowling his first over of the day and in a desperate hurry to get to the course before the odds shortened.

That day Hammond scored 187 in three hours – four 6's, twenty-four 4's. He hooked Macdonald mercilessly, yes, 'Wally' hooked during the first careless raptures of his youth.

As the years went by, he became the successor to Hobbs as the Monument and Foundation of an England innings. Under the leadership of D. R. Jardine he put romance behind him 'for the cause', to bring into force the Jardinian theory of the Survival of the Most Durable. At Sydney, he wore down the Australians with 251 in seven and a half hours (on the 1928–29 tour); then, at Melbourne, he disciplined himself to the extent of six and three-quarter hours for 200, with only seventeen 4's; and then, at Adelaide his contributions with the bat were 119 (four and a half hours) and 177 (seven hours, twenty minutes). True, the exuberant Percy Chapman was Wally's captain in this rubber, but Jardine was the Grey Éminence with his plotting already spinning fatefully for Australia's not distant future. In five Tests of this 1928–29 rubber, Hammond scored 905 runs, average 113.12.

Walter Reginald Hammond was born in Kent at Dover on June 19, 1903, the son of a soldier who became Major William Walter Hammond, Royal Artillery, and was killed in action in the first world war. As an infant, Walter accompanied the regiment with his parents to China and Malta. To the bad luck of Kent cricket, when he was brought back to England he went to Portsmouth Grammar School in 1916 and two years later moved with his family to Cirencester Grammar school, rooting himself for such a flowering as Gloucestershire cricket had not known since the advent of W. G. Grace.

In all first-class games, Hammond scored 50,493 runs, average 56.10, with 167 centuries. Also he took 732 wickets average 30.58. In Test matches his batting produced 7,249 runs, average 58.45.

As a slip fieldsman his easy, lithe omnipresence has not often been equalled. He held 78 catches in a single season, 10 in one and the same match. He would stand at first slip erect as the bowler began to run, his legs slightly turned in at the knees. He gave the impression of relaxed carelessness. At the first sight, or hint of, a snick off the edge, his energy swiftly concentrated in him, apparently electrifying every nerve and muscle in him. He became light, boneless, airborne. He would take a catch as the ball was travelling away from him, leaping to it as gracefully as a trapeze artist to the flying trapeze.

Illness contracted in the West Indies not only kept him out of cricket in 1926; his young life was almost despaired of. His return to health a year later was a glorious renewal. He scored a thousand runs in May 1927, the season of his marvellous innings against Macdonald at Whitsuntide at Old Trafford. I am gratified that after watching this innings I wrote of him in this language: – 'The possibilities of this boy Hammond are beyond the scope of estimation; I tremble to think of the grandeur he will spread over our cricket fields when he has arrived at maturity. He is, in his own way, another Trumper in the making.'

Some three years before he thrilled us by this Old Trafford innings he astounded Middlesex, and everybody else on the scene, by batsmanship of genius on a terrible wicket at Bristol. Gloucestershire, in first, were bundled out for 31. Middlesex then could edge and snick only 74. In Gloucestershire's second innings Hammond drove, cut and hooked no fewer than 174 not out in four hours winning the match. By footwork he compelled the bowlers to pitch short, whereupon he massacred them. He was now hardly past his twentieth year.

Like Hobbs, he modulated, as he grew older and had to take on heavier responsibilities as a batsman, into a classic firmness and restraint. He became a classical player, in fact, expressing in a long innings the philosophy of 'ripeness is all'. It is often forgotten that, on a bad wicket, he was also masterful. At Melbourne, in January 1937, against Australia, on the worst wicket I have ever seen, he scored 32 without once losing his poise though the ball rose head-high, or shot like a stone thrown over ice.

He could, if he had given his mind constantly to the job, have developed into a bowler as clever as Alec Bedser himself with a new ball. Here, again, he was in action the embodiment of easy flowing motion – a short run, upright and loose, a sideway action, left-shoulder pointing down the wicket, the length accurate, the ball sometimes swinging away late. I never saw him besmirching his immaculate flannels by rubbing the ball on his person, rendering it bloody and hideous to see.

He was at all times a cricketer of taste and breeding. But he wouldn't suffer boredom gladly. One day at Bristol, when Lancashire were scoring slowly, on deliberate principle, he bowled an over of ironic 'grubs', all along the ground, underhand.

As a batsman, he experienced only two major frustrations. O'Reilly put him in durance by pitching the ball on his leg-stump. Wally didn't like it. His batting, in these circumstances, became sullen, a slow but combustible slow fire, ready to blaze and devour – as it did at Sydney, in the second Test match of the 1936–37 rubber. For a long time Hammond couldn't assert mastery over O'Reilly. For once in his lifetime he was obliged to labour enslaved. In the end he broke free from sweaty durance, amassing 231 not out, an innings majestic, even when it was stationary. We could always hear the superb engine throbbing.

The other frustration forced upon Wally occurred during this same 1936–37 rubber. At Adelaide, when victory at the day's outset – and the rubber – was in England's reach at the closing day's beginning, Fleetwood-Smith clean bowled him. Another of Wally's frustrations – perhaps the bitterest to bear – befell him as England's captain. At a time of some strain in his life, he had to lead in Australia, in 1946–47, a team not at all ready for Test matches, after the long empty years of world war. Severe lumbago added to Hammond's unhappy decline.

Those cricketers and lovers of the game who saw him towards the end of his career saw only half of him. None the less they saw enough to remain and be cherished in memory. The wings might seem clipped, but they were wings royally in repose. Wally had a quite pretty chassé as he went forward to drive; and, at the moment his bat made impact with the ball his head was over it, the Master surveying his own work, with time to spare. First he played the game as a professional, then turned amateur. At no time did he ever suggest that he was, as Harris of Nottinghamshire called his paid colleagues, 'a fellow worker'.

Wally could have batted with any Prince of the Golden Age at the other end of the pitch – MacLaren, Trumper, Hobbs, Spooner, 'Ranji' – and there would have been no paling of his presence, by comparison.

Tributes to Hammond included:
A. V. Bedser (Surrey and England): I rate him the greatest all-rounder I have ever known.

C. J. Barnett (Gloucestershire and England): I played with Wally for 20 years and consider him the greatest athlete I ever knew.

W. E. Bowes (Yorkshire and England): Wally was a naturally-gifted player of most games. Tennis, golf, swimming, boxing, soccer and billiards all came alike to him.

Sir Donald Bradman (Australia): I have never seen a batsman so strong on the off-side and as a slip fieldsmen he ranked as one of the greatest. He was usually too busy scoring runs to worry about bowling, but when he did take a hand at it he caused plenty of concern. He was a much better bowler than he was given credit for.

Sir Learie Constantine (West Indies): Those of us who were fortunate enough to have watched him and played against him will always remember him.

G. Duckworth (Lancashire and England): He hardly played in a game without leaving his imprint as batsman, fielder or bowler.

T. W. Goddard (Gloucestershire and England): He was the greatest batsman of them all, ahead of Bradman and the rest. A brilliant bowler, he was incomparable as a fielder.

H. Larwood (Nottinghamshire and England): He was a magnificent cricketer. We used to expect a 'Ton' from him every innings and more often than not he seemed to get it.

S. J. McCabe (Australia): Everything he did he did with the touch of a master. One could refer to him as the perfect cricketer.

A. Melville (South Africa): He was the greatest all-rounder I ever played against. He was a magnificent fielder and as a bowler I think he underestimated his capabilities.

W. A. Oldfield (Australia): Wally was majestic on the field – the perfect batting artist.

W. J. O'Reilly (Australia): He was certainly the greatest English batsman of my time, tough, hard, but always a brilliant player.

SOBERS – THE LION OF CRICKET [1967]

No sooner had the old lion departed than it was time to herald the advent of the young one. By the time of the publication of the 1967 almanack there was little doubt in anyone's mind who was the world's most outstanding cricketer. The like of Gary Sobers had never been seen before. A left-handed batsman of pantherine grace touched with genius, Sobers was also a world-class opening bowler, an equally gifted purveyor of assorted spin and a dazzling fielder in the spectacular West Indies tradition. In attempting a comparative assessment of this paragon, Cardus takes some care to warn the modern reader not to forget too easily that there have been phenomenally gifted all-rounders in the past, including W. G. Grace, Aubrey Faulkner and, of course, the Yorkshire comrades from the West Riding village of Kirkheaton, Wilfred Rhodes and George Hirst. Hammond and Woolley are also invoked before Cardus gets down to the aspect of the case which has never failed to fascinate him; style as it relates to the man.

In addressing himself to the enigma of Sobers' quintessence, Cardus concludes that the Barbadian lacks MacLaren's serenity, which is merely another way of admitting that MacLaren lacked Sobers' exuberance. Nearer the mark is the observation that Sobers is not a classic grammarian of batsmanship in the mould of Martin Donnelly but rather a player whose overriding impression is one of lyricism. Here follow the musical analogies involving Mozart and Wagner, followed by the final canny deduction that because the one hint of fallibility in Sobers' batting technique may be a tendency to be cavalier with the outswinger, the great Sidney Barnes could well have relished the challenge of bowling at him had the opportunity ever arisen.

The essay then proceeds to the larger consideration of environment. In writing that the subject of his essay is 'a natural product of the West Indies' physical and climatic environment, and of the condition of the game in the West Indies, historical and material, in which he was nurtured', Cardus comes to the heart of the issue which, throughout the career of Sobers, so exasperated the English cricket fancier; why were the English apparently incapable of producing a like paragon? Returning for the umpteenth time to the old Cardusian tenet concerning the relationship between a society and the artists it produces, it ought to have been clear to connoisseurs of the period that the extraordinary flowering of Barbadian cricket in the time of Sobers, an exfloriation so luxuriant that this tiny island was able to stage a match between itself and the Rest of the World, had no more relevance to the self-expression of a Geoffrey Boycott or a Peter May than the tides of the Gulf Stream do to those of the North Sea. The point is so obvious as to hardly seem worth making and yet it seems not to have been perceived by commentators whose vocation it was supposed to be to see beneath the surface of things. In 'The New Statesman' at around the time of the Cardus essay on Sobers, there appeared a comically wrongheaded assault by J. B. Priestley on English society at large for lacking the flair to accept the challenge of life with the flair of a Sobers. The readers who were diverted by this twaddle were too polite to write to the editor asking why Priestley lacked the flair to accept the challenge of the novel with the flair of a Turgenev.

GARFIELD ST. AUBRUN SOBERS, thirty years old in July 1966 – the most renowned name of any cricketer since Bradman's high noon. He is, in fact, even more famous than Bradman ever was; for he is accomplished in every department of the game, and has exhibited his genius in all climes and conditions. Test matches everywhere, West Indies, India, Pakistan, Australia, New Zealand, England; in Lancashire League and Sheffield Shield cricket. We can safely agree that no player has proven versatility of skill as convincingly as Sobers has done, effortlessly, and after the manner born.

He is a stylish, prolific batsman; two bowlers in one, fastish left-arm, seaming the new ball, and slow to medium back-of-the-hand spinner with the old ball; a swift, accurate, slip fieldsman in the class of Hammond and

Simpson, and generally an astute captain. Statistics concerning him speak volumes.

Sobers holds a unique Test double, over 5,500 runs, and close on 150 wickets. Four years ago he set up an Australian record when playing for South Australia by scoring 1,000 runs and taking 50 wickets in the same season. To emphasize this remarkable feat he repeated it the following summer out there.

Only last January he established in India a record for consecutive Test appearances, surpassing J. R. Reid's 58 for New Zealand. He is also amongst the select nine who have hit a century and taken five or more wickets in one Test, joining J. H. Sinclair, G. A. Faulkner, C. E. Kelleway, J. M. Gregory, V. Mankad, K. R. Miller, P. R. Umrigar and B. R. Taylor.

Is Sobers the greatest all-round cricketer in history? Once upon a time there was W. G. Grace, who in his career scored 54,896 runs and took 2,876 wickets, many of which *must* really have been out; also W. G. was a household name, an eminent Victorian, permanent in the National gallery of representative Englishmen. Aubrey Faulkner, South African, a 'googly' bowler too, scored 1,754 runs in Test matches, average 40.79, and took 82 wickets, average 26.58. In 1906, George Hirst achieved the marvellous double performance of 2,385 runs and 208 wickets. When asked if he thought anybody would ever equal this feat he replied, 'Well, whoever does it will be tired.' But Hirst's record in Test matches was insignificant compared with Sobers', over a period. (All the same, shouldn't we estimate a man by his finest hour?)

There was Wilfred Rhodes, let us not forget. In his career he amassed no fewer than 39,802 runs, average 30.83, and his wickets amounted to 4,187, average 16.71. In first for England with Jack Hobbs at Melbourne in 1912, and colleague in the record first-wicket stand against Australia of 323; and in last for England in 1903, partner of R. E. Foster in a last-wicket stand of 130. Again, what of Frank Woolley, 3,283 runs in Tests, 83 wickets?

It is, of course, vain to measure ability in one age with ability in another. Material circumstances, the environment which moulds technique, are different. Only providence, timeless and all-seeing, is qualified to weigh in the balance the arts and personality of a Hammond and a Sobers. It is enough that the deeds of Sobers are appreciated in our own time, as we have witnessed them. He has, as I have pointed out, boxed the compass of the world of present-day cricket, revealing his gifts easefully, abundantly. And here we touch on his secret: power of relaxation and the gift of holding himself in reserve. Nobody has seen Sobers obviously in labour. He makes a stroke with moments to spare. His fastest ball – and it can be very fast – is bowled as though he could, with physical pressure, have bowled it a shade faster. He can, in the slips catch the lightning snick with the grace and nonchalance of Hammond himself. The sure sign of mastery, of genius of any order, is absence of strain, natural freedom of rhythm.

In the Test matches in England last summer, 1966, his prowess exceeded all precedents: 722 runs, average 103.14, twenty wickets, average 27.25, and ten catches. In the first game, at Manchester, 161 and three wickets for 103; in the second, at Lord's, 46 and 163 not out and one wicket for 97; in the third, at Nottingham, 3 and 94, five wickets for 161; in the fourth, at Leeds, 174 and eight wickets for 80; in the fifth, at The Oval, 81 and 0, with three wickets for 104. A writer of highly-coloured boys' school stories wouldn't dare to presume that the hero could go on like this, staggering credulity match after match. I am not sure that his most impressive assertion of his quality was not seen in the Lord's Test. Assertion is too strenuous a word to apply to the 163 not out scored then; for it was done entirely free of apparent exertion, even though at one stage of the proceedings the West Indies seemed beaten beyond salvage. When the fifth second-innings wicket fell, the West Indies were leading by nine runs only. Nothing reliable to come in the way of batsmanship, nobody likely to stay with Sobers, excepting Holford. As everybody concerned with cricket knows, Sobers and his cousin added, undefeated, 274. It is easy to argue that Cowdrey, England's captain, did not surround Sobers with a close field. Sobers hinted of no technical flaw, no mental or temperamental anxiety. If he slashed a ball when 93, to Cowdrey's hands, Cowdrey merely let us know that he was mortal when he missed a blistering chance. Bradman has expressed his opinion that few batsmen of his acquaintance hit with the velocity and strength of Sobers. And a sliced shot can travel at murderous pace.

At his best, Sobers scores as easily as any left-handed batsman I have seen since Frank Woolley. He is not classical in his grammar of batsmanship as, say, Martin Donnelly was. To describe Sobers' method I would use the term lyrical. His immense power is concealed, or lightened, to the spectator's eye, by a rhythm which has in it as little obvious propulsion as a movement of music by Mozart (who could be as dramatically strong as Wagner!). A drive through the covers by Sobers sometimes appears to be quite lazy, until we see an offside fieldsman nursing bruised palms, or hear the impact of ball striking the fence. His hook is almost as majestic as MacLaren's, though he hasn't MacLaren's serenity of poise as he makes it. I have actually seen Sobers carried round, off foot balance, while making a hook; it is his only visibly violent stroke – an assault. MacLaren, as I have written many times before, dismissed the ball from his presence. The only flaw in Sobers' technique of batsmanship, as far as I and better judges have been able so far to discern, is a tendency to play at a dangerously swinging away off-side ball 'with his arms' – that is to say, with his bat a shade (and more) too far from his body. I fancy Sydney F. Barnes would have concentrated on this chink in the generally shining armour.

He is a natural product of the West Indies' physical and climatic environment, and of the condition of the game in the West Indies, historical and material, in which he was nurtured. He grew up at a time when the first impulses of West Indies' cricket were becoming rationalised; experience was being added to the original instinctive creative urge, which established the general style and pattern – a creative urge inspired largely by Constantine, after George Challenor had laid a second organised basis of batting technique. Sobers, indeed, flowered as West Indies' cricket was 'coming of age'. As a youth he could look at Worrell, at Weekes, at Walcott, at Ramadhin, at Valentine. The amazing thing is that he learned from all these superb and definitely formative, constructive West Indies cricketers; for each of them made vintage of the sowings of Challenor, George Headley, Constantine, Austin, Nunes, Roach, and Browne – to name but a few pioneers. Sobers began at the age of ten to bowl orthodox slow left-arm; he had no systematic coaching. (Much the same could safely be said of most truly gifted and individual cricketers.) Practising in the spare time given to him from his first job as a clerk in a shipping house, he developed his spin far enough to win a place, 16 years old now, in a Barbados team against an Indian touring side; moreover, he contrived to get seven wickets in the match for 142.

In the West Indies season of 1953–1954, Sobers, now 17, received his Test match baptism at Sabina Park, Kingston. Valentine dropped out of the West Indies XI because of physical disability and Sobers was given his chance – as a bowler, in the Fifth game of the rubber. His order in the batting was ninth but he bowled 28 overs, 5 balls for 75 runs, 4 wickets, when England piled-up 414, Hutton 215. In two innings he made 14 not out, and 26. Henceforward he advanced as a predestined master, opening up fresh aspects of his rich endowment of gifts. He began to concentrate on batsmanship, so much so that in 1955, against Australia in the West Indies, he actually shared the opening of an innings, with J. K. Holt, in the fourth Test. Facing Lindwall and Miller, after Australia had scored 668, he assaulted the greatest fast bowlers of the period to the tune of 43 in a quarter of an hour. Then he suffered the temporary set-back which the fates, in their wisdom, inflict on every budding talent, to prove strength of character. On a tour to New Zealand, the young man, now rising twenty, was one of a West Indies contingent. His Test match record there was modest enough – 81 runs in five innings and two wickets for 49.

He first played for the West Indies in England in 1957, and his form could scarcely have given compensation to his disappointed compatriots when the rubber was lost by three victories to none. His all-round record then was 10 innings, 320 runs, with five wickets costing 70.10 each. Next he became a professional for Radcliffe in the Central Lancashire League, where, as a bowler, he relied on speed and swing. In 1958/9 he was one of the West Indies team in India and Pakistan; and now talent burgeoned prodigiously. On the hard wickets he cultivated his left-arm 'googlies', and this new study did not in the least hinder the maturing of his batsmanship. Against India he scored 557, average 92.83 and took ten for 292. Against Pakistan he scored 160, average 32.0 and failed to get anybody out for 78.

The course of his primrose procession since then has been constantly spectacular, rising to a climax of personal glory in Australia in 1960–1961. He had staggered cricketers everywhere by his 365 not out v. Pakistan in 1958; as a batsman he has gone on and on, threatening to debase the Bradman currency, all the time swinging round a crucial match the West Indies' way by removing an important opposing batsman, or by taking a catch of wondrous rapidity. He has betrodden hemispheres of cricket, become a national symbol of his own islands, the representative image on a postage stamp. Best of all, he has generally maintained the *art* of cricket at a time which day by day – especially in England – threatens to change the game into (a) real industry or (b) a sort of out-of-door 'Bingo' cup jousting. He has demonstrated, probably unaware of what he has been doing, the worth of trust in natural-born ability, a lesson wasted on most players here. If he has once or twice lost concentration at the pinch – as he did at Kennington Oval in the Fifth Test last year – well, it is human to err, occasionally, even if the gods have lavished on you a share of grace and skill not given to ordinary mortals. The greatest ever? – certainly the greatest all-rounder today, and for decades. And all the more precious is he now, considering the general nakedness of the land.

J. B. STATHAM – GENTLEMAN GEORGE
[1968]

Sometimes he bowled too superbly

In 1968 the editor of Wisden did something unique in more than a hundred consecutive editions by publishing the same essay twice. In the centenary edition of 1963, in selecting his six giants of the Wisden century, Cardus had, predictably enough, included Sydney Barnes who, by general agreement, including that of Cardus, was the most gifted bowler in the history of the game. Five years later Barnes died at the age of 96, as formidable in extreme old age as he had once been as a minatory young man stalking the batsmen of the world. He had indeed remained as remarkable as ever to the end, continuing to be a working man by lending his unimpaired copperplate hand to the production of illuminated addresses for the Staffordshire County Council. His death clearly called for a leading essay and there was nobody better qualified to provide it than Cardus, who had been singing Barnes' praises for half a century. But it had been only five years since he had written his definitive piece on Barnes for the almanack. And so the editor, preferring pragmatism to the conventions of journalism, did the simple thing and republished the 1963 essay.

The connection between Barnes, born at Smethwick in Staffordshire and Cardus's home county had been tenuous, ending on an acrimonious note with the editor of Wisden committing one of the more amusing gaffes of critical history by writing, on the occasion of Barnes' departure from Old Trafford for the more easeful life of the Leagues: 'If only Barnes had possessed the enthusiasm for the game that characterised Barlow and Johnny Briggs he might have made a great name for himself'. In 1969 Lancashire cricket was again the theme of Cardus's essay, on a subject as unlike Barnes as could be imagined. Barnes had never been very impressed by the obligation of a cricketer to remain loyal to his county. Instead he sensibly remained loyal to himself and was the diametric opposite of a man like Brian Statham, that epitome of one cricketing ideal, the loyal servant of his club. Statham laboured long in the service of Lancashire and, although his career was studded with great performances and unstained by a single controversy, it was his destiny to suffer as well as profit from his participation in one of the most effective opening bowling partnerships of the century. The combination of Trueman and Statham was formidable indeed, but the flamboyance of Trueman abetted by a talent for finding the nearest body of hot water and then flinging himself into it caused very nearly an eclipse of Statham's status in the public eye. Yet Statham had his own qualities which balanced the very different ones of Trueman, most importantly his unwavering accuracy. The batsman facing Trueman might get the occasional gift as consolation for all that naked aggression but Statham, although he looked much the milder of the two, was never known to give any batsman anything for nothing.

Once again Cardus uses the device of historical allusion to place Statham in his niche. Parallels are drawn with Ted MacDonald and, just as the Gregory-MacDonald alliance was bludgeon and lance, so Trueman-Statham was thunder and lightning. A more telling analogy comes later with a typically Cardusian resort to the larger cultural context, with his likening of the young Statham, dashing from the ration books of his home to the land of plenty in Australia in the 1950–51 series, to a character in a Lowry painting. The comparison is inspired as well as perfectly accurate; the gangling Statham always did look rather like one of Lowry's stick-men. The lead offered by Cardus is taken up by one of Statham's other partners who usurps Cardus's role with an amusing musical analogy of his own. The last few lines of Cardus's appreciation hint at years of easeful retirement for one of England's finest and most modest fast bowlers. Sadly, twenty seasons later, the English cricket world was mustering support for a Brian Statham broken by illness.

LANCASHIRE COUNTY CRICKET has enjoyed a long and sequential lineage of fast bowlers, though one or two of those in the succession were, so to say, born under a *bar sinister* – in other words, two of them, Crossland and Mold, blotted the escutcheon because they were throwers or 'chuckers' of the ball. Two Lancastrian fast bowlers satisfied the severest tests of breeding and deportment, Brearley and Brian Statham;

but only one fast bowler playing for my native county could stand comparison, in point of classic poise and action, against Brian Statham, and he was an Australian, none other than E. A. McDonald.

I make a great compliment both to Statham and to the ghost of Ted McDonald by coupling their names. McDonald's action was as easy and as rhythmical as music, and so was Statham's. Purist critics, during Statham's first seasons, suggested that as his right arm swung over, the batsman was able to see too much of his chest; the left shoulder didn't point the way of the flight down the wicket.

The truth about Statham's action is that it was so elastic and balanced (and double-jointed) that there was no forward shoulder rigidity possible; his movement, from the beginning of his run to deliver, to the final accumulated propulsion, had not an awkward angle in it at all. The whole man of him, from his first swinging steps of approach to the launching of the ball from the right foot, was the effortless and natural dynamo and life-force of his attack. He wasn't called 'The Whippet' for nothing.

Fast bowlers, as a rule, are aggressive by nature, rough-hewn and physically overbearing. Statham, like McDonald, was unruffled of temper, almost deceptively pacific. I have seen McDonald lose control and let fly a fusillade of unbeautiful 'bouncers', wasting fuel, or petrol, like a perfectly engineered car back-firing going up hill. Never have I seen the equanimity of Statham's temperament or technique rendered out of harmony for a minute.

Again, resembling McDonald, he found, in Test cricket, his ideal foils and contrasts. McDonald came to the front when J. M. Gregory was his collaborator in pace; he was the piercing lance to the bludgeon of Gregory. Likewise Statham was the flash of lightning to the thunder of Trueman or the typhoon of Tyson.

Did Statham ever send down a 'wide'? He was marvellously accurate in direction; not even Larwood equalled Statham's persistent certainty of length and direction. To describe him as a 'seamer' is libellous. He could bring the ball back viciously – and the Press Box would tell us that he 'did it off the seam', which is a phrase that is meaningless; moreover, it is a phrase which would have us believe that a bowler can, while achieving rare velocity of flight, drop the ball's seam exactly where he would like it to drop.

I imagine that Statham's break-back was, like Tom Richardson's, caused by body-swing, with the right arm sweeping across the ball's direction at the last split-second of release. I have been told by more than one batsman – in two hemispheres – that Statham has cleaned bowled them, middle or leg stump, by balls pitching outside the off – and during flight tending to swing away to the slips. There is no answer to this trick, as the South Africans were obliged to admit at Lord's in the Test match of 1955; Statham on this occasion bowled 56 overs: two for 49 first innings, seven for 39 second, relieved by a two-hour weather break.

At the age of twenty, Statham provoked some sensation in the Lancashire v. Yorkshire match at Old Trafford, 1950, by taking five wickets
for 52, in the ancient enemy's first innings. On the strength, maybe, of
this performance he was flown out, with Tattersall, as reinforcements
for F. R. Brown's gallant team in Australia, 1950–51.

These two Lancashire lads arrived in what must have seemed to them
then a truly foreign climate; for they had been rushed out of an English
winter, still unnourished in a post-rationed environment, to a land of
plenty. They came to Sydney looking as though each had escaped from
a Lowry canvas, lean and hungry. Statham did not play in a Test match
during this rubber; in fact he found the Australian air rather a strain on
his breathing apparatus. Nonetheless, he took eleven wickets at 20 runs
each against State and Country XI's and in New Zealand.

Back in England he began to foretell the quality soon to come; he had
90 Championship wickets for Lancashire, average 14.65; and in two Test
matches v.South Africa his contribution as a bowler was four wickets for
78. Invited to play for England in India and Pakistan, in 1951–52, his
record was merely modest, eight wickets costing 36.62 runs each in the
important engagements. Though in 1952 he harvested 100 wickets for
Lancashire at 17.99 runs each, he was not asked to play for England v.
India; and next summer he was chosen only once for England v. Australia
– at Lord's – where he took one for 48, and one for 40, though he came
sixth in the season's bowling averages, with 101 wickets at 16.33 each;
easily the best figures of any English fast bowler that year.

His time was at hand; his place in an England XI became almost a
permanency after the Test matches in the West Indies of 1953–54. Now
he headed the England bowling averages, 16 wickets for 460 runs.

He was a fairly certain selection for Sir Leonard Hutton's conquering
contingent which won the rubber in Australia, 1954–55. This was the
rubber in which Frank Tyson achieved a hair-raising speed, so fast that
Arthur Morris told me that Tyson was 'through you almost before you
had picked up your bat'. Tyson stole all the limelight, but he was
indebted for much of his blinding efficiency to Statham. And most generously has he acknowledged this indebtedness, in print, for he has written:
'The glamour of success was undoubtedly mine. When in the second
innings of the Sydney Test I captured six for 85, few spared a thought
for Statham, who on that day bowled unremittingly for two hours into
a stiff breeze and took three for 45.'

Tyson adds that he 'owed much to desperation injected into the batsmen's methods by Statham's relentless pursuit. To me it felt like having
Menuhin playing second fiddle to my lead.'

This is the most generous tribute paid by one cricketer to another
since MacLaren maintained in a conversation with me, 'Talk about class
and style? Well, I was supposed to be a batsman of some majesty but,
believe me, compared to Victor Trumper I was like a cab-horse side by
side with a thoroughbred Derby winner.'

The Statham-Trueman collaboration of speed is recent history. Trueman in Test matches took 307 wickets, average 21.57. Statham in Tests took 252, average 24.84. It is useless to measure one against the other. As well we might try to assess Wagner and Mozart on the same level. Trueman, on occasion, nearly lost a big match by loss of technical (and temperamental) control; Statham never.

I particularly like Frank Tyson's story of the West Indies bowler who hit Laker over the eye. When subsequently the West Indies 'bouncer' came in to bat and reluctantly took guard, somebody asked Statham to retaliate in kind and explosive 'kick'. 'No', said Statham, 'I think I'll just bowl him out.'

Here, in a phrase, is the essence of Statham's character. Gentleman George.* Sometimes he bowled too superbly to tail-end batsmen, they were not good enough to get into touch. It is rare for a fast bowler to play all round the world for nearly twenty years and not suffer animosity or verbal abuse from the opposition.

In his first-class seasons of the game, Statham overthrew no fewer than 2,259 batsmen, and each of them were glad to call him a friend. What is more, he could use a bat himself (left-handed) on occasion. At Sydney, in December of 1954, Statham, in number 11, scored 25 at the moment of high crisis and, with Appleyard, added 46 for England's last wicket. And England won the match by only 38 runs.

At the game's end Statham waved aside congratulations. 'When I bat and miss I'm usually out. When I bowl and they miss, well – *they* are usually out.' He has been an adornment to the game, as a fast bowler of the classic mould, and as a man and character of the rarest breed and likeableness. Also he is amongst the select company of fast bowlers who could field and catch. Cricket will for long have a gap without him.

His benefit of 1961 against the Australians at Old Trafford realised £13,047 and is second only to that of Cyril Washbrook who received £14,000 in 1948. Lancashire in further appreciation of this 'model example for all to copy', as they put it, 'modest, unassuming, ever-willing to shoulder the burden of the attack or to 'rest' in the outfield where speed of foot and unerring accuracy of throw made him a man to be feared', have organised a Testimonial for him this year. I feel sure that again the response will be generous from his legion of admirers.

---

* *To his friends he has been 'George' through his cricketing career.*

EMMOTT ROBINSON [1970]

The death in November 1969 of the Yorkshire all-rounder Emmott Robinson posed in its starkest form the problem of what Cardus might have referred to as his own aesthetic morality. Was he or was he not guilty of cooking the facts in the cause of poetic truth? If he did not exactly cook them he certainly stretched them further than the circumstances sometimes merited, but because in the final reckoning Cardus was a creative writer first and a critic second, the issue which each of his readers must decide for himself is not whether Emmott Robinson was a fine cricketer but whether Cardus, stimulated by the spectacle of Robinson, is a fine writer.

The facts of the case are that Robinson came into the Yorkshire side at just about the revelatory moment in Cardus's life when he was transmuting himself into 'Cricketer' of 'The Manchester Guardian', a time when the Wars of the Roses between Makepeace's Professors and the enemy from across the Pennines took on the aspect of tribal rituals. In his career Robinson took just under 900 wickets with his outswingers and scored nearly ten thousand runs, including a modest total of seven centuries. Humble achievements indeed. But Cardus happened to see in Robinson's quirky, often whimsical temperament something indigenous to the county of Yorkshire and proceeded as the years passed to build up a portrait owing as much to his own sensibilities as to Robinson's. In 'The Manchester Guardian' in his early, effusive years Cardus went as far as he ever did along the road of excess which, however, led him in the end to the palace of wisdom so far as the character of Robinson was concerned. Here is the over-zealous 'Cricketer' on the subject of the modest Robinson:

> . . . a grizzled, squat, bandy-legged Yorkshireman, all sagging and loose at the braces in private life, but on duty for Yorkshire he was liable at any minute to gather and concentrate his energy into sudden vehement leaps and scuffles. He had shrewd eyes, a hatchet face and grey hairs, most of them representing appeals that had gone against him for leg-before-wicket. I imagine that he was created one day by God scooping up the nearest acre of Yorkshire soil at hand, then breathing into it saying, 'Now lad, tha's called Emmott Robinson and tha can go on with new ball at t'pavilion end.'

To the reader for whom Emmott Robinson is no more than a name from the past, long gone from the playing field, the effusiveness of this notorious passage tends to cause unease, not so much through the invocation of God Almighty, but at the very idea that the Creator of the Universe should turn out to be a provincial with a cricketer's perceptions. The brand of loony pantheism which selects God for the eleven had already been introduced by Lord Harris; Cardus, by making the Deity a denizen of the pavilion at Headingley had gone much further, dangerously close to the bathetic. Later in his career he was to disown his early greenery-yallery effusions in the cricket columns of 'The Manchester Guardian', and he took care not to quote the famous passage concerning God and Our Emmott when compiling the obituary.

But forgetting Robinson in the moment of his own demise and reading his obituary as a piece of prose, how delightfully the central figure leaps off the page into the portrait gallery of memorable cricketers. It is easy to see that the rich sap of the portraiture springs directly out of the soil of the Roses matches when Cardus, privy to the tankards as well as to the tactics of the Lancashire side, caught glimpses of the players he was never to forget. Robinson was one who engaged his imagination at an unusually deep level and Cardus repaid the debt of revelation by transforming a journeyman county player into a vivid regional archetype. The exchange between Robinson and Rhodes while examining the pitch one rain-soaked lunchtime at Headingley comprises one of the best of all cricketing jokes, so revealing of the type of man represented by Robinson and Rhodes that the reader really cares very little whether in narrating it Cardus was reporting an actual exchange or bowing to the Higher Truth.

On the occasion of Cardus's 70th birthday celebrations, Emmott Robinson had the rare opportunity to return the compliment, which he did in this style:

> Ah ewsed to think 'at he took t'mickey aht o' me sometimes be what he said abaht me when we wor laikin' Lenkysheer, but noabody injoyed it mooee nor Ah did. They wor reyt happy days, and noabody did moore nor Neville Cardus to mak 'em happy days. Ah'm reyt glad he's got ta 70 not aht, and Ah do hooap he makes it a hundred.

And with the thought that Cardus by writing about games of cricket contributed to the general contentment of players and spectators alike, the case for the Higher Truth rests.

Emmott Robinson, who was born on November 16, 1883 and died on November 17, 1969, played for Yorkshire from 1919 to 1931 and afterwards became a first-class umpire.

EMMOTT ROBINSON was as Yorkshire as Ilkley Moor or Pudsey. He was the personification of Yorkshire cricket in one of its greatest periods, the 1920s, when the county appeared to look forward towards winning the Championship by a sort of divine right. He came to first-class cricket in his late thirties – and 'thrive he did though bandy'.

Statistics tell us little of his essential self; in twelve seasons he scored 9,444 runs and took 892 wickets. Many cricketers have surpassed these figures; few have absorbed the game, the Yorkshire game, into their systems, their minds, nerves and bloodstreams, as Emmott did. Yorkshire cricket was, for him, a way of living, as important as stocks and shares.

With Rhodes he established the unwritten Constitution of Yorkshire cricket, the skipper content to serve in a consultative capacity. Nowadays we hear much of the supposition to the effect that first-class cricket in recent years has become 'more scientific' than of yore. To speak the truth, there are few players of our latest 'modern' times who would not seem to be as innocent as babes talking tactics and know-how in the company of Rhodes and Emmott.

It was these two shrewd men who evolved – with rival competition from Makepeace and Co. in Lancashire – the protective philosophy: how to close a game up, how to open it out, how to stifle the spin on a 'sticky' wicket with the 'dead' bat. 'Loose grip on top of 'andle', said Emmott.

The shrewdness, humour, uninhibited character of North of England life was marvellously revealed and fulfilled in Yorkshire v. Lancashire matches of the 1920s. Gates closed at noon; 30,000, even 40,000, partisan spectators watching. Watching for what? 'Bright cricket'? Not on your life.

'We've won the toss', Harry Makepeace would announce in the Lancashire professionals' dresssing-room. 'Now lads, no fours before lunch.' And Emmott Robinson was already polishing the new ball, holding it up to the light of day, as though investigating an egg. He bowled outswingers; for in his heyday the lbw rule rendered inswing more or less harmless. He swung the ball from middle and leg, compelling a stroke of some sort.

He was shocked if anybody 'wasted new ball'. After he had bowled the first over, he would personally carry the new ball, in cupped hands, to the bowler at the other end.

At Bradford in 1920, he took nine wickets in an innings against Lancashire. At a crisis for Yorkshire too! Lancashire needed only 52 to win, six wickets in hand. Then Emmott turned the game round violently. For some reason or other, I did not, in my report of the match, praise Emmott in generous enough language. I was not a convert to seam bowling in those days; and am not a bigoted convert yet. When Emmott next met me he said, 'Ah suppose if Ah'd tekken all ten Lanky' wickets, tha'd have noticed me.'

As a batsman he exploited pad-play to perfection. Remember the lbw law of Emmott's halcyon years permitted a batsman to defend with his pads a ball pitching outside the off stump. If any young greenhorn, batting for Yorkshire or Lancashire, were to be bowled by an off break, he received severe verbal chastisement. 'What dos't think thi pads are for?' was Emmott's outraged inquiry.

Emmott was one of the pioneer students of the 'green wicket' and its habits. One day, at Headingley, rain soaked the field, then the sun shone formidably. After lunch Emmott and Rhodes walked out to inspect the pitch. Arrived there, Rhodes pressed the turf with a forefinger and said, 'It'll be sticky at four o'clock, Emmott.' Whereat Emmott bent down and also pressed the turf with a forefinger. 'No, Wilfred,' he said, 'half-past.'

These grand Yorkshiremen in general, and Robinson in particular, never were consciously humorous. Emmott was a terribly serious man. He could not, as Freddie Trueman did, play for a laugh. One summer at Lord's, Yorkshire got into dire trouble against Middlesex. During a tea interval I ran into Emmott. 'Hey dear,' he growled, 'fancy, just fancy Yorkshire getting beat by Middlesex. And wheer *is* Middlesex? Is it in Lundin?' A far reaching question; because London swamps county boundaries and identities. We know what county means in Yorkshire and Lancashire.

Emmott merged his ability as cricketer into the Yorkshire XI entirely; by sheer power of will he added a technical stature which, elsewhere, might not have amounted to much. A celebrated Indian batsman, intro-duced to Rhodes in Rhodes's wonderfully blind old age, said he was honoured to meet so 'great a cricketer.' 'Nay,' said Wilfred, 'Ah never considered myself a Star. I were just a good utility man.'

Thus might Emmott have spoken; no part, no individual, was greater than the part of any Yorkshire team. 'Aye,' Emmott once reminded me, 'and we are all born and bred Yorksheer. And in thy county, tha's tekken in Ted McDonald. A TASMANIAN, mind you', as though a Tasmanian was beyond the pale.

He maintained an average of round about 24 while compiling more than 9,000 runs in his years of active service. The point about his use of the bat, aided and abetted by the broadest pads procurable, is that every stroke he ventured to make was part of a plan, designed to win the match for Yorkshire or save it.

I imagine that in all his days in the sun and rain, his keen eyes were as constantly on the clock as on the score-board. But, in the field, crouching close to the bat, he missed nothing. A lordly batsman who could hit, asked Emmott to move away a little, for the sake of self-preservation. 'Thee get on with thi laikin', and Ah'll get on with mine', retorted Emmott – and for the benefit of the uninitiated I herewith translate: 'laikin' means playing; 'get on with thy playing.'

As I write this tribute to Emmott Robinson, with as much affection as admiration, I am bound in fairness to memory of him, to recount an incident at Old Trafford in 1927. The wicket prepared in those days, for the Lancashire and Yorkshire match, was a batsman's sleeping bed stuffed with runs. Match after match was unfinished – none the less, a grim fight for first-innings points (78,617 rabid Lancastrians and Yorkshi-remen paid to watch the Lancashire v. Yorkshire match at Old Trafford in 1926, fours before lunch or no fours).

Over after over did Emmott resist on this occasion in time and space, when he was, with Rhodes, salvaging his county. Suddenly, for no reason, in fact, as he later admitted, against all reason, he indulged in a most elegant late-cut towards third man. So transfixed was he by this stroke that he stood there contemplating it. And when he emerged from the realm of aesthetic contemplation to the world of unescapable reality, Wilfred Rhodes was on his doorstep and was run out. Consequently Yorkshire lost. 'Fancy,' he said sorrowfully to me (years after), 'fancy.

What could Ah'ave been thinkin' about? Me and mi cuts? But, mind you, Wilfred should never 'ave come runnin' down the pitch. Runs didn't matter with the game in that sta-ate. They counted for nowt.' He was an economist. Must not waste new ball.

One Saturday Yorkshire batted all day at Lord's, scoring 350 or thereabouts. Sunday morning was drenching, a thunderstorm cleared up by noon, followed by dazzling sun. In Hyde Park near four o'clock I came upon Robinson and Rhodes. 'A lovely afternoon,' I said to them, in greeting. 'Aye,' snapped Emmott, 'and a sticky wicket wa-astin' at Lord's.'

He was richly endowed by native qualities of character, and gave himself, heart and soul and with shrewd intelligence, to Yorkshire cricket. That's why he is remembered yet; that's why no statistics can get to the value of him. The score-board cannot reflect human nature, Yorkshire human nature, in action. He was not named Emmott Robinson for nothing.

HERBERT STRUDWICK [1971]

Born at Mitcham, January 28, 1880
Died February, 1970

As one by one the demigods of his youth passed away, Cardus was confirmed in his role of official obituarist to the great. Several of the old heroes lived on into an era sadly inimical to their style, of living as well as of cricket. Sydney Barnes had remained active into his nineties. Andy Sandham was to do the same. Sandham's teammate Herbert Strudwick just managed to reach ninety, dying a fortnight after reaching the mark. Strudwick belonged to that era of Cardus's boyhood when professional cricketers had to watch their step when in the presence of their employers, the gentlemen-captains of the first-class game. In referring to Strudwick's tendency to convert himself into a deep fielder at moments of crisis, Cardus evokes recollections of a day when the editors of the almanack, seeing themselves as part of the amateur establishment, reprimanded Strudwick for his antics and advised with the unconscious comicality of patrician condescension:

Strudwick has a regrettable habit of chasing the ball to the boundary. I would suggest to the Surrey captain a system of modest fines, the amount being increased for each offence.

Strudwick is not known ever to have responded to this extraordinary intrusion into his professional affairs but, given the social structure of

Edwardian cricket, he could perhaps have considered himself fortunate not to be sent to the Tower. Because his career, as international wicket-keeper and then county scorer, extended over so vast a period, he was a priceless source of wisdom when it came to comparative judgements, such as his revealing disclosures about Lockwood measuring himself against Tom Richardson.

H ERBERT STRUDWICK (hereinafter to be known, as he was affectionately always known, as 'Struddy') served Surrey County Cricket faithfully for some sixty years; wicket-keeper for thirty years, then as a diligent scorer. He died a few days after his ninetieth birthday, and with his death a whole and lustrous chapter of cricket history at The Oval was ended.

Amongst wicket-keepers in my own experience of the game, I count Struddy with the best, in the company of 'Tiger' Smith, Duckworth, Ames, 'Jock' Cameron, the South African, W. A. Oldfield, Tallon, Cornford, Godfrey Evans and our present and gifted Knott. But before all else, I count Struddy as a man – in fact, to use discarded language nowadays, as a gentleman.

Few cricketers – and there have been many of rare warmth and character, off and on the field – have shared Struddy's gentle way of showing his friendliness. He was modest, often shy. With just a look in his eye he would greet you in passing; yet in a moment, he would find in you your wave-length of affection.

As wicket-keeper he was courteous as Oldfield himself. If he appealed for a catch at the wicket, it was an *appeal*, a question. An appeal emanating from, say, the mouth of George Duckworth was a denunciation of a batsman's delinquency, an order, even a command to the umpire.

Struddy seemed to appeal almost apologetically, as though saying to the errant batsman, 'So sorry. Pains me as much as yourself. But Law 42 must be observed. Better luck next time.' Which reminds me that Struddy in his prime before the first world war thought nothing of standing up to the fastest of bowlers like Neville Knox or Bill Hitch. The batsmen only advanced from the crease at their peril. Struddy was part and parcel, image and embodiment of Surrey cricket, in a hey-day of the county's and The Oval's renown, when Hayward, Hobbs, Hayes, Holland and Hitch strained East-Enders' powers of the accurate response to the aspirate.

I have heard it said that wicket-keeping was an easier job technically in Struddy's period than it is today – wickets were truer in texture for one thing, when the attack concentrated on the off side, giving the keeper a closer view of the ball than he can have if the ball veers to leg, the batsman's body impeding the view.

It is true that The Oval pitches were invariably firm in Struddy's high noon. Also they were very fast, enabling bounce. Struddy told me of a severe bruise he suffered from a good-length ball from J. N. Crawford, fast-medium through the air, but after pitching, it lifted explosively, and nearly cracked Struddy's breast-bone. 'I once moved to the off side to take Jack Crawford, but the ball broke back inches, missed the leg stump and went for four byes.'

How did Tom Richardson achieve this famous breakback, fast and acutely angular? Body action, explained Struddy. Struddy had to cope with 'sticky' wickets, not generally known nowadays. The marled polished surface of lawn in dry weather became viciously collaborative with spin after rain and sun. Wickets were not covered in Struddy's years. 'Razor' Smith, on a 'sticky' wicket, could pitch, right fingered, on the leg stump and miss the off. Struddy taking the ball shoulder high. In 1910, 'Razor' Smith took 247 wickets in the season, average 13.05. But nobody ever dreamed of asking him to play for England. The currency had not then been devalued.

Struddy played 28 times for England, between 1909 and 1926. In his career he was the cause of no fewer than 1,493 batsmen's dismissals, to use the beautiful formal phrase of the Victorians. He was one of the England team in Australia in 1911–12, 1920–21 and 1924–25. Twice he went to South Africa, with M.C.C. teams, 1909–10, 1913–14.

It is interesting to recall the players in Struddy's first England XI v. South Africa, at Johannesburg, January 1909 – Hobbs, Rhodes, Denton, F. L. Fane, Woolley, Thompson (G. J.), M. C. Bird, Buckenham, H. D. G. Leveson Gower, G. H. Simpson-Hayward, and Struddy himself. A curious fact of this England XI is that Simpson-Hayward bowled 'lobs', underarm spin; and in this Johannesburg Test took six for 43 and two for 59, confounding batsmen such as Aubrey Faulkner, J. H. Sinclair, J. W. Zulch and L. A. Stricker, each as skilful as the next best of 1971. Faulkner, in fact, was a truly great batsman. Struddy always remembered Simpson-Hayward's off-spin (yes, off-spin from a right-handed lob bowler), as well as his flight and leg-break. It was later in South Africa that Struddy performed his most skilful and versatile work in Test matches. This happened in 1913–14, when in the five Tests he held fifteen catches and had eight stumpings.

The point of this achievement is that it was done coping with Sydney Barnes on a *matting* wicket. Barnes caused the ball to go through all manner of gyrations, off-spin and leg-spin, rising sharply from a good length, the pace from the mat red hot. Barnes in four Tests (he did not play in the fifth) took 49 wickets, at 10.93 each. He was quite unplayable, yet Herbert Taylor, for South Africa, scored 508 runs, average 50.80, a miracle of resourceful batsmanship against the most dangerous bowling ever.

As resourceful as Taylor in front of the wicket was Struddy behind. He was for a stumper, the right height. He was quick on his feet without demonstration and waste of physical energy. On fast grounds in England, the attack, as I have mentioned, invariably concentrated on, or outside the off-stump, with no fieldsman behind the wicket on the leg-side. Struddy would often be seen in the swift chase (despite his flapping pads) of a hit to leg, throwing off his gloves, picking up on the run, and returning the ball rapidly and accurately. I once described him, in a report, as amongst the best outfields in the land.

On his first tour of Australia, 1903–04, he did not appear in any of the Tests and his second tour, 1911–12, engaged him in only one Test, the first of the rubber. 'Tiger' Smith was then the brilliant keeper to Barnes and Frank Foster. Struddy's subsequent two visits to Australia were with unfortunate teams, captained in 1920–21 by J. W. H. T. Douglas, and by Arthur Gilligan in 1924–25. Douglas's contingent lost all five Tests, each played to a finish (as, I think, *all* Tests should be played; for, from the bowling of the first ball, we know that one team is doomed, with no chance of escape; every ball a nail in somebody's coffin!).

In the 1924–25 rubber Australia won four games, against an England XI containing Hobbs, Sutcliffe, Woolley, J. W. Hearne, Hendren, A. P. F. Chapman, Roy Kilner, J. W. H. T. Douglas, A. E. R. Gilligan, Maurice Tate and Struddy. He was in the great kill of the ancient enemy at Kennington Oval in August, 1926. England and Chapman regained the Ashes after years. On a turning pitch Hobbs and Sutcliffe amassed 172 for England's first wicket in the second innings, after Australia had led by 22. More than 100,000 watched this famous victory. Rhodes, called back to International cricket in his forty-ninth year, took six wickets in the two innings for 79. So the curtain fell on a wonderful career splendidly, even as it did on Strudwick's – as a player.

In the scorer's box, Struddy was as vigilant as ever – nobody in those days to help with the statistics. His influence on the field did not diminish in helpfulness when he was obliged to submit to increase of years. Many a young cricketer was all the better for his advice, which was never pompously or schoolmasterly given. He was a dedicated cricketer, a dedicated man, generous in praise of the Masters he had grown up with, season after season, 'from W. G. Grace to Peter May'.

He was always certain that Tom Richardson was the fastest and best of all fast bowlers. (In four consecutive seasons here Richardson's wickets amounted to 1,005.) Struddy would tell a rare story of a tribute to Richardson, from none other than Lockwood, regarded by Ranjitsinjhi as the 'very greatest' of fast bowlers. Struddy met Lockwood, now aged and in a wheel-chair, and asked, 'Bill, who was the best fast bowler of your time?' And Lockwood unhesitatingly pronounced the name of Richardson. 'What about yourself?' asked Struddy, whereat Lockwood shook his head, saying, 'No, I wasn't in the same parish as Tom, never mind the same street.'

Naturally, Struddy regarded Jack Hobbs as the first of all batsmen of his acquaintance. He was a friend of Sir Jack, a close and abiding friend. I can say nothing better than that of Struddy of Surrey, England and Kennington Oval.

PERCY HOLMES – A TRUE YORKSHIREMAN [1972]

Born at Oakes, Huddersfield, November 25, 1887
Died September 3, 1971

The next oak to fall was Strudwick's contemporary Percy Holmes, the Yorkshire opening batsman who in less plentiful times would have walked into the England side and remained there for many years. But he shared with Andrew Sandham of Surrey the fate of being eclipsed by the twin deities of Hobbs and Sutcliffe. Even so, Holmes did represent England, enjoyed a long, successful and even record-breaking career. The obituary necessarily becomes a study in twin yet contrasting temperaments because Holmes' career can hardly be seen to have happened at all without the constant presence of Sutcliffe. To conceive one without the other would be like imagining Mr. Dodson without Mr. Fogg or Laurel without Hardy. Each man served as a backdrop for the style of the other and few of Cardus's metaphors are more dazzling than the one in the Holmes obituary which is stimulated by the hint of another gifted writer on the game, R. C. Robertson-Glasgow. Having picked up Robertson-Glasgow's allusions to an ostler, Cardus embellishes the theme with witty imagery and then, persisting, as the Pardon brothers might have said, with the equine, he flings Holmes astride the horse he has been brushing and transforms him into the artist-jockey. Sutcliffe in contrast, keeps both suede-shoed feet firmly on the ground, maintains his hauteur and goes about the business of the partnership as the senior partner should, grave to the brink of self-parody. It might have been interesting to see how Cardus, having shot his bolt regarding Sutcliffe in the obituary of Holmes, would have approached the obituary of Sutcliffe. But the challenge was never to be met, for Sutcliffe was to outlive Cardus by three years.

OVER decades a Yorkshire batsman has been one of the two opening an England innings in Test matches, Rhodes with Hobbs, Sutcliffe with Hobbs, Hutton with Washbrook; now Boycott sustains the great tradition. But one of Yorkshire's most accomplished Number One (or Number Two) batsmen only once raised the curtain of an England innings v. Australia; his name Percy Holmes, a name as famous in Yorkshire during the 1920's and early 1930's, as Brown or Tunnicliffe, or Sutcliffe or Rhodes, or Boycott.

Holmes opened for England at Trent Bridge against Gregory and McDonald, the fearsome bowlers of Warwick Armstrong's rough-riding team, which arrived in England in 1921, having defeated J. W. H. T. Douglas's hapless England contingent five times in five Test matches, in Australia, each played to a finish. And in 1921, blessed by a glorious

English summer, Armstrong's conquerors proceeded to annihilate England in the first three Test matches, three-day engagements. And the victories were settled well within the allotted time span.

Percy Holmes walked jauntily to the wicket at Trent Bridge on May 28, 1921, accompanied by D. J. Knight. England were all out for 112 and Holmes defended stoutly for ninety minutes, making top score, 30. Next innings he made no more than 8. The match was all over on the second afternoon. And this was the end of his Test match appearances until the South Africa season of 1927–28. He then went in first with Sutcliffe in five consecutive Test matches, at Johannesburg, Cape Town, and Durban; his scores were 0 and 15 not out; 9 and 88; 70 and 56; 1 and 63; and in the fifth game of this rubber 0 and 0.

In 1932, ten days after Holmes and Sutcliffe had made 555 together at Leyton, Holmes once again, and for the last time, received recognition from the English Selection Committee; he went in first with Sutcliffe at Lord's v. India, scoring only 6 and 11. So altogether this superb batsman played for England on seven occasions, and his modest record of 14 innings, 357 runs, average 27.46, is a complete falsification of what manner of cricketer and what manner of Yorkshire character Percy Holmes was, season after season.

His name was household in Yorkshire, as closely and proudly linked with Sutcliffe's as Tunnicliffe's with Brown's. As everybody knows – or should know – Holmes and Sutcliffe surpassed the first-wicket stand and aggregate of 554, incredibly achieved by Brown and Tunnicliffe v. Derbyshire, at Chesterfield in 1898. Holmes was 44 years and troubled with lumbago in 1932, when he and Sutcliffe belaboured the Essex attack and after what the politicians call a recount, went beyond the Brown-Tunnicliffe scoreboard marathon.

Holmes, seven years to the day older than Sutcliffe, technically was perhaps Sutcliffe's better. His range of strokes was wider; he was the more versatile and impulsive batsman of the two. But Sutcliffe knew that very rare secret, which is revealed to few men, whatever their vocation. Mastery comes to him who knows his technical limitations. Again, Holmes as a temperament, was at Sutcliffe's extreme; he was volatile, unpredictable of mood, always alive by instinct, so to say, intent on enjoyment on the cricket field, or off it. He was always first to admit that, like the rest of humans, he was fallible.

Sutcliffe seldom, if ever, admitted, as batsman, to ordinary mortal frailty. In other words, Sutcliffe found it hard to imagine that any bowler could get him out, whatever the state of the game or the wicket. One day, I saw Maurice Tate clean bowl Sutcliffe, at a game's outset – Yorkshire v. Sussex. The ball was good enough to overwhelm Bradman. As Sutcliffe returned to the pavilion, I commiserated with him. 'Unlucky Herbert, to get such a ball at the beginning of the morning.' But Sutcliffe reacted to my sympathy with high dudgeon. 'I could have played it,' he asserted, 'but a man moved in the stand, unsighting me.' 'I could have played it', he repeated. I felt that I had offended Sutcliffe family pride.

Holmes, as I say, was different. At Lord's, in 1925, he actually accumulated 315 v. Middlesex, in ten minutes under seven hours, with thirty-eight boundaries, as comprehensive an exhibition of stroke play as well could be imagined, all round the wicket, brilliant with late cuts and enchanting flicks to leg. Yet, when later he talked of this innings – it broke a century-old record at Lord's – and a year afterwards it was beaten by the Master Batsman of All (Sir Jack Hobbs) – Holmes could not account for it, at least not for the first half hour of it. He exaggerated by reckoning he was 'morally out' half-a-dozen times in the first few overs. One of the Middlesex bowlers who had to cope with Holmes, in 'these first few overs', confessed to me that he hadn't 'so and so noticed' Holmes's insecurity. 'He never missed a ball he intended to play.'

Holmes was a great Yorkshire cricketer in one of the most historical periods of the county's many triumphant summers. From 1919, his real baptism to top-class cricket, till his last year of 1933, Yorkshire won the County Championship eight times. And in his prime, Yorkshire were more or less invulnerable – 1922 to 1925. These were the halcyon years, when Old Trafford, Leeds, Bradford and Sheffield would close gates at noon for a Yorkshire v. Lancashire match. Nearly 80,000 people watched Lancashire v. Yorkshire at Old Trafford, in 1926.

Holmes was one of the 'characters', identifiable as soon as he took guard, twiddling his bat. Robertson-Glasgow, brilliant as observer as with his wit, rightly discerned in Holmes a certain aspect of 'an ostler inspired to cricket'. There was a curious 'horsey' stable-boy air about him; he seemed to brush an innings, comb it, making the appropriate whistling sounds. He was not of the broadly soily nature of Emmott Robinson and Rhodes. I doubt if Rhodes, in his heart of hearts, really approved of Holmes's delight in a late-cut. 'Cuts were never business strokes,' quoth Wilfred. Roy Kilner, lovable as Maurice Leyland, would describe Percy as 'a bobby-dazzler'. (By nature's law of compensation, there are usually one or two rich genial spirits in the Yorkshire XI, to allow cheerfulness occasionally to creep in.)

Holmes really played cricket for fun. In a word, he was an artist, revelling in his batsmanship for its own sake. If he was furthering 'The Cause' – the Yorkshire will-to-win, all very well. But he set himself to drink deeply from the sparkling wine distilled in most innings he played. In his career he scored 30,574 runs, average 42.11, including sixty-seven centuries; and I'm pretty certain that the bulk of them, the ripe bin of them, were vintage stuff.

Holmes and Sutcliffe made a most fascinating conjunction and contrast of character and technical method: Holmes was as spruce and eager to begin a Yorkshire innings as a jockey to mount his horse, using his bat as a sort of pliant persuasive whip to urge his innings along the course to the winning-post of a first-wicket century partnership.

Sutcliffe was all relaxed as he took guard. Then, very likely, he would wave, with his bat, some obtrusive member in the pavilion, even at Lord's, out of his way, wave him into crawling oblivion – and the poor exposed movable spectator could easily have been our Lord Chancellor. But, as soon as the bowler began his attacking run, Sutcliffe became almost stiff and angular with concentration. He scored with the air of a man keeping an appointment with a century, and must not be late.

Holmes often appeared to improvise; he could change stroke whenever his first glance at a ball's length had deceived him. He might move forward anticipating a half-volley; if the ball dropped shorter than its first flight advertised, he would, on swift feet, move back and cut late exquisitely. There was a certain light-footedness in his batsmanship; he could defend as obstinately as most Yorkshiremen, but even then, he gave the impression that he was defending by choice, not compulsion. He was an artist, as I say, expressing himself through cricket.

Sutcliffe, of course, was also an artist expressing himself in a different temperamental way. Never let it be thought that Sutcliffe was a tedious batsman; whether or not he was moving the score ahead, he remained an individual, lord of all that he surveyed. He was the image of supreme confidence, basking in it.

Holmes was prepared to risk the mercy and indulgence of fortune. Sutcliffe was not only surprised but scandalised, if he was bowled; Holmes accepted such a downfall as part of the common lot of cricketers and of human nature in general.

Some sixty-nine times Holmes and Sutcliffe rounded the hundred mark for Yorkshire's first wicket. Undoubtedly Holmes would, but for the omniscient presence of Hobbs, have opened for England with Sutcliffe against Australia, not once but perennially. Most of the achievements batsmen dream about came to Holmes – a century in each innings v. Lancashire at Old Trafford in 1920; one thousand runs in a single month, June 1925, average 102.10; two thousand runs in a season seven times, over thirty thousand runs in his career.

But the scoreboard could not tell of his personal presence and animation. He seldom seemed static; he was always in the game. Between overs, and in the field, he was, as they say, eye-catching; but not self-consciously 'producing' himself. He was as natural as could be, not aware that, as Percy Holmes, he 'signed' everything he did.

His end as a cricketer arrived with an abruptness which, I am sure, tickled his mellow sense of humour. In 1932, he took part in the gigantic 555 first-wicket stand. The summer following, in 1933, he batted for Yorkshire 50 innings, scoring only 929 runs, average 19.25. This was the fall of the curtain for him. True, he was in his forty-sixth year; but somehow none of us suspected that age was on his heels or shoulders. He is a permanent chapter, not to say a whole volume of Yorkshire's cricket history.

He had the talent – not always nurtured in the North country – to play hard for Yorkshire and, at the same time to spread over our cricket fields flashes of pleasure by his batsmanship, his nimble fielding and – best of all – by his infectious, though not demonstrative, Yorkshire nature.

WILFRED RHODES – YORKSHIRE PERSONIFIED [1974]

Born at Kirkheaton, West Riding, October 29, 1877
Died near his home in Dorset, July 8, 1973
He had been blind since 1952

For the first time in more than a decade, the Cardus essay in Wisden was conspicuous only by its absence, although there must have been many thousands of regular readers of the almanack who opened the 1973 edition in the expectation of reading Cardus on the subject of Charlie Hallows, the Lancashire opening batsman who scored all fifty-five of his first-class centuries in the years when Cardus was 'Cricketer' in 'The Manchester Guardian'. In his key essay 'Myself When Young', Cardus had told one of his best stories, featuring Hallows, Makepeace and Frank Watson, 'deputy stonewaller to Makepeace'. But the Hallows obituary appeared not as a feature but as an item in the columns at the back of the almanack, signed by John Kay. Pessimists might have taken this as a sign that the President of the Lancashire County Club was getting past the age when he could meet a deadline. But there he was once again in the following year, lamenting the passing of yet another nonagenarian, the great Wilfred Rhodes. The essay was however, reproduced from 'The Guardian' and may well have been lying in the 'Pending' files for some years. In the appreciation of Rhodes Cardus paraphrases his own famous description of how Rhodes would use the various balls of an over, remembering with each delivery his own dictum, 'You can't flight a ball, only an over'. In 'Autobiography' Cardus nominates the description of Rhodes going about his business as 'one of the best bits of prose of my life' and, because he felt constrained to shorten it in the obituary, it should be reproduced here and appended to the 1974 essay:

> Flight was his secret, flight and the curving line, now higher, now lower, tempting, inimical; every ball like every other ball, yet somehow unlike; each over in collusion with the others, part of a plot. Every ball a decoy, a spy sent out to get the lie of the land; some balls simple, some complex, some easy, some difficult; and one of them – ah, which? – the master-ball.

WILFRED RHODES was Yorkshire cricket personified in the great period of the county's domination, shrewd, dour, but quick to seize opportunity. For Yorkshire he scored more than 30,000 runs, averaging 30 an innings: for Yorkshire he took 3,608 wickets at 16 runs each. When he was not playing for Yorkshire, in his spare time, so to say, he played for England and amassed 2,000 runs, average 30, and took 127 wickets, at the cost of 26.96 apiece. In his first Test match he was last in the batting order, and at Sydney in the 1903–4 rubber he took part in the most persistent and prolific Test match last-wicket partnership to this day; he helped R. E. Foster to add 130 for the tenth wicket, his share 40 not out. Eight years afterwards he went in first for England at Melbourne, and against Australia he was the partner of Hobbs in the record first-wicket stand of 323.

His career is already legendary; it does indeed read like a fairy tale. He was not 21 years old when he first bowled for Yorkshire in a match against M. C. C. at Lord's. In the first innings he accounted for Trott and Chatterton; in the second for Trott, Chatterton, C. P. Foley, and the Hon. J. R. Tufton – six wickets for 63, a modest beginning, true. But at the season's end he had established himself as the greatest slow left-hand bowler in England with 154 wickets, average 14.60.

During the period in which Rhodes and Hobbs opened every England innings by prescriptive right, Rhodes put aside his bowling. In the Australian rubber of 1911–12 he contributed only 18 overs. But then the war came, reducing the Yorkshire attack. In 1919 Yorkshire needed again the spin and flight of Rhodes, so he picked up his bowling arts exactly where years before he had laid them down, picked them up as though he had not lost touch for a moment. He headed the bowling averages of 1919, 164 wickets, average 14.42 in 1,048 overs. He was nearly 42 by the calendar. In 1902 he had gone in last for England at Kennington Oval when 15 runs were wanted to beat Australia; George Hirst, with whom he always opened Yorkshire's attack, was holding the wicket at the other end. England won by one wicket.

Twenty-four years afterwards, Rhodes in his forty-ninth year was recalled to the England XI and was one of the main causes of Australia's defeat and England's emergence from years in the wilderness. On this, his last appearance for England, Rhodes took the wickets of Woodfull, Ponsford, Richardson (twice), Collins, and Bardsley for 79 runs. He had probably lost by then much of his old quick vitally fingered spin; but as he explained to me: 'If batsmen thinks as I'm spinnin' them, then I am' – a remark metaphysical, maybe, but to the point. At Sydney, in December 1903, on the shirt-fronted polished Bulli soil pitches of that distant halcyon day for batsmen, Australia scored 485, and the might of Australia's champions commanded the crease – Trumper, Hill, Duff, Armstrong, Gregory. Rhodes bowled 48 overs for 94 runs, five wickets. It was on this occasion that Trumper, most brilliant of all batsmen, alive or dead, made his famous remark to Rhodes – 'for God's sake, Wilfred, give me a minute's rest.'

Rhodes could not turn the ball on the Australian grounds of half a century ago. He prevailed by length, variations of flight, but chiefly by unceasing accuracy of pitch, always demanding close attention from the batsman, the curving arc through the air, the ball dropping on the same spot over by over, yet not on quite the same spot, each over in collusion with the rest, every ball a decoy, some balls apparently guileless, some artfully masked – and one of them, sooner or later, the master ball. He was economical in action, a few short strides, then a beautifully balanced sideways swing of the body, the arm loose and making a lovely arc. He could go on for hours; the rhythm of his action was in its easy rotation, hypnotic, lulling his victims to the tranced state in which he could work his will, make them perform strokes contrary to their reason and intention. Batsmen of Rhodes's heyday frequently succumbed to his bait for a catch in the deep field. David Denton had safe hands at long-on; and the score-sheets of the period repeated day by day the rubric – 'c Denton b Rhodes.' In rainy weather, 'c Tunnicliffe b Rhodes' was familiar proof that Wilfred was at work on a 'sticky' pitch, for Tunnicliffe was the best slip fielder of the century, a long giant with a reach into infinity.

Rhodes really was a slow bowler, not quick and low flight to the pitch, after Lock's manner. At the end of his career he proudly maintained that 'Ah were never hooked and Ah were never cut,' a pardonable exaggeration considering the proportion of truth in it. Rhodes seldom pitched short. 'Best ball on a "sticky" pitch is a spinnin' half-volley,' such was his doctrine. And he bowled to his field with the precision of high mathematics. Ernest Tyldesley once told me that he often had no alternative but to play at least three balls an over, on a batsman's wicket, straight to mid-off, an inch off the spot where Rhodes had planted mid-off.

Rhodes made himself into a batsman by practice and hard thinking. He was one of the first batsmen to adopt the full-fronted stance, left shoulder pointing to forward leg. But it is a mistake to suppose that his batting was perpetually dour and parsimonious in strokeplay. In the Test match against the Australians at Lord's in 1912, England had first innings on a rain-damaged pitch. 'Wisden' relates that Rhodes, with Hobbs as company, 'so monopolised the hitting that his share of 77 runs amounted to 52.' On the whole and naturally enough, Rhodes distrusted the romantic gesture. One day in conversation with him, I deplored the absence in modern cricket of the cut. 'But it were never a business stroke,' he maintained.

While he was actively engaged in the game he was not a man given to affability. He was known as a 'natterer' on the field; and to natter in the North of England means to talk naggingly, mostly to oneself, with the intention of being overheard. At Old Trafford in the 1930s Lancashire reached a total of 500 against Yorkshire. The Lancashire captain, Leonard Green, was about to take the bowling of Rhodes when the score was 499. Green was sure in his mind that a total of 500 would never again, or not for decades, be achieved by Lancashire against Yorkshire. He therefore determined that come what may he would himself score the five hundredth run. So he blocked a ball from Rhodes, then ran like the wind. The ball was picked up by Emmott Robinson at silly-point, and hurled to the bowler's end, where it struck Rhodes on the wrist even as Green got home by the skin of his teeth. And in all the scurry and excitement Wilfred was heard to mutter, while he retrieved

Robinson's violent throw, 'There's somebody runnin' up and down this wicket. Ah don't know who it is, but there's somebody runnin' up and down this wicket.'

He was a great player, one of the greatest in cricket's history, not only for his all-round performances denoted by the statisticians: nearly 40,000 runs scored in 37 seasons and 4,184 wickets taken. He was great because his cricket was redolent and representative of Yorkshire county. In his old age he lost his eyesight and found his tongue. He accepted his affliction philosophically, and consoled himself by a flow of genial chatter never before heard from him. He attended cricket as long as health would permit. With an acquired sense he was able to follow the play. 'He's middlin' the ball right.' But it was his delight in his last years to recall the old days. I asked him what he thought of Ranjitsinhji. 'He were a good bat were "Ranji". But I always fancied myself getting him leg before doin' that leg glance of his.' I tried again. 'What did you think of Trumper?' "E were a good bat were Victor.' There was no advance on a 'good' bat in Wilfred's vocabulary of praise. Once, though, he let himself go. I asked him his opinion of Sidney Barnes as a bowler. 'The best of 'em today is half as good as Barnie.' He intended this as a compliment to the champions of today.

I last saw him as his daughter, Muriel, and her husband Tom Burnley, led him out of Trent Bridge at the close of play of a Test match. More than fifty years ago he had first played for England, on this same ground in 1899, when he was 21. Now he was going home to Canford Cliffs, Bournemouth, white stick in hand, arm in arm with his son-in-law, his face ruddy after hours sitting and listening to cricket, and whether he knew it or not, himself a permanent part of the game's history and traditions.

This memoir first appeared in The Guardian *and is reproduced by kind permission of the Editor.*

OLD TRAFFORD HUMILIATED [1975]

The best and greenest turf anywhere

It was by a most fitting turn of fate that Cardus's last essay for the almanack should, like his first, be about his home county. Half a century before, he had celebrated the bringing of the County Championship to Old Trafford. Now he had sterner duties to perform. The competition for Test matches had become so fierce that Old Trafford was to go on a rota and not necessarily get a Test match by right, as had been the case throughout the century. In the event, Old Trafford continues to see its Test Matches but Cardus used the occasion as an excuse to wax more eloquently than ever on the lustrous past. The anecdotes are the same ones, the heroes unchanged, the great matches those we have been told of before. Why then is all the reiteration not tiring? For the same reason that a long innings by a great master is not tiring, because it consists of an expression of style. There is one mysterious and beautiful touch, one of those moments when we are reminded yet again that there has never been a writer on cricket, or indeed on any game, who can approach Cardus for the sudden vivid glimpse of humanity caught in a pregnant moment lost beyond recall and therefore affecting and mysterious. Now halfway through his eighties, Cardus still cannot resist looking back at A. C. MacLaren and, in writing a charming passage describing the purlieus of Old Trafford in his boy-hood, he suddenly sights his hero in the Manchester Botanical Gardens: '. . . but he was not, I think, studying botany'. And we, having clung to the coattails of a great writer for so long, may be pardoned for concluding that while he was often seen at a cricket ground, he was not, we think, studying cricket.

OLD TRAFFORD has now to stand in a queue, with other county cricket grounds, to receive the privilege of staging a Test match between England and Australia. This is a humiliation which would surely have provoked A. C. MacLaren to a purpled vocal indignation. For ninety years Old Trafford has enjoyed the Royal Warrant; in other words, Old Trafford has taken it for granted that England and Australia would join issue on the greenest turf anywhere.

The first of all England v. Australia Test matches at Old Trafford occurred in 1884, July 10, 11 and 12. The opening day was ruined by rain. Six summers later, in 1890, the England v. Australia match at Manchester was entirely blank, rain throughout three days. In 1938 rain also prevented a single ball bowled at Old Trafford in the England v. Australia engagement.

'Typical Manchester weather' is a familiar saying. Will it be believed that in 1934 the sun blazed down on Old Trafford with so much regal heat and splendour that three Australians were affected so that each could not do justice to his skill in the Test match – Bradman, Chipperfield and Kippax. In four days in and under this Manchester furnace of sun-shine, 1307 runs were scored, and only twenty wickets fell. It was at the outset of this match that Walters and Sutcliffe, in first for England scored at ease, 68 runs in the first hour. Walters as imperial of poise and style as ever was Maclaren – which is saying much. Only Ted Dexter, in these modern times, has enthroned the crease with the disdainful command of MacLaren.

England 60 for none, the temperature, in the shade of the Press Box 88. So we all took what seemed a perfect opportunity to go down from our writing and typing seats for drinks. So, for a while, the Press Box was more or less vacant, and during our absence from the Press Box, while we were refreshing throats of parched sand, Bill O'Reilly took three wickets in one over, Walters caught at forward short-leg; Wyatt bowled middle stump; and Hammond, clean bowled too. In extenuation of the Press Box's diversion from duty, on this historic occasion, it must be recorded that before O'Reilly bowled his famous over, the players themselves ceased scalding action, to imbibe refreshment. The ball, having gone out of shape, too, was being changed.

History murmurous and memorable has been made at Old Trafford by England and Australia; not Lord's, even, has inspired more illustrious deeds. Shades of great cricketers will revisit the glimpses and wonder why, with England and Australia in ball by ball issue elsewhere, Old Trafford is vacant. At Old Trafford, in 1902, Victor Trumper scored his immortal century before lunch. England lost the toss. The wicket was damp and soft, but would surely become helpful to bowlers later on, as the sun baked the pitch. As a fact, after lunch, Lockwood took 6 wickets for 48. Australia, 173 for 1 at lunch, were all out for 299. MacLaren, the England captain, went into the field with one plan – 'We must keep Victor quiet before lunch; then we'll get into them.' All the skill and strategy of MacLaren, and of his bowlers, Rhodes, Tate (the father), Braund, Jackson and Lockwood, were concentrated on one purpose – 'to keep Trumper quiet'.

As every schoolboy knows, or should know, England lost this match by three runs. Poor Fred Tate missed a catch at the crisis, then last man to bat, with Rhodes at the other end, he came to the wicket, eight to win, snicked a sightless four, then was catastrophically bowled. If he could have blindly snicked again his name would today be heroically acclaimed.

In 1896, six years in advance of Fred Tate's match of heartbreak, Ranjitsinhji conjured at Old Trafford one of the magical innings of his life. England, following on, 181 behind lost three wickets more or less cheaply, then Ranjitsinhji scored 154 not out, sheer necromancy of batsmanship. He glanced the bouncers of Ernest Jones to leg with Oriental ease and grace. In his last years he told me that he missed aim to one of Jones's high flyers, and the ball grazed 'Ranji's' left ear. 'I could not have been seeing the ball with my usual sharpness of vision', explained 'Ranji'. Well, six years later, the ironic gods mocked Ranjitsinhji at Old Trafford, in the three-run Test match referred to above. Hugh Trumble, the Australian off-spinner, exorcised the genius from Ranjitsinhji, rendered him impotent, immobile, reduced the magician to mortality, and got him out twice, l.b.w. for 2 and 0. A sinful transformation – and inexplicable.

The procession of illustrious ghosts of England and Australian cricket at Old Trafford is almost endless. Not at Kennington Oval did Jim Laker choose to perform his miracle – 19 wickets in the same Test match, v. Australia. No author of romantic fiction would expect his readers to believe in a hero who bagged 19 wickets in the same game – even in a preparatory school match.

It was not at Lord's that Ted Dexter produced an innings clean out of Debrett (or, in this context, should I say Ruff's Guide to the Turf?), an innings blue blooded, on August 1, 1961. England, on the closing day, needed 256, in three hours, fifty minutes. Dexter, with strokes of royal command, scored 76 in eighty-four minutes, placing England on the doorstep of victory, 150 for one wicket.

And it was at Old Trafford, this very afternoon, that Richie Benaud achieved the bowling performance of his much too abruptly curtailed career. He went round the wicket, dropping his spin into rough earth caused by Trueman's thunderous stampings or thuddings; and taking six for 70 he wrecked the England innings to defeat by 54 runs.

Not at Lord's, but at Old Trafford, R. B. Simpson amassed 311 for Australia against England. Not at Kennington Oval, but at Old Trafford, did Tom Richardson send down 110 overs and 3 balls (five balls to the over in 1896) and, but for a dropped catch from him, would have scaled heights to snatch victory for England. This was the noblest, the most sacrificially arduous, the most nobly Spartan bowling known in all the annals of cricket. It ennobled Old Trafford turf for all time.

Old Trafford was, once in a time, when I was a little boy, situated in 'the country', surrounded by green fields. From the top of the pavilion could be seen the meadows of Cheshire. No smoke, except from the adjacent railway; no trace of industry. At the top of Warwick Road, approaching the county ground, was the Botanical Gardens. One night I actually saw A. C. MacLaren in these Botanical Gardens, but he was not, I think, studying botany.

The Old Trafford scene in those days was quite suburban. At the Manchester end of the ground reposed a Ladies' Pavilion, black-and-white timbered. Afternoon tea was served there by white-laced maids. When drinks were requested by the cricketers in the field they were not carried out by the twelfth man but by Old Trafford's ancient retainer, the original Jeeves; and he served the drinks from a silver tray.

The scene and background suited the presence at the wicket of A. C. MacLaren, R. H. Spooner and J. T. Tyldesley. No cricket team has had three opening batsmen as wonderfully diversified in style as these – MacLaren blue-blooded and Caesarian, Spooner all graceful curves and lyric ease and flow, Tyldesley, a swordsman with a square-cut as though executed by a battle-axe. The crowd represented the social structure of the period; the 'working class' in the sixpenny seats, the middle-class (upper) in the Ladies' Pavilion and adjacent enclosure, the aristocrats on the main Pavilion, wealthy shipping merchants, lawyers, bankers, etc.

I first entered Old Trafford as far back as 1900, on June 4, at the age of eleven. Lancashire were playing Kent; and Kent won the toss. The Lancashire attack began with Mold, very fast, and Briggs, slow left-hand. The new ball was never mentioned then; only one ball was at the bowlers' service throughout the longest of a side's innings. Mold and Briggs threatened to destroy in quick time the Kent batting on this morning of June long, long ago. Alec Hearne, W. H. Patterson and B.

D. Bannon were out for next to nothing. We young Lancashire urchins crowed with ravenous delight. Then J. R. Mason came in; and he looked helpless, sightless, facing Mold. The truth is that he stayed in with C. J. Burnup while 110 were added. At close of play Kent's total, all out, was 420, Burnup 200 exactly. It was a sad young Cardus that walked home, nearly four miles, that sunny evening. Burnup, by the way, was taken to task by *The Times* cricket correspondent for slow play; but the critic relented by adding 'maybe Mr Burnup's dilatory progress could be excused because of Kent's disastrous start to the innings'. Mark you, 200 in a day, single-handed . . . but 'dilatory'.

At Old Trafford, in 1906, a tall, rather gawky young man from Tonbridge played for the first time at Old Trafford for Kent. Lancashire won the toss; and at six o'clock, J. T. Tyldesley was fielding at third-man but he had scored 295, and Lancashire totalled 531 in five and a half hours. He was missed by the gawky Tonbridge lad with his score in the thirties. Next day this Tonbridge novice was l.b.w. for 0. Then, when Kent followed-on, he drove and glanced effortlessly for 50 or so; and we all knew, now, that a rare batsman was here in the bud, ready to blossom bountifully. His name was Frank Woolley and it was his first county match.

In the summer of 1920, or thereabouts, the Manchester Guardian contrived to gather together a cricket team, of which I was captain. One of our matches was against Manchester Club and Ground; and it actually took place on the, for me, legendary turf of Old Trafford, trodden over the ages, by all the great cricketers, from Grace to Bradman. What is more, the captain of the Manchester Club and Ground was none other than A. C. MacLaren, then cricket coach for Lancashire. He opened the Club's innings. I could not believe my eyes. The hero of my boyhood was standing there, taking guard white haired, but none the less, A. C. MacLaren. I could not resist the temptation. I put myself on to bowl, praying to myself – 'Please God, let me get him out. If I can get him out, with Your help, I shall remember the event all my life.' After an over or two, I bowled an off-break at MacLaren. He played forward, majestic as ever, missed the ball, which missed his leg stump by half-an-inch; and went for one bye. When MacLaren had lazily run to my end of the wicket, he said, 'Well bowled, Cardus, well bowled. I didn't realize that you could turn the ball back. But, so long as we know.' Next time, and every ball, he didn't push forward to me. He went back on his right foot and – whoosh! – he dismissed my off-breaks from his presence, to the boundary.

Not only Australian Test matches have contributed to the ripe harvest of cricket lore at Old Trafford. Lancashire v. Yorkshire are part of the historic harvest. During the 1930's, the wicket at Old Trafford was so much a batsman's heaven that seldom did a Lancashire v. Yorkshire match completely finish. Each team played to gain first innings points. If Lancashire should win the toss, Harry Makepeace would say to his colleagues 'We're in first. Now play steady. And no fours before lunch.'

The match was a comedy of North country character. The score-board told you little of the subtle show of character going on 'in the middle'. The joke was that the batsmen were not refraining from strokes because they couldn't make them. They were not making strokes *on principle*. Roy Kilner, lovable Yorkshire cricketer, once said, 'In Lancashire and Yorkshire matches, Mr Cardus, we should have no umpires – and fair cheatin' all round.' Vast crowds looked on; gates closed at eleven o'clock. In a Lancashire v. Yorkshire match at Old Trafford a spectator was seen and heard to applaud everything. 'Ah, well played!' 'Well bowled!' 'Well fielded, sir!' Dour Lancashire (and Yorkshire) men, cloth-capped, noted this indiscriminate applause; and at last, one of them said, 'Hey, tha seems to be enjoyin' thisself impartial. Does tha coom from these parts?' 'Oh, no,' replied the impartial spectator, 'I've come up from Brighton.' 'Well then', retorted the cloth-capped native, 'keep thi tongue quiet. This match has nowt to do with thee.'

Australia or no Australia in a Test match at Old Trafford, the ground, the place, the accumulated history remain. And amongst the visiting ghosts lovingly haunting Old Trafford is a small boy once myself, poor as a church mouse in his pocket but rich in vision as he looked upon his Lancashire heroes. 'O, my Hornby and my Barlow long ago!' But these famous lines are getting a little out of date. For myself, I change them to.

'MacLaren and my Spooner long ago' – not forgetting Cyril Washbrook and Brian Statham, not so long ago.

SIR NEVILLE CARDUS [1976]

Born April 2, 1889; Died February 27, 1975
C.B.E. 1964; knighted 1967

BY ALAN GIBSON

When the 1976 edition of Wisden was almost ready to be sent to the printers, Sir Neville Cardus died, mercifully after only the briefest of illness. He died in his sleep, which he once suggested to me was the ideal way to go, when bad light had stopped play. His death provoked in those who had drawn pleasure from his books a deep and abiding sadness. For those who had enjoyed even a little of his company, there was the anguish of irremediable loss. I believe that my acquaintance with him was beginning to ripen into a sort of friendship, largely, I suspect, because he saw in me one of those rough diamonds whose genesis interested him. He regarded me as one of the last custodians of regional speech, which was a charming way of dubbing me a cockney, and said that he was warmed by the sound of my laughter. Better than a tonic, he once called it, after which fulsome flattery he told me that there was an excellent little restaurant just off Marylebone Road, round the corner from his flat, where it would please him to wine and dine me and listen to my laughter. He died just before I could partake of that great pleasure.

Perhaps wisely, Wisden attempted no formal obituary. Instead it reproduced an account of the Memorial Service followed by the text of a tribute delivered by the writer Alan Gibson who perceptively defines 'Autobiography' as Cardus's greatest achievement. Gibson suggests, quite rightly, that Cardus was one of the finest writers of English prose of his generation and provides, as one example among hundreds, the wonderful reportage of an encounter with Frederick Delius at the old Langham Hotel. Gibson also implies something else. In describing his first encounter with Cardus's writing, he gives the reader the suspicion that if one man can have inspired another to write as well as Gibson does, then that man was Cardus. My own first experience was in the last year of my teens, the year of Denis Compton's apotheosis, the year when 'Autobiography' was published as a three-shilling paperback. I was deeply affected by every page but especially by the account of the long love affair with 'The Manchester Guardian'. It was this aspect of his life which helped me focus my own ambition. I had been bowled over by all sorts of writers whose work seemed to say that the best life was the writing life – I was, after all, very young and very callow – but it was Cardus who first brought the vague dreams of composition down to earth, provided a target and set a mark. I too would lay siege to the newspaper and, by achieving the mark, would be able to claim at least one thing in common with him. It took me fifteen years and when I told Cardus this, it was his laughter which warmed me. 'Don't work it out per annum whatever you do', he said. So I never did.

Sir Neville Cardus died in his sleep after a very short illness. Regular readers will remember a special tribute by John Arlott to Sir Neville which appeared in the 1965 edition.

At a Memorial Service in St. Paul's, Covent Garden, over 720 people joined in an occasion brimming over with joyous music and amusing talk.

The Royal Philharmonic Orchestra, conducted by James Loughran of the Hallé, offered Elgar – Serenade for Strings, and Mozart – the 2nd movements of both the Piano Concerto in A Major, and the Clarinet Concerto. Clifford Curzon played the former.

A Lancashire cricket match was recalled by Miss Wendy Hiller, who rose from a sick bed to read Francis Thompson's poem 'At Lord's', and Dame Flora Robson read 'Shall I Compare Thee to a Summer's Day'.

The Service had great warmth and style, as had Cardus himself. Alan Gibson set the tone on the day with this tribute.

M.H.

SINCE we are in a church, I thought it proper that we should have a text. Hear then these words from the prophet Blake (I am not sure whether Blake was one of Sir Neville's favourites, though he has recalled how enthusiastically he would join in 'Jerusalem' in his days with the Ancoats Brotherhood). Blake wrote, in *Auguries of Innocence*:

> 'Joy and woe are woven fine,
> A clothing for the soul divine;
> Under every grief and pine
> Runs a thread of silent twine'.

On an occasion such as this, joy and woe are inseparable companions: thanksgiving for such a life, sadness that it has ended. But more than that: it was the mingling of joy and woe that made Sir Neville such a writer – the sensitivity to the human condition, not least his own; the ability to observe it, and to communicate what he saw, with detachment and yet with passion. His books are full of humour: rich comedy, sometimes almost slapstick, and yet he keeps us hovering between tears and laughter. For always he is conscious, and makes us conscious, of the fragility of happiness, of the passing of time. He loved the good moments all the more avidly because he knew they were fleeting.

There is no need to recite his achievement. His autobiographical books, the crown of his life's work, have done that already. His early cricket books gave him a reputation for 'fancy' writing. The words 'lyrical', 'rhapsodical', were sometimes applied to him, usually by people who would not know a lyric from a rhapsody. These terms were still jostled about long after they had any possible justification, to Sir Neville's wry amusement. His mature prose was marked by clarity, balance, and indeed by restraint, thought he never shrank from emotion or from beauty. Perhaps George Orwell was as good a writer of prose; or you may think of P. G. Wodehouse, or Bernard Darwin – everyone has his own favourites – but in this century it is not easy to think of many more in the same class.

I remember clearly how I was introduced to Cardus's writing. It was in August, 1935. We were on holiday in Cornwall, at St. Ives, and my father was buying me a book, because of some small family service I had done. I said I would like a cricket book, and the choice narrowed to two: a book of reminiscences attributed to Hendren, I think it was, and 'Good Days', by Neville Cardus. I doubt if I had heard of Cardus then, because it was difficult to get *The Manchester Guardian* in the south of England. I was inclined to Hendren, but father was inclined to Cardus. Father won. We bought 'Good Days'. Father read it before I did, though I have more than made up for that since. Most of us, perhaps half a dozen times in our lives, read books – not always famous books – which change us, change our thinking, books which open doors, revelatory books. That was one of mine. It was the essay on Emmott Robinson that did it – do you remember it? – when Cardus imagined 'that the Lord one day gathered together a heap of Yorkshire clay, and breathed into it, and said 'Emmott Robinson, go on and bowl at the pavilion end for Yorkshire.' And then the next bit, about how Emmott's trousers were always on the point of falling down, and he would remember to grab them just in time.

All cricket writers of the last half century have been influenced by Cardus, whether they admit it or not, whether they have wished to be or not, whether they have tried to copy him or tried to avoid copying him. He was not a model, any more than Macaulay, say, was a model for the aspiring historian. But just as Macaulay changed the course of the writing of history, Cardus changed the course of the writing of cricket. He shewed what could be done. He dignified and illuminated the craft.

It was, it has occurred to me, fortunate for cricket that Bradman and Cardus existed at the same time: fortunate for them, too, since the best of batsmen was recorded by the best of critics. Each was worthy of the other.

In the music of Sir Neville's time, at least in English music, there was never one figure quite so dominant as Bradman. Elgar, Delius and Beecham were, he wrote, 'the three most original spirits known in English music since Purcell, if we leave out Sullivan'. He said it with a shadow of a wink, as if to say 'and take it out of that'. You remember how he described Delius, when he met him in what now seem the improbable surroundings of the Langham Hotel: 'His attendant carried him into the sitting-room of his suite and flopped him down on a couch, where he fell about like a rag doll until he was arranged into a semblance of human shape. There was nothing pitiable in him, nothing inviting sympathy in this wreck of a physique. He was wrapped in a monk-like gown, and his face was strong and disdainful, every line on it grown by intrepid living'. There is a picture for you; there is a piece of prose for you.

As for Sir Thomas Beecham, he is always bursting out of Cardus's pages and making his own way. It was with some difficulty that Cardus stopped his splendid Aunt Beatrice from conquering his first autobiographical book. He never quite stopped Beecham, any more than Shakespeare ever quite stopped Falstaff taking charge of Henry the Fourth.

Perhaps the most remarkable episode in the life of Cardus, going by what he said himself, and one to which we should refer here, was his conversion. I think the word is properly used: I mean his conversion to music. It was achieved by one of the minor saints: Edward German. He was watching a production of a light opera, *Tom Jones*, at the Prince's Theatre, Manchester. He had gone there because he was reading Henry Fielding, but, he says, 'the music of Edward German got past my ears and entered into my mind behind my back'. Only twenty months after that first experience, he was listening to the first performance of Elgar's Symphony in A Flat, and wondering, with the other musicians in the audience, how Elgar was going to cope with such a long first subject.

He used to say that he was baffled that it should have been Edward German who had first revealed the light: yet he should not have been.

It was all of a piece with the man and his thought. When Beecham and MacLaren, and Bradman and Ranjitsinhji, and Elgar came within the experience of Cardus, he rose to them and did them justice – but he was capable of being moved, such was his sense of humanity, by men who were no more than good county bowlers, Emmott Robinson or Edward German.

'Joy and woe are woven fine'. They are not alien, they are complementary, 'A clothing for the soul divine'. And in another part of that poem, Blake says

> 'It is right it should be so,
> Man was made for joy and woe,
> And when this we rightly know,
> Safely through the world we go'.

I am not sure whether Sir Neville Cardus would approve of that as an epitaph: but he is probably too busy to bother just now, arguing with Bernard Shaw.